# TELL IT TO THE WORLD

# TELL IT TO THE WORLD

INTERNATIONAL JUSTICE AND
THE SECRET CAMPAIGN TO
HIDE MASS MURDER IN KOSOVO

## ELIOTT BEHAR

DUNDURN
TORONTO

Editor: Dominic Farrell
Design: Courtney Horner
Printer: Webcom
Cover Design: Ingrid Paulson
Map: Andrew O'Driscoll

**Library and Archives Canada Cataloguing in Publication**

Behar, Eliott, author
Tell it to the world : international justice and the secret campaign to
hide mass murder in Kosovo / Eliott Behar.

Includes index.
Issued in print and electronic formats.
ISBN 978-1-4597-2380-1

1. Kosovo War, 1998-1999--Atrocities. 2. Albanians--Crimes against--
Serbia--Kosovo. 3. War crime trials--Netherlands--Hague. 4. International
Tribunal for the Prosecution of Persons Responsible for Serious Violations
of International Humanitarian Law Committed in the Territory of the
Former Yugoslavia since 1991. I. Title.

DR2087.6.A76B43 2015          949.7103'15          C2014-906780-1
                                                    C2014-906781-X

1   2   3   4   5        18   17   16   15   14

We acknowledge the support of the **Canada Council for the Arts** and the **Ontario Arts Council** for our publishing program. We also acknowledge the financial support of the **Government of Canada** through the **Canada Book Fund** and **Livres Canada Books**, and the **Government of Ontario** through the **Ontario Book Publishing Tax Credit** and the **Ontario Media Development Corporation**.

Printed and bound in Canada.

**Visit us at**
Dundurn.com | @dundurnpress | Facebook.com/dundurnpress | Pinterest.com/Dundurnpress

Dundurn
3 Church Street, Suite 500
Toronto, Ontario, Canada
M5E 1M2

*For my parents*

# CONTENTS

# AUTHOR'S NOTE

There are a few things I should address before we start.

First, the views expressed here are entirely my own. They do not represent the Tribunal or anyone else.

Second, there is no confidential information contained in this book. Where I have recounted specific events, they have been intensively sourced from public materials — events in open court, transcripts of witness testimony, public witness statements, a range of physical exhibits that were tendered into evidence, and final judgments. I have been very careful not to write about anything confidential and I did not (and could not) review any confidential materials in writing this book. Where witnesses were codenamed or had other protective measures imposed, what I have written here is based only on what was provided in open testimony, public exhibits, or the public final judgment — in many cases all three. For this reason, there are certain witnesses I have not written about, who might otherwise have added to this account.

This book is not an attempt to re-argue these cases. That job has been done and the resulting evidentiary and documentary records are enormous, numbering many thousands of pages and covering a scope of material, at a level of granularity, that I could never hope to replicate here. One of the great advantages of writing about a trial is that there is an incredible wealth of well-tested material to rely on; one of the main purposes of a trial, after all, is to ensure truth and accuracy. I have, therefore, been careful to keep my descriptions either consistent with findings made by the judges or with evidence that wasn't really disputed.

Finally, a brief note on place names. The cities, towns, and villages in Kosovo have names in both Serbian and Albanian. As with many other things in the Balkans, language and place names can be a sensitive issue. For the purposes of this book I have generally used the Serbian names, if only because these cases were prosecutions of Serbian nationals. This was not a political decision but a practical one.

# WHERE THE DEAD MEN LOST THEIR BONES

I think we are in rats' alley
Where the dead men lost their bones.
                                    — T.S. Eliot, *The Waste Land*, 1922

The fisherman saw it first, the low waves of the Danube rippling across what appeared to be a large crate. The white roof stood out sharply from the blue-black river, hard and immobile against the shifting water. The morning sky was overcast and there was a damp chill in the air. He brought his boat in close for a better look.

The object became clearer as he approached. A container. The back corners were protruding out of the water and the front, he guessed, was stuck in the ground. It was April 4, 1999, and Serbia was at war. But in the small village of Tekija, located in a remote corner of Northeastern Serbia, life had remained relatively quiet thus far. The fisherman returned to shore and called the police.

At around noon, police in the nearby town of Bor dispatched Boško Radojković, who drove out to the scene. Radojković was a senior crime technician for the Serbian Ministry of the Interior. His job was to attend crime scenes, gather evidence, and investigate. Now forty-three years old, he had a wealth of experience under his belt, having been a police officer and a crime technician since he was eighteen. He brought a scuba diver with him, a man named Živojin Đorđević, also known by the nickname Zika.

As a policeman, Radojković was used to waiting. He stared out at the white box, only about twenty or thirty metres from the bank. Some sort of vehicle. He watched as Živojin put on his aquatic gear and then slipped into the water. He circled near the surface at first but soon disappeared from sight.

Radojković was still watching when Živojin's head finally broke the surface. He swam back to shore, then turned and looked back out. He took his time removing his gear.

When Živojin's equipment was off he walked over to Radojković, who was staring out at the water. The men didn't look at each other.

"Yes, it's a truck — a refrigerator truck I think," Živojin said. "There is no trace of the driver. And no passenger."

Radojković waited.

"The front window is missing," Živojin added. "And there's a large stone on the accelerator pedal."

He paused.

"There is something protruding from the rear of the truck," he finally said. "It looks human."

Živojin looked to Radojković for guidance. He took a moment, then asked the obvious question.

"What do we do?"

Radojković took a moment to answer. "There is nothing we can do," he said. "Let's pull it out and see."

Radojković called for a crane and more personnel. Then the men left the scene for the night, marking the area with a buoy and tying the truck to a tree to hold it steady. Radojković returned to the police station. The police issued a dispatch reporting that a citizen had made a finding in the river, that a team had been assigned to investigate, and that it appeared to be a traffic accident.

The crane arrived the next day, along with about fifteen men from the nearby hydro plant. The men set to work trying to pull the truck from the river. A number of officials had arrived on scene: the deputy municipal prosecutor, an investigative judge from the town of Kladovo, the chief of the Crime Prevention Squad, and a coroner. The officials milled around the scene and looked on as the team worked.

It was not a large crane. The truck seemed deeply embedded in the muddy bottom and the crane strained against its weight. Živojin geared up and re-entered the water, swimming into the truck's cab and turning the wheels in an attempt to orient them in the direction the crane was pulling. The truck eventually began to move, edging its way to the shore. As it emerged, the men saw that it had no licence plates.

It was around noon when the truck began to rise from the Danube in earnest. As it rose, dripping with water, the men could see the sign on the side: "Pik Progres, Exportna-Klanica Prizren" — the Pik Progres export slaughterhouse. The lower right-hand corner of the rear cargo door was broken and something was protruding through. Radojković moved closer and his stomach turned. It looked like human legs, and an arm.

The men continued to work, uneasy. Radojković took photographs as they managed to pull the freight box completely out of the water. Held firm by the crane, the rear box of the truck was on the beach while the bottom chassis and the front of the cab were still in the water.

The men moved to open the freight box and the various officials on scene gathered around. Živojin used a pair of iron-cutting shears to break the chain securing the door, then opened the latch and pushed the door up. Sunlight abruptly lit the cargo. The truck was piled high with human bodies, a heavy mass of men and women, intertwined. Amongst the intact bodies, too many to count, were individual heads and body parts.

The door was closed almost as quickly as it had been opened. Some men retched. Others simply turned away.

The gathered men stood in silence for a moment. The signs were plain to read. The country was at war in Kosovo. The bodies were dressed in the clothing of rural ethnic Albanian villagers. The truck itself was clearly from Kosovo, the inscription on the door identifying it as having originated in Prizren. A piece of something larger had washed up on their shore.

The officials quickly left the scene, the investigative judge apparently telling Radojković that it was actually the district court that had jurisdiction and that he should inform them instead. Radojković sent a dispatch back to headquarters and waited. The chief of the Bor police secretariat eventually sent a message back: suspend all activities and close the area. The police closed the freight box, secured the site, and managed to pull the truck the rest of the way onto the riverbank, the bodies still inside.

The police held a meeting that night. It was agreed that Radojković would repaint the truck, covering the inscription that showed it was from Kosovo. He would attach new licence plates, from the Serbian town of Bor.

After the meeting, Radojković went to work. He painted over the truck's inscription, covered the back door with tin, and concealed the crack through which the human cargo had emerged. He even banged up the new local licence plates he had attached, smearing them with mud so they would look as weathered as the truck.

A larger crane was brought to the scene and the men pulled the truck all the way out of the river. It sat strangely on the shore, damp and hulking.

The question, of course, was what to do with the bodies.

# 1

# TO WRITE ABOUT A TRIAL

I

## Events and Ideas

This book was born from a desire to look simultaneously at the strange and ambitious international criminal trial process and at a particular set of events that were prosecuted: the ethnic cleansing of the small and scarcely-known territory of Kosovo in 1999, and the secret operation that was conducted to hide these crimes from the eyes of the world.

The structure of the book flows from a deeply held conviction that the international criminal justice system is equally about events and ideas. The system is premised on grand and ambitious conceptions of truth, justice, and fairness. It both begins and ends, at least ideally, with a view of how things ought to be. At the same time, it lives and breathes in the real world. It is applied to real people, in real situations. Some come to the process willingly, others come unwillingly, but all come with high expectations. Dealing as it does with acts of mass violence, crimes against humanity, war crimes, and genocide, the acts that the international justice system addresses, the pronouncements it makes, and the consequences it imposes have inescapably historical dimensions.

The stories in this book are told through the accounts of witnesses who came to the International Criminal Tribunal for the Former Yugoslavia (ICTY), where I worked as one of a team of prosecutors, to testify about what they saw, heard, and experienced. Alongside the telling of these stories, I have tried to explore three important and interrelated questions: how these events came to pass; how it is that we could find ourselves descending into such unimaginable violence; and how our efforts at international criminal justice actually fit within this broader context.

Listening to the accounts of the victims and witnesses who survived these atrocities, and reflecting on the admissions and denials of the perpetrators who committed them, I came to see that the ways in which we understand such acts of injustice, and the ways in which we speak about them — or, to put it another way, the stories that we tell — can pull us in two very different directions.

On the one hand, there was — and is — something crucially important about the need many of these victims had to speak out about what had happened to them. For these witnesses, seeking justice at an international tribunal meant being given the opportunity — if not also the burden — of telling their stories to the world. Responding to such staggering acts of inhumanity meant not just prosecuting the perpetrators but also, crucially, ensuring that these stories were heard. I came to see something essential in this: a powerful and very human desire to explain what had taken place, within a context that could see the wrongness of these acts formally declared.

Considering these events from a broader perspective, however, it became equally apparent that notions of justice, and the *pursuit* of justice, had also been used to motivate and perpetuate these atrocities in the first place. In this, the events that unfolded in Kosovo and across the Balkans reflected what I came to see as a much larger pattern — a pattern that has been apparent across many of the darkest events of the past century and that continues to manifest itself today. Understanding the ways in which such staggering violence can unfold, and the role of the international justice system within this broader context, means understanding that the stories we tell about injustice can also be used to enable and perpetuate large-scale violence in the first place.

To address these events and ideas, and the relationship between them, we will sometimes need to move back and forth, from one to the other.

## II
# The Other Face of Justice

The standard narrative used to frame our international justice system says that we are bringing justice to the darkest corners of the globe and the darkest moments of humanity. We are identifying victims and holding perpetrators accountable, and, as the promoters of international justice and human rights love to declare, we are putting an end to a culture of impunity. In short, we are bringing justice into the void, across the lines of the nation-state. We are introducing justice where it did not exist before.

This is the lens through which international justice and war crimes prosecutions are typically seen. It is the framework for the media who report on war crimes and call for international prosecutions. It is a largely unquestioned assumption for many of the academics who write about the international criminal process. And it is the essential prism through which most well-meaning citizens of the world view our responsibility as global citizens. This framework tells us that in the face of murderous actions by foreign governments who are slaughtering portions of their citizenry we must introduce justice where it did not exist before and shine its light into the darkness.

This is a tempting narrative and an alluringly simple construction. It is also, I think, fundamentally wrong.

Spend time listening to the men who directed these atrocities, and listen to the collective narratives and beliefs of the citizens who either carried out these acts or endorsed them from the sidelines, and you begin to see that they were themselves, even before the bloodshed began, driven to act by their own sense of injustice and victimhood. When we impose our international criminal justice system onto these events, we are *not* bringing justice into the void, because a sense of injustice and victimhood, and the language and rhetoric of pursuing justice, were there all along. The human drive for justice — provoked, mobilized, and directed outward as an entitlement to violence — is often what enabled, motivated, and then perpetuated the killing in the first place.

It can be hard to hear this, I think. It sits strangely with our notion of victimhood, seems somehow at odds with the shining regard in which we hold the pursuit of justice and the pride with which we normally wield it. It is difficult to imagine a context in which invoking or pursuing justice could be negative. The connotations of the word seem inherently positive; it is really only the failure to pursue justice, or the failure to achieve it, that we permit ourselves to find fault with. We say that justice was frustrated, that justice was abandoned, or that justice was denied, and it is clear that we mean to convey by this that something wrong has happened. The implication is that justice must always be pursued.

But the human *reaction* to injustice has a power that can also be wielded by perpetrators and that can spur and perpetuate terrible violence in itself. Look to the commission of mass violence, and to genocide and crimes against humanity in particular, and you start to see, everywhere, that the men who directed these acts and the men who committed them were themselves rallied and motivated by a well-stoked sense of injustice, and enabled by a seemingly righteous sense of victimhood. It is not necessarily that they thought they would never be held to account and could therefore act with impunity — they may, or may not, have thought themselves to be immune from eventual punishment. What such perpetrators and cheerleaders tend to believe, or at least convince themselves of, is that history is on their side; that a broader and more righteous struggle justifies acts that they would otherwise never countenance.

It takes more than a lack of immediate consequences to motivate large groups of human beings to commit acts they would otherwise find utterly unconscionable. This is even more so when what is demanded involves personal sacrifice — joining an army, signing up for a militia, risking their lives. More likely than not, the men and women who committed or supported genocide and crimes against humanity were driven by what they allowed themselves to see and feel as an imperative to commit violence. Whether they came to define themselves by a group identity formed along lines of religion, ethnicity, or nationality, it is as if they were made to think and feel that history, and moral rightness, was on their side. At the root of this, I think, tends to lie a core conviction that their actions — the most brutal, inhumane, and unconscionable deeds imaginable — were *justified*.

Look to the major acts of genocide in recent times and you can see certain striking commonalities in the psychology and the narrativizing that enabled acts of appalling inhumanity. In case after case, the perpetrators of these acts — not just those who directed the acts from the top, but also those who either enacted or facilitated them on the ground — were in thrall to narratives of injustice and victimhood that made them feel entitled to act as they did, and that seemingly silenced the demands of their individual consciences. This pernicious mindset has the power to quell the individual and collective consciences that would otherwise be ashamed of such abhorrent acts. It is a mentality with the power to infect not just the leadership but also the facilitators and willing executioners amongst the general population.

This feeling of entitlement to justice — this impulse — is a powerful prerequisite to collective violence. It provokes anger and invokes an enabling sense of self-pity to go along with it. It stokes fear of an enemy and can activate a corresponding and collectively shared sense of pride and duty. These are dangerous combinations, ones that can readily breed the notion that violence is acceptable and necessary. The stories we tell ourselves — our collective narratives — can be all too easily contorted under the right circumstances to serve these goals. They transform how we see ourselves, how we see others, and what we choose not to see at all.

III
# How I Got Here

As I asked the first question to my first witness, waited for it to be translated into Albanian, waited for her to understand and answer, and then waited for that answer to be translated back into English, I found myself looking around the courtroom and wondering how I had ended up here and what exactly we were attempting. The well-established routines of the courtroom — the slow formality of the proceedings, the distinctive cadence of the speech, the sombre quiet of the room, the robed men and women all playing defined roles — seemed somehow surreal. What were we doing here, and what were we hoping to achieve?

Not of the post–World War II baby boom like my parents, nor defined by the war itself like my grandparents, I am old enough to have experienced the final stages of the Cold War and the collapse of Communism, but too young to have appreciated the significance of that change as it unfolded. Mine was a generation that grew up to find the fear of war between global powers rapidly dissipating, only to see that fear replaced by the uncertainties of asymmetrical combat and the proliferation of global terrorism. We assumed there would be an ever-increasing acceptance of diversity along the lines of race, religion, and ethnicity, but then witnessed the rampant propagation of ethnic nationalism and the spread of inter-ethnic civil war.

The new ideology for my generation — the "last utopia," as some have called it — has been the identification and protection of human rights.[1] Though many point to the movement as beginning in the wake of World War II, the embrace of human rights as a concept only really began in the 1970s, and its influence didn't assert itself meaningfully until the 1990s.[2] In a global climate where the sources of violence and instability seem ever more uncertain, we seem to have looked increasingly to the law to identify right and wrong and to order the world. It was against this backdrop that I became a prosecutor, and then found myself prosecuting war crimes at the first international criminal tribunal since Nuremberg.

That I ended up at the ICTY seems on the one hand strange and on the other somehow inevitable. Growing up in Toronto in the 1980s, mass murder, oppression, even divisive politics seemed far from the door. We travelled often as a family, and my father had a favourite ritual that he would perform every time we came home. "How nice," he would say, thumbing through the seldom-changing headlines of the local newspaper, "to live in a place where this is the news." We were living in a time and place of almost unprecedented peace.

I grew up unquestionably Canadian, but with roots that extended — and tugged — from outside the country. My father grew up in Istanbul, our family part of a minority Jewish population of about twenty thousand that lived amongst an overwhelming majority of Muslims. Though it's easy to forget in the often hostile contemporary climate of Muslim-Jewish relations, the Ottoman Empire was a relative safe-haven for Jews in an otherwise oppressive world. After Mustafa Kemal Ataturk founded the modern Turkish republic in the wake of World War I, living in the newly modernizing and secular Turkey allowed the Jews there to avoid the horrors of European pogroms and then the Holocaust. Being Jewish in Turkey meant identifying proudly, on one hand, with Turkish life and culture, and yet somehow, inevitably, also being set apart.

My father and his older brother were amongst the first in the family to leave, departing for an Israel that had recently and surprisingly emerged victorious from the Six Day War in 1967. Israel was then a country whose very existence seemed precarious, with the potential for war lurking around every corner and the loss of any war meaning the likely disappearance of the country. Politics in Israel, and its surroundings, could quickly and suddenly shift the ground beneath one's feet. For a country formed in the wake of the Holocaust, that fear has always been difficult to discount.

Both my father and his older brother met the women they would marry — a Canadian and an American, respectively — in Israel. Within several years, they found themselves resettled in North America. My father and mother moved to Toronto, where my father became an architect, and my uncle and aunt moved to New York, where my uncle went into business. Their youngest brother stayed in Istanbul and raised his family there. Later, as tensions in Turkey increased and eruptions of violence became more common, many of the other members of our family began to leave Turkey as well.

Like many Jewish families, my mother's side, originally from Poland, was deeply scarred by the Holocaust. Their stories, and the broader facts underlying them, would be recounted from time to time — as a child these experiences felt at once immediate and yet lifetimes away. As I look back now, the events of the Holocaust seem closer in time, the Second World War having ended a mere thirty years before I was born. My mother, a family therapist who sometimes used family trees in working with her clients, would on occasion take me through our own family tree, where the legacy of the Final Solution was all too apparent in the broad swathes of the chart marking relatives who had died in concentration camps or simply disappeared.

The events of the Holocaust provoked no small amount of curiosity in me as I grew up and I read a lot about them. There were survivors like Elie Wiesel and Primo Levi, who seemed able to capture the raw inhumanity of what took place, and there were numbing black-and-white videos shown in the classroom, which painted cruelty and suffering on a scale that seemed impossible to comprehend. I have never forgotten one of the first video images I saw, a bulldozer pushing what must have been hundreds of Jewish bodies from a concentration camp into an enormous mass grave.[3] To see such things seemed important, but they also seemed entirely disconnected from the life and the people that I knew.

Sometimes the accounts came from closer to home. There was the story of my aunt Ruth's father, Sam Berger, who survived the camps and later chronicled his experiences in the book *The Face of Hell*.[4] For a high-school project, which soon became much more, my brother Mark conducted detailed interviews of my mother's cousin Perry, who had survived Auschwitz as a child along with his brother Saul. The stories were hard to comprehend, not simply for the picture they painted of growing up in the camps but also for the depiction of surrounding events, including the execution of Saul and Perry's father. The project forged a deep and lasting bond between Mark and Perry and the report remains a moving record for our family.

Despite all of this, there always remained some sense of disconnection between the events of the Holocaust and the reality of my life in Canada. I wondered how such things could actually come to pass and how they could be prevented. In retrospect, I can see how these thoughts shaped what was to follow. I studied psychology, travelled whenever I could — including time spent volunteering in Guatemala in the wake of the cease-fire that ended their brutal civil war — read as much as I could about human rights, then wrote the LSAT and went to law school. Following my graduation, I would spend ten years as a prosecutor, running trials and arguing appeals on cases of child abuse, sexual assault, domestic violence, and murder. I worked with the Province of Ontario's hate crimes unit and later spent two years in a specialized unit that oversaw the prosecution of police officers charged with committing criminal offences.

When I was hired to prosecute war crimes at the ICTY in 2008, it already felt like the culmination of *something* — though of what I wasn't quite sure. As our case progressed, I began to see the overriding influence of many of the same historical antecedents that had cast shadows in my own life — the Holocaust and the history of the Ottoman Empire chief among them — and of many of the same core questions about narrative and group identity, the psychology of victimhood and fear, and the power of the human drive for justice, that I had been grappling with for years.

# 2

# THE HUMAN AND THE BUREAUCRATIC

I

## Against All Odds

The ICTY was established by the United Nations Security Council in May of 1993, a direct response to the worsening spiral of inter-ethnic atrocities that were then being committed in Croatia and Bosnia and Herzegovina. The decision was portrayed immediately as both timid and bold. Timid because it was a "solution" that did not require the use of force and seemed to hold little prospect of actually stopping the escalating violence. Bold because the ICTY would be the first international war crimes tribunal since the Nuremberg and Tokyo tribunals were set up following World War II — a sudden and ambitious act of faith in international law and the principles of human rights.

Given its significance to the world of international criminal law — a field that didn't really exist yet — the ICTY appeared rather suddenly. The United Nations had appointed a commission in 1992 to examine and document the ongoing events in the former Yugoslavia. The commission's report led the Security Council to pass Resolution 827 on May 25, 1993, establishing the "International Tribunal for the Prosecution of Persons Responsible for Serious Violations of International Humanitarian Law Committed in the Territory of the Former Yugoslavia since 1991" (such an exhaustively long title that I've never actually heard it said out loud). The ICTY's ongoing mission would be to prosecute the individuals responsible for the most serious crimes committed in the former Yugoslavia, including acts of large-scale murder, torture, rape, mass deportation, and destruction of religious and cultural property. It would draw on core principles of international law to prosecute four broad categories of crime: "grave" breaches of the 1949 Geneva Conventions (Article 2), violations of the laws or customs of war (Article 3), genocide (Article 4), and crimes against humanity (Article 5).[1] These were, and are, the most serious crimes known to the law.

The question on everyone's mind when the ICTY was established was whether, and how, the fledgling institution might actually be able to *do* any of this. Imagine a domestic justice system trying to work without a police force to actually stop crimes or arrest offenders and you have some idea of what the ICTY faced after its formation. The Tribunal had no direct mechanism to bring anyone to court; for this it had to depend on concrete action from the member states of the United Nations.

The first employees reporting to work in the empty and echoing offices of the Tribunal faced no easy task. They had to set up the entire structure of the institution: create the rules of procedure and evidence that would dictate the basic procedures to be followed, set up the internal organizations to deal with witnesses and fund and support defence counsel, and recruit all of the necessary employees. As the first investigators set out to identify the perpetrators of crimes in Croatia and Bosnia, and to provide the Tribunal with actual perpetrators to prosecute, they confronted numerous obstacles. The inability to actually arrest anyone and put them on trial quickly emerged as the central and defining struggle of the Tribunal's early years.

Unfolding on the ground in the early years after the Tribunal's creation was a story of the abject failure of the international community to use force to stop violence. With the world looking on, the city of Sarajevo endured a brutal siege for almost four years. Supposed United Nations "safe areas" in Bosnia were attacked and their protected civilians were slaughtered by the thousands. Campaigns of ethnic cleansing were redrawing maps through acts of murder, rape, and intimidation. If the events in the former Yugoslavia were not enough, 1994 saw the slaughter of some 800,000 people in Rwanda, with the United Nations and its member states refusing to intervene or to support the tiny and hopelessly outmanned peacekeeping force on the ground.

Against this backdrop, the ICTY was struggling to take its first wobbly steps. Early investigations and prosecutions focused on low-level and intermediate-level perpetrators. With both Serbia and Croatia obstructing the Tribunal at seemingly every turn — at least when it sought to investigate or prosecute their own nationals — the ICTY struggled to get any significant perpetrators before the court.

In the early 2000s, however, things began to shift dramatically. Since that time, and despite its inauspicious beginnings, the Tribunal has exceeded nearly everyone's wildest expectations for the range and scope of its prosecutions. Against all odds, it has brought the major surviving perpetrators of the worst crimes in the former Yugoslavia to trial.

It is in the trail blazed by the ICTY that the world of international criminal law has flourished: since its formation, the world has seen the creation of ad-hoc tribunals for Rwanda, Cambodia, Sierra Leone, and Lebanon, among others, as well as the establishment of the International Criminal Court, with jurisdiction over the entire world. These are significant achievements. But they say little about what is actually happening in the cases themselves, and how these events fit into, and impact, the broader context of violence in which they occurred.

II

# The Kosovo Trials

The ethnic cleansing of Kosovo Albanians by Serb forces was prosecuted in three separate but related trials at the ICTY. The first, and most well known, was *Prosecutor v. Slobodan Milošević*, which ran from 2002 to 2006. The Milošević trial, monumental though it was in the history of international law, was never finished — Mr. Milošević passed away before the case could be concluded. Many witnesses told their stories, and many documents were tendered, but no findings were ever made.

The second case was *Prosecutor v. Milan Milutinović, Nikola Šainović, Dragoljub Ojdanić, Nebojša Pavković, Vladimir Lazarević, and Sreten Lukić,* which I will refer to here as the "Kosovo 6" trial. The Kosovo 6 case prosecuted members of the senior Serbian leadership for participating in what international criminal law refers to as a "joint criminal enterprise" against the ethnic Albanians of Kosovo. Milan Milutinović was the president of the Republic of Serbia, Nikola Šainović the deputy prime minister of the Federal Republic of Yugoslavia, Dragoljub Ojdanić the chief of the General Staff of the Yugoslav National Army, Nebojša Pavković the commander of the 3rd Army, Vladimir Lazarević the commander of the army's Priština Corps, and Sreten Lukić the head of the "MUP Staff" within the police.

The third and final prosecution for the ethnic cleansing of Kosovo was *Prosecutor v. Vlastimir Đorđević*. Mr. Đorđević was the chief of the Public Security Department (RJB) of the Serbian Ministry of the Interior. In shorthand, he was the chief of police, responsible for all units and police personnel in Serbia, including Kosovo, during the events of 1999. It was Mr. Đorđević who was charged with overseeing the operation to cover up the evidence of the ethnic cleansing of Kosovo, perhaps the most surprising, and telling, of any of the events that took place there. When the Kosovo 6 trial began, Mr. Đorđević was still on the run from the Tribunal. When he was finally captured, he was tried on his own.

It was the Đorđević trial on which I was a prosecutor; I was brought in shortly before the case began and saw it through to its completion just under two years later. Much of what I have written here is based on that trial and the testimony that was given there. To tell the story of the ethnic cleansing of Kosovo, however, I have also relied on testimony and experiences from the Kosovo 6 trial, and occasionally on evidence from the Milošević case. The cases were extensively intertwined.

The Tribunal also prosecuted members of the Kosovo Liberation Army (KLA) for their actions in 1998. Ramush Haradinaj, Idriz Balaj, and Lahi Brahimaj were charged with unlawfully removing, mistreating, and killing Serb civilians along with ethnic Albanians and others who were seen as collaborators. The Tribunal also prosecuted KLA members Fatmir Limaj, Haradin Bala, and Isak Musliu for their alleged involvement in detaining approximately thirty Serb civilians and ethnic Albanian collaborators at a prison camp on a farm in Llapushnik and murdering fourteen detainees.

There were, without question, serious crimes committed by the KLA against Kosovo's Serbian population. There were crimes committed before the Kosovo War, during the fighting, and — perhaps most notably — after the war had concluded. This book does not tell that story; it is not the account of the Haradinaj or Limaj trials at the ICTY, which would warrant a book of their own, nor is it the story of some rather disturbing allegations that have yet to be proven. In many ways, and as many across the Balkans would be quick to tell you, that is a chapter that history, and the international justice system, have yet to write.

January 27, 2014 marked the end of all of the Kosovo prosecutions at the ICTY. The end of the final chapter came with the pronouncement of the Appeal Judgement in the Đorđević case, delivered on a rainy Monday morning in The Hague by a panel of five appeal judges. I watched from the gallery with the public, sitting amongst television and print reporters, NGO observers, and a mix of Serbs and Albanians. Although I had been a trial prosecutor on the case, working inside the courtroom that I was now peering into through six adjacent panes of reinforced glass, I had not been part of the appeal process and was no longer working at the Tribunal. A year earlier I had stepped away from my ten-year career as a prosecutor entirely. It was strange to be sitting on the outside.

The end of the Kosovo cases, and the close of this remarkable chapter in both history and international law, was met with little public fanfare. By the time of this final conclusion, a significant amount of time had passed and the headlines had shifted. Yet it was events in Kosovo that had led directly to Slobodan Milošević's ascendency to power and then to the shocking and brutal violence that unfolded across the former Yugoslavia. It was events in Kosovo that saw NATO go to war in mainland Europe at the turn of the twentieth century — a new type of "humanitarian war," a war that too few Westerners ever appreciated or understood. It was events in Kosovo that had formed the basis of Slobodan Milošević's international indictment and arrest — the charges later broadened to include his other actions across the former Yugoslavia — with the case marking the new emergence of international criminal law on the global stage. It was events in Kosovo that served as a closing bracket for the inter-ethnic violence in the former Yugoslavia, that saw the formation of a new and controversial nation-state, and that still serve as a lightning rod for tension and anger amongst both Serbs and ethnic Albanians.

We marked the close of the Kosovo cases with a skeleton crew of prosecutors in a small office at the Tribunal. There were maybe twelve of us in all. A number of the original prosecutors had already returned to work in their home countries, or left for other international tribunals, but in their stead there were a handful of new faces. Some champagne was poured, a few words were said, and glasses were raised. The mood was not celebratory, exactly, but nor was it sombre. Having returned as an outsider, I could acutely feel how privileged I had been to walk this intense, strange, sometimes rewarding, and sometimes discouraging path. The first sip of champagne brought a surprisingly strong tug of emotion.

III

# Ridiculous Robes

Working at the ICTY, it turns out, is an office job.

You work in a large grey industrial building that used to house an insurance company. You live in The Hague — or Den Haag, as the Dutch call it — which is about an hour outside of Amsterdam and the home of most of the world's international courts. You probably ride your bike to work, in a dedicated bike lane with dedicated bike traffic lights, and then lock your bike inside the Tribunal's sliding steel gate along with hundreds of other bikes belonging to Tribunal employees. You often ride through the rain, because the rain seems ceaseless in this town on the North Sea, and the weather is never quite warm. Whatever direction you're riding in (or walking in, for that matter), the wind always seems to be blowing directly into your face. You more than likely live fairly close to the Tribunal, since this is a relatively compact city, and if you're like me you find yourself in a top-floor apartment that somehow brings to mind Anne Frank's attic, even if you enter through a regular door and not a secret bookcase.

You enter the Tribunal through metal detectors, typically from the basement, tossing your wallet and keys into a bin and collecting them when you emerge on the other side. You sit two to an office, across from another lawyer who more than likely works on a different case. Like many office workers, you spend most of the day with your face buried in a computer. This is true whether you're at your desk, with a witness, in court, or at home. It's both the blessing and the curse of the modern digital litigation environment at the ICTY, where millions of pages of evidence have been digitized, transcripts scroll live while court is in session, and the judgments that you rely on as precedents will sometimes run more than a thousand pages.[2]

When you're in court, or on your way to court, you wear long black flowing robes with a white dickey tied across the front. If you're American, this seems ridiculous. If you're British, you probably feel underdressed. If you happen to be Canadian, these robes look and feel a little more (okay, a lot more) like wearing a dress than the robes you wore in the high courts back home. Wherever you're from, you probably grow to appreciate the fact that you can wear these legal coveralls overtop whatever else you happened to be wearing that day — most likely business casual — so long as your shoes look respectable. You may even wonder, after you pay your one and only visit to the curious robing room in the bowels of the Tribunal and are brusquely handed your assigned robe, if the person who used it before you was a sumo wrestler, because it would comfortably hold three or four regular-sized people.

Throughout the day you drink espressos and cappuccinos from a Lavazza machine that reminds you you're actually in Europe. At lunch you grab a tray and line up in the cafeteria like a high-school student, often standing shoulder to shoulder with the defence lawyers, judges, or court staff from your case. You eat lasagna, Dutch tosti sandwiches, or the special of the day. Friday means fish and chips. If you're lucky, your friends and co-counsel will join you at one of the long tables, where you'll try not to speak too loudly or talk too much about work, because you never know who else might be within earshot. If you're really lucky, and this is one of those ultra-rare days when it's nice enough to eat outside, you might find yourself on the balcony, overlooking the courtyard and fountain out front. If you're not in court that day, and are willing to grant yourself clemency from the backlog of catch-up work that invariably awaits you, you might even leave the building for lunch and eat in a real restaurant — reminding yourself, if only for a short time, that there's an entire world outside of this Tribunal.

What could easily go unnoticed to any casual observer dropped into the corridors of this building in the middle of a workday is that this industrial grey building is also the place where the world has sat in judgment of some of its darkest moments. The three courtrooms in this building have heard accounts of mass murder and rape, of families destroyed, of entire populations displaced or deported. They have also been the site of formal, historical pronouncements purporting to decree whether these things did or did not actually happen. These three small, windowless rooms are where a small group of representative individuals — lawyers and judges, acting in accordance with certain rules and procedures — have tried to bring justice to faraway places where human beings were dramatically and catastrophically wronged.

What happens in this building is not merely symbolic. The decisions made in these courtrooms determine whether real people will be held accountable, condemned with the full force of law, and sentenced to serve their remaining days locked in a prison with common criminals. If they are acquitted they will find themselves set free; sometimes to return to a quiet, solitary life and sometimes to be met at their hometown airport by thousands of cheering patriots who believe they should be celebrated and memorialized as heroes. The individuals who have stood indicted before this tribunal were not ordinary civilians. They were high-ranking soldiers, army generals, and bureaucrats, and in some cases they were the presidents and prime ministers of entire nations.

But what happens here is also deeply symbolic. The words uttered inside this building can transform a historical legacy, stoke anger, or redress wrongs — sometimes all at once. They can promote peace, understanding, and stability, or they can provoke rage, retribution, and violence. They can see a man condemned as a criminal or they can exonerate him from any accountability at all.

This process, and this responsibility, is entrusted to a system that was optimistically, perhaps even naively, cobbled together from domestic systems, built upon an always-controversial and sometimes precarious foundation of "international criminal law," and then handed over to a few hundred people, most of them foreigners and outsiders to the conflict, to put into practice. They have all been figuring it out as they go.

IV

# Burden of Proof

The prosecutor's job in an international criminal trial is to positively prove each and every charge against the accused beyond a reasonable doubt. Unlike your typical domestic criminal case, however, proving a war crimes case tends to require two different levels of proof. The first level involves evidence establishing that the crimes themselves actually happened and who directly perpetrated them. The second involves evidence that connects the accused himself to the crimes that took place on the ground — showing that he directed the acts of these immediate perpetrators, or was otherwise responsible for them. The need to satisfy these two levels of proof has implications.

The first level of proof is relatively straightforward; it consists of what most people tend to expect from criminal trials. It involves calling victims and eyewitnesses to testify — the survivors of mass murders and executions, the victims of sexual assault, the people who endured mass deportations, and the witnesses who saw and heard these events unfold with their own eyes and ears. Identifying these witnesses and taking statements to establish their experiences is no small task. It requires locating them, often in circumstances where they may be afraid or unwilling to talk. In many cases these witnesses were first identified by NGOs on the ground or in nearby refugee camps. The Kosovo trials owed much to the work of Human Rights Watch, which first interviewed many of the victims in Kosovo.

Proof on this first level — often referred to informally as "the crime base" in international trials — also tends to involve physical evidence to corroborate these live accounts, and forensics to show who was killed and how. Proving deaths and matching up described victims to found bodies can be an immense administrative task in a case involving thousands of murders. Nonetheless, this first level of proof is not usually where the challenge lies. From an evidentiary perspective, this is the easy part.

The challenge tends to lie at the second level of proof, which requires establishing that the accused before the court, who was likely a political, military, or police leader — a bureaucrat, in other words, stationed far from the crimes that were committed — knew what was going on and was directing or overseeing the operations on the ground. This is often a tremendous challenge, and is more often than not where cases are won or lost. This second level of proof is typically met with counter-arguments that the accused didn't know such heinous crimes were being committed, didn't actually exercise the power or influence alleged, and wouldn't have wanted these things to happen. Such knowledge and intent is not something to be presupposed. It has to be proven.

Evidence of criminal responsibility for leaders at the top of the pyramid typically involves reliance on two different types of evidence. The first is documents: hundreds, if not thousands, of documents. Documents showing that soldiers or police were deployed to particular areas and establishing what they were tasked to do. Documents showing that militias were formed. Documents showing the broad strokes of a concealment operation.

Rare indeed would be the document that makes any explicit reference to crimes being intended. People are usually smarter than that — too self-aware. This is particularly so in the case of crimes committed in Kosovo in 1999, when the ICTY had been in existence for six years and the world was watching closely for human rights abuses. Without a smoking gun, these documents are most often used in conjunction with the evidence of what actually happened on the ground. You prove that these units of the police and military were deployed to this particular town, on this particular date, and arrayed in these particular formations. Then you call evidence from eyewitnesses to show what these units actually did on the ground. Then you look across multiple operations, in area after area, and search for patterns. As you look at the details of what happened — who was deployed, how they were deployed, and with what instructions — the cryptic but nonetheless telling directions in the various deployment orders can become increasingly clear.

What you really require to prove these cases, alongside the documents and eyewitnesses, are *insider* witnesses: witnesses from inside the administration who can tell you how things actually worked, who was in charge, how events were orchestrated on the ground, and what information was being fed back up to the top. They can tell you what the people in charge were actually doing, what they knew, what was going on behind the scenes, and what was never written down.

Insider witnesses, not surprisingly, are hard to find. When you do find them, their motives tend to be varied and difficult to discern. Sometimes they choose to testify. Other times, you compel them to attend court. Sometimes you don't know whether they're going to help your case, or try to sabotage it, until they're on the witness stand.

# 3

# HIDING BODIES

Man is not what he thinks he is, he is what he hides.

— Andre Malraux

I

## Operation Dubina II

Caslav Golubović, the chief of the Police Secretariat in Bor when the truckload of bodies washed ashore, was seventy-two years old when he arrived in The Hague to testify in the Đorđević case. His bureaucrat's suit hung loosely now, but he still carried an air of authority.

Mr. Golubović had been through this process before. He had been summoned to testify against Slobodan Milošević, recounting his story there for the first time. Years later he would be summoned again, this time to testify against the Kosovo 6, the men directly under Milošević who were the central architects of the Kosovo campaign. His testimony in the

Đorđević trial would almost certainly be his last at the Tribunal. But this time he had been summoned to testify against his former colleague — in fact, his direct superior — who we were alleging had personally overseen the operation to conceal the bodies of murder victims. His evidence had been peripheral in the other trials and little had come of it. The defence had not bothered to cross-examine him in the Kosovo 6 trial. Now, however, this was the main event.

This was probably the last place Mr. Golubović wanted to be. He had found himself in The Hague as a result of that all-important concept in military and police bureaucracy, and thus in international criminal prosecutions: "chain of command." As with a great many war crimes trials, much of our case would depend on establishing that chain of command. Much of Mr. Đorđević's defence would depend on refuting it; casting himself alternately as an impotent pawn of the minister above him or as an out-of-the-loop bureaucrat who was unaware of the men below him committing crimes across Kosovo.[1]

Mr. Golubović would presumably need to walk a delicate line, between minimizing the damage to his former colleague and to himself, and not saying anything that stood too brazenly in contradiction to the increasingly mounting evidence.[2]

He sat there in this small room, carefully and quietly reading through statements he had provided years ago about events that took place over a few days in 1999. He consumed cigarettes voraciously on every break, standing on the Tribunal's balcony and looking far into the distance before dutifully returning to the small room to continue. When he had finished, the table was piled with small, empty coffee cups.

When he testified, Mr. Golubović's evidence was that he first thought the truck ended up in the river after a traffic accident. There was, after all, a dangerous bend in the road nearby. He acknowledged that he was brought up to speed on the findings of Radojković and the diver. He admitted that at the time he was informed of the situation the bodies found in the truck were already thought to be those of Kosovo Albanians. They were clad in traditional clothing and they consisted of men, women, and some children.[3]

He adamantly denied that he had attended the scene where the truck and the bodies were found, although his answers over the course of his testimony seemed to suggest otherwise. Asked whether the district prosecutor or investigating judge had attended the scene, he responded, "No, I don't think so. When I was there they never showed up, and I don't think they showed up the next day either."[4] When asked about when the truck was first opened, he answered: "As soon as it was opened, I realized there were bodies inside so the door was shut. The public prosecutor and the investigating judge were there. They saw this too."[5]

Nonetheless, Golubović admitted to phoning Vlastimir Đorđević after he learned about the bodies in the truck. He told him everything he had learned and he sought instructions on how to proceed. Đorđević called him back, instructing him to keep the case quiet and to ensure the media didn't report on it. Then he told him to try to bury the bodies somewhere nearby.

Đorđević and Golubović spoke multiple times that night, discussing how to ensure that the bodies would never be found.


It was left to the men on scene to conduct the gruesome work of unloading the decomposing bodies and body parts. They waited until nightfall. They assembled the necessary workers, arranged for another truck, and brought blankets and gloves to the scene. The men retrieved the bodies, wrapping them in sheets before unloading them. The work was grotesque: dividing and emptying this intertwined and decomposing human mass, the sheer rotting bulk of it, the need to put out of mind the individuated humanity at all costs.

But Radojković was looking, perhaps overcome by his police training, perhaps as some act of conscience, or perhaps because he couldn't turn away. He saw the bodies of children, at least two. He counted about ten women; the rest of the bodies were men. They wore no uniforms, he noticed. These were civilians. By his estimation, these were people who had been dead for not longer than three or four days. He could see and identify their injuries easily enough: blunt force trauma, at least three decapitated heads, and a body with its hands tied by wire, blown open by a short-range gunshot wound. These were the marks of executions.

As the men laboured to unload the human cargo, it became increasingly clear that they had badly underestimated the number of bodies in the truck. What they initially guessed were thirty bodies now looked more like eighty. It also became clear that they wouldn't be able to conceal the bodies by burying them at the site. Golubović called Đorđević at about 10:30 p.m., explaining the situation and letting him know they wouldn't be able to finish by morning.

Đorđević directed that the bodies be loaded into a new truck. Golubović asked his driver, Ljubinko Ursuljanović, to pick up a dump truck from the Komunalac public utility and to bring it to the scene. By 2:30 a.m. the men had loaded about thirty of the bodies into that truck.

At Đorđević's direction, Ursuljanović drove the truck off towards Belgrade, accompanied by a police escort. Đorđević gave instructions that a man would call to ask for the truck's licence plate number, and that someone would meet up with the truck and escort it to a new location from there. As Ursuljanović arrived with the truck at the outskirts of Belgrade, he was met by men driving a Volkswagen Golf and escorted through the city. Eventually, the truck was directed to the side of the road. Ursuljanović was asked to get out and several men he didn't know — or wouldn't identify — got in and drove away.[6]

Back at the scene, the remaining fifty-three bodies were loaded into a second truck, a Mercedes with a tarpaulin cover. With the remaining human cargo on board, that truck was driven off towards Belgrade as well.

Portions of Mr. Golubović's testimony were clear, particularly the parts that were consistent with other evidence. Other portions seemed intended to be exculpatory, if only in a limited way.[7]

Golubović claimed that he told Đorđević they had no experts to carry out autopsies. He said he recommended that the bodies be taken to a place with forensic facilities. He made the rather curious suggestion that the police "wanted to take the bodies somewhere where they could be examined by a pathologist, not just one but a team of pathologists" — as if policemen who were actually interested in solving a crime or preserving evidence would work in the middle of the night to evacuate evidence from a crime scene.[8]

The Trial Chamber identified concerns with Golubovic's reliability on certain issues, in particular in his attempts to minimize his own culpability and that of his co-workers. Addressing his testimony along with that of several other "co-conspirators," including Radojković, the Chamber concluded:

> Some aspects of the evidence given by several of these witnesses appeared to the Chamber to be unreliable or dishonest and to be consciously aimed at minimizing the witness's own role and culpability in the events described. There were also times when the Chamber was left with the impression that a witness's departure, in the present trial, from evidence given in prior proceedings was motivated by desire to minimize the role of the Accused. This was apparent from the demeanour of the witnesses concerned, variations in their accounts of material matters for which the explanations offered were not satisfactory, as well as other available evidence about the matter.[9]

In the end, however, the court accepted the core of Mr. Golubović's evidence about the bodies, particularly as it was supported by a range of corroborative evidence and testimony.

Several days after the final truck had driven off from the scene, Ursuljanović was sent to a Ministry of the Interior parking lot in Belgrade, where he was instructed to pick up the first truck, now empty. The truck was delivered to a special police base in Petrovo Selo that was not in active use. There, a number of the men, including Radojković, set about destroying it. They lit the truck on fire, and when that proved ineffective, they rigged it with explosives and blew it up.[10]

The men involved in the operation were paid a total of ten thousand dinars for their efforts. The paper trail showed that Đorđević approved the payments, which were sent through Golubović. The operation was cryptically codenamed "Dubina (Depth) II."[11]

The workers at the scene knew that this lone truck and the bodies it contained had been re-concealed. What they didn't know was where the bodies had been taken. Nor did they know — though they must surely have wondered — whether this lone truck was part of something much larger.

II

# Behind Bulletproof Glass

International criminal trials are at the same time both intensely human and inescapably bureaucratic. Their size and scope makes them distinct from domestic trials in ways that tend to amplify the feeling that you're a cog in a bureaucratic machine.

Trial judges at the ICTY sit three to a trial. Behind these judges is a fully staffed "Trial Chamber" apparatus, which includes a number of lawyers working on each case behind the scenes. From the outset of each trial, these Chamber lawyers are helping to sift, sort, and organize the evidence, supporting the judges as they write pre-drafts of what will almost certainly be an enormous final judgment. It can sometimes feel as if the role of both prosecution and defence is simply to funnel evidence into the court. You organize and pre-process that evidence, and argue about how it should be interpreted, but you also recognize that the court's internal machinery has been independently processing the evidence all along. If you're going to persuade the Trial Chamber then you need to persuade them as you go, not in a big flourish when you put all the evidence together, because the judgment is being constructed from the day the trial starts.

A corollary of this is that a substantial amount of evidence is adduced in documentary form, outside of the courtroom, as part of a written process that proceeds in parallel to the activities in open court. Though witness testimony forms a key part of the evidence, a significant volume of documents, witness statements, and previous testimonies are tendered into evidence through various legal motions that are seldom argued orally or even mentioned in the courtroom.

While some aspects of the proceedings take place unseen, others have been set up precisely to speak to the watching world. Tucked away behind soundproof glass is a staff that records and live-produces multi-camera videos of the court proceedings, which are then broadcast over the Internet, occasionally shown on live television, and also screened on monitors in the Tribunal's foyer. The proceedings are always broadcast on a tape delay — the better to catch accidental slips that could reveal the identity of a confidential or protected witness. This can lead to some strange moments, however, particularly if you walk out to the foyer on the court break and are confronted with a digital ghost of yourself still speaking in the courtroom.

Behind bulletproof glass, directly behind the witness chair, is the courtroom gallery, which is sometimes empty and sometimes packed. The glass is tinted, but not so much that you can't see school groups shuffling in and out, reporters or NGO monitors taking notes, or even, on one strange morning in the middle of the Đorđević case, the Reverend Jesse Jackson walking in, standing up at the front of the glass and pointing around the room, then striding out again thirty minutes later with a nod to the prosecutors.[12] Sometimes spectators are treated to fascinating and dramatic moments of live testimony and sometimes they find themselves enduring hours of impenetrable legal jargon or seemingly interminable testimony about institutional command structure. Sometimes they find themselves with nothing to see or hear at all as the court clerk lowers the blinds and turns off the audio channel to the gallery so the court can go into "closed session" to protect the confidentiality of certain witnesses, usually with no indication of when or whether the blinds will come up again.

Walking the halls of the Tribunal, with all of its machinery, people, and infrastructure, it is hard not to think about what it costs to create and maintain this self-contained world. Though the ICTY opened with an annual budget of $276,000 in 1993, fifteen years later the institution had grown exponentially and the budget had more than followed suit, expanding to well over $100 million per year (the ICTY does its budgeting in two year increments; the biennial budget for 2012 and 2013 was $250,814,000).[13]

The costs are certainly high, but an international tribunal has to function not merely as a courtroom but as an entire justice system. Because there is no international police force, no international jail, no international legal aid program, and no system of either administration or physical security to draw on, the Tribunal has had to supply all of these. In addition to the court facilities, lawyers, judges, and staff, the Tribunal has had to support its own investigations and evidence-gathering initiatives, its own detention unit, its own legal aid program, its own victim-witness assistance unit, its own security and administration, and its own translation services. These things are expensive — and also particularly hard not to think about when you're dealing with witnesses struggling to live on dollars a day and communities trying to rebuild from the ground up. But these costs pale in comparison to the costs of war.

The size of the cases mean that as a prosecutor you work as part of a team of lawyers, with maybe five or ten of you working on a case at any given time. Your co-counsel are likely from all over the world, although there's a good chance your team leader (or leaders) are from the United States or England.[14] The Đorđević team was from Jamaica, Chile, Malaysia, Germany, Norway, Italy, Denmark, the United States, and Canada.

Prosecuting by committee takes some adjustment, particularly when the members of your team come from such dramatically different backgrounds and legal systems. But working on a team with other lawyers also greatly diffuses the weight and the stress of a task that would otherwise be crushing. In some cases, this forges bonds of respect and affection that can last for a lifetime. In others, it leads to clashes and resentment. It depends on the team.

The learning curve for each case is remarkably steep. Working within an entirely new legal regime turns out to be the easy part, however; for someone grounded in the common law system and the core principles underlying the laws of evidence, the Tribunal's rules of evidence are fairly intuitive. The real challenge is to learn the labyrinthine factual world of your case well enough to navigate within it.

In this respect, the practical reality is that you can only really pick things up on the fly. You likely read what you could before the case started — history of the conflict, media coverage of the events, perhaps even judgments from other cases — but that only scratches the surface. What must eventually become second nature are things like the command structure of the Yugoslavian and Serbian military and the bureaucratic infrastructure of the Ministry of the Interior. How were these structures ostensibly controlled and how were they *actually* controlled; who wielded the real power and how? How did these institutions collaborate, how were orders provided to the men on the ground, and what role did the politicians play? In Serbia there were often vast differences between the rules and procedures as formally established and what was actually taking place.

Litigating a war crimes case means immersing yourself in a world that you likely knew next to nothing about and learning it to a level of detail that allows you to function like an expert — if only in short bursts, for particular aspects of the case — and to challenge or outflank people who lived the events that you could only read about.

You do this — as everyone does, at least in the beginning — mostly by focusing on your next witness and by reading all the evidentiary materials you can. There isn't time for much else, because once the cases start they tend to run at full throttle.[15] So you speak to and rely on your team members, investigators, and analysts, who thankfully tend to know a lot more than you do at the outset, and then you read some more. As the case progresses, each member of the team develops expertise in certain areas and the work is divided along those lines.

Despite these challenges, the process is often surprisingly smooth; you can learn what you need to learn. But you never quite lose sight of the fact that for someone who grew up in the region you're dealing with a great many of the things you spent weeks or months trying to understand as an outsider were already second-nature. Facts that surprised you, and the names and roles of various people involved in the more notorious incidents, are often known to locals — even in other parts of the country — at a depth you can only envy. More than once in Serbia I encountered people who had no direct involvement with the events of our case, including a driver who mentioned one of the incidents unprompted, who clearly knew the details and the names of the people involved at a level that had taken us weeks to achieve. Sometimes, surely, they knew things we didn't.

Working at the Tribunal has its range of peculiarities, including accustoming onself to the court's strange proclivity for the use of acronyms. Making this all the more confusing is the fact that the words being abbreviated often began in another language. The Serbian police are the MUP, and the MUP are divided into local OUP offices, which report to broader SUPs.[16] All of this is relevant to proving a JCE (Joint Criminal Enterprise) involving the MUP and the VJ (army). With time it starts to become second nature — at which point you forget just how unintelligible these acronyms are for anyone else.

Language itself is also a frequent obstacle to understanding, and an ever-present issue of your workday. If you're working on one of these Kosovo cases, most of your victims speak Albanian. Your "insider witnesses," and the defence witnesses, mostly speak what the Tribunal calls "B/C/S," an abbreviation for Bosnian/Croatian/Serbian that deals bluntly with the fact that, although the ethnic divisions within the former

Yugoslavia have resulted in stubborn claims for the existence of three separate languages, they are all essentially the same.[17] You thus spend a lot of your time working with, and through, interpreters. Your documents have hopefully been translated for you, but often that's been done in a hurry. You prepare witnesses with an interpreter who sits with you in the "proofing room" and are often left wondering about the differences between how something was originally voiced and how it emerged.[18] Different languages mean that you wear headphones in court, choosing the channel for the language of your choice, and talking with headphones over your ears takes time to get used to. So does the slow and beyond-your-control pace engendered by the inevitable wait for interpretation.

With time it all starts to feel natural. You stop thinking about the interpreters sitting behind soundproof glass and speaking directly into your ears, or the strangeness of the courtroom, or the robes, or the glowing screens, or the Tribunal itself. You focus, instead, on the evidence.

III

# Lake Perućac

> Sing, sing, Drina, tell the generations,
> How we bravely fought,
> The front sang, the battle was fought
> Near cold water
> Blood was flowing,
> Blood was streaming:
> By the Drina was freedom!
> — "The March on the Drina"[19]

Less than two weeks later, on the opposite side of Serbia and more than four hundred kilometres away, it happened again.

Serbia's western border with Bosnia follows the Drina river, which cuts a jagged path between the two territories. In 1966, the Drina was dammed near the village of Perućac, its powerful flow harnessed through the Bajina Bašta hydro-electric power plant. That dam created Lake Perućac, an artificial lake that sits tucked amongst Serbia's western mountains, bordered by the scenic Tara National Park to the south. In the summer months, Lake Perućac has long been a popular recreational spot, the lush lakeside surroundings full of men, women, and children swimming and lying in the sun.

For all of the lake's scenic beauty, however, the waters that pool there have travelled a course through some of the most blood-soaked lands of the twentieth century. On its way to Lake Perućac, the River Drina winds through the Municipality of Višegrad, which in the summer of 1992 was the site of some of the darkest acts of the Bosnian War. In a ruthless campaign of ethnic cleansing by Bosnian Serb militias, thousands of the town's Bosnian Muslims were murdered, raped, or tortured. Many were shot and then thrown into the river, often from the picturesque sixteenth-century Ottoman bridge that spans the town.[20] From Višegrad, the Drina cuts north through the municipality of Srebrenica, now notorious as the area where Bosnian Serb and other forces executed thousands of Bosnian Muslim prisoners over a single week in July of 1995 — the worst massacre in Europe since World War II and now a well-established act of genocide.[21]

By the end of the twentieth century, the Drina had seen its share of bodies. It may have seemed a good place, then, to dispose of murdered Kosovo Albanians.


The corpses began to appear individually, floating in the water around the Perućac dam. It's not clear who saw them first; civilians, probably, who in turn called the local police. The responding officers who arrived at the scene could see six or seven bodies drifting in the lake.

The findings were reported up the chain of command, no one quite sure what to do. The chief of the local police station in the closest Serbian town, Bajina Bašta, called the acting police superintendent for Užice, a man named Đorđe Kerić. Kerić called Vlastimir Đorđević directly, in Belgrade. As a result, Mr. Kerić would subsequently find himself testifying in The Hague, as a prosecution witness against Mr. Đorđević — a man who had been his boss and who he had known for fifteen years. Like Golubović, Kerić would seemingly need to walk a difficult and delicate line, between allegiance to his former colleague, concern for his own liability, and a need to remain at least somewhat internally consistent.[22] In the end, however, the basic facts were clear enough.

Đorđević directed that the chief of the crime police in Užice, Zoran Mitricević, should go to the site to conduct an inspection and then report back. Once again, he made clear that no one else was to be informed.

Mitricević made for the lake, bringing other officers with him. They could see bodies drifting in the water: both men and women, dressed in civilian clothes. As the men watched from the shore, the number of bodies seemed to be multiplying, growing by the hour.

"It frightened them," Kerić said of the increasing appearance of new corpses, "and created a kind of psychosis."[23]

The men took boats out onto the water for a better look. Ten to twenty metres from the dam they saw what looked like the crate from a refrigerator truck in the lake. Pulling closer, they saw that there were decomposing bodies inside, gradually drifting out into the lake and then floating away.[24] They estimated there were between thirty and forty bodies in the water.

Mitricević reported back to Kerić, who conveyed the information to Đorđević. Đorđević ordered him to "clean the terrain" by engaging officers and civilians to collect the bodies from the lake. The men were ordered to bury the bodies in a mass grave on site, near the dam.[25] Kerić relayed the instructions to Mitricević, who put a team together to carry out the task.

Over the next two days a group of men collected the decomposing bodies floating in Lake Perućac and dumped them into a mass grave they had dug nearby. When the work was done — the hole filled back in and the bodies re-concealed — Mitricević reported up to Kerić and Kerić reported to Đorđević.

By May 1, Kerić was transferred to Belgrade, where he commenced a new position with the Federal Ministry of the Interior. It would be more than two years, he said, until he heard any mention of these bodies again.

4

# TWO MEN TO SPEAK FOR A VILLAGE

Tahir Kelmendi had been waiting to meet me. I saw him first through the windows of a small interior room where he was sitting with coffee in a paper cup. An older villager with a thick white moustache, slightly yellowed at the lips, he was wearing a qeleshe, a traditional white woolen skullcap. His eyes were bloodshot and he looked lost deep in thought. Mr. Kelmendi was to be our next witness at the Đordević trial, here to provide an eyewitness account of the massacre that took place in his small hometown of Ćuška (Qyshk), Kosovo.

It struck me, as I approached, how much he stood apart here. The hallways were busy — people typing at their computers, talking on the telephone, criss-crossing the patterned blue-grey carpeting, moving briskly in and out of rooms. He was instantly recognizable as an outsider here and would garner the occasional double-take look. But witnesses like him are the very reason the ICTY exists.

Mr. Kelmendi nodded respectfully as I entered the room, then looked down again at his hands. This was just to be an introduction; since he was in the building I wanted to say hello before we started preparing him to testify. But when our interpreter explained in Albanian that I was the prosecutor who would question him in court, he shot suddenly to his feet, taking my hand in a crushing grip, his qeleshe almost falling to the ground in the fluster. He wasn't letting go, speaking hurriedly, shouting almost, and as he continued to pump my hand up and down the on-the-fly translation struggled to keep up. He told me it was an honour — a great, great honour — and that the work we were doing was important. His grip was alarmingly strong and there was an almost wild look in his eyes.

He could scarcely get his words out fast enough and our interpreter did his best to keep up the translation. He told me again that the trial was important for his village. He said repeatedly that he was here to tell the truth. Then, without warning, he grabbed my hand and pulled it towards him. He was speaking too quickly for the interpreter to match his pace; his words were no longer clear but the intensity of his emotion was all too apparent.

As he was speaking he locked eyes with me, then pulled down his lower eyelid. He grabbed my hand, tight, then pulled it towards his exposed eye. I didn't understand. As I realized he was pulling my hand to his eyeball I recoiled, trying to pull away and yet not wanting to struggle. But he was insistent, his grip like a vice, pulling my hand in anyway as if imploring me to trust him, not understanding my reluctance. I let go and he redirected my hand, at the last second, to the flesh underneath his eye. I could feel something hard there. He released my hand and his eyes went wide.

He was looking at me, hard. I turned to our interpreter for the explanation, but he was shaking his head, apparently as confused as I was. We sat there for a moment as Mr. Kelmendi looked on at me expectantly.

"What was he trying to show me?" I asked the interpreter.

The men conferred, Kelmendi gesturing and pulling on the skin underneath his eye, retelling the story. The interpreter nodded in understanding and turned back to me.

"He's showing you there's a bone chip in the skin under his eye," he said. "He was assaulted, at an earlier time, by the Serb police."

I was relieved to finally understand. Such was the nature, sometimes, of communicating across cultural and linguistic lines.

I had spent the past several days sifting through hundreds of pages of materials about the massacre in Ćuška. I would have spent weeks, if we had them, but the pace of the trial wouldn't allow it; different witnesses from across Kosovo were following one after the other. We didn't yet have a translation of Mr. Kelmendi's statement into his native Albanian. Without it, he would need to sit and listen to the interpreter translate each line of the statement and read it aloud to him. It is standard practice — at the Tribunal, and in most Western courtrooms — to ensure that witnesses have the chance to reread their previous statements so they can refresh their memories before testifying. Across different languages it can be an exhausting process.

Mr. Kelmendi and his fellow villager and friend Hazir Berisha would be our only two witnesses to address what had become known as the Ćuška massacre — the mass execution of forty-one Kosovo Albanian civilians by Serb forces on May 14, 1999. As a Canadian prosecutor, I was trained in a system that would routinely call upwards of a dozen witnesses, often many more, to prove a single murder, allocating days to scrutinize everything from tire-track evidence to the chain of continuity of a significant piece of evidence. In my new role, however, I'd come to realize that we would need to prove our case with a significantly condensed list of witnesses. Our indictment was forty-eight-pages long and read like a book, alleging criminal responsibility for massacres across Kosovo and the systematic deportation of close to half the total population. It would be virtually impossible to prosecute a case of this scope and complexity in Canada, where it can take months to prosecute a single murder.

Mr. Kelmendi's evidence represented a very small part of the case against Mr. Đorđević. In fact, the Ćuška killings were not specifically charged against him in our indictment. The deportations there were part of the larger scheme of deportations across the municipality of Peć;[1] the operation was being established to demonstrate the pattern of actions by Serb forces. But Mr. Đorđević could not himself be found culpable for these killings.

We would not bring justice to the citizens of Ćuška as a result of our trial. But the case represented a beginning, not just because the Tribunal was seeking to hold one of the individuals at the top responsible for orchestrating the systematic campaign that brought the killings to their doorstep, but also because of the role we would play in the context of a multifaceted international justice system. This system, with its component parts of United Nations institutions, national legal systems, and non-governmental human rights organizations, would slowly work its way towards exposing and prosecuting the individual men who had stormed this village one day in May, more than ten years ago. That process would begin with the accounts of Tahir Kelmendi and Hazir Berisha.

May 14, 1999 began like any other day in the small village of Ćuška. The sun rose early this time of year, at about 5:20 a.m., and the town was quiet but for the crowing of roosters. Some of the villagers were already rising to tend to their small fields, while others stayed sleeping. It was late in the war. Ćuška had somehow stayed relatively untouched by the Serbian offensive that had begun in earnest on March 24, for reasons not entirely clear. It may have been sheer happenstance. Some have speculated that money changed hands.[2]

Ćuška sits on the outskirts of Peć, a town of about sixty thousand people that in many ways epitomizes the historical tensions between Serbs and Albanians. Strategically located in western Kosovo, Peć was conquered by Serbian forces in the late twelfth century and ruled by the Serbs for the next three hundred years. The town is the site of the Patriarchate of Pec, a Serbian Orthodox monastery that serves as the spiritual seat of the Serbian patriarchs and archbishops and remains sacred ground for the Serbs to this day. In 1455, Peć was captured by the Ottomans, bringing an influx of Turks and an Islamic character to the city, along with the construction of a number of mosques. The city remained under Ottoman rule for almost five hundred years, seeing the struggle for Albanian autonomy flare at the end of the nineteenth century. The city's modern history has seen it occupied by nearby Montenegro, taken by Austria-Hungary during World War I, made a part of the Kingdom of Yugoslavia (then known as the Kingdom of Serbs, Croats, and Slovenes), and then occupied by Albania during World War II. By the time the town became a part of the new Yugoslavia following the war, a significant majority of its people were ethnic Albanian — a balance that would shift upwards of 75 percent in the early 1990s and accelerate from there.

Situated just off of the main road from Peć, Ćuška seems scarcely recognizable as a distinct village; to an outsider there is little to distinguish it from the surrounding towns and houses. Not so for a local. In

1999, there were about two hundred houses in the village, most characteristically large and spartan. Backed by a mountain range, the houses are spread liberally and separated by fields — some cultivated, with high stalks of corn; others open, with grass; some bare. The townspeople were predominantly Albanian and knew each other well. By May of 1999 there were somewhere in the neighbourhood of seven hundred people still living in the village.

On the morning of May 14, Mr. Kelmendi had been outside since 6:00 a.m., taking his cattle out to the field. He could see members of what looked like the police and the army surrounding the village, arriving from the direction of Peć.

It wasn't the first time Serb forces had descended on the area. They had come as recently as mid-April and set fire to a number of the Albanian houses, leaving the Serb houses untouched. Now, a month and a half later, the Serbian regime was well into its intense and well-orchestrated campaign of deportation, destruction, and murder. Some of the villagers would by now have heard talk of what Serb forces were doing in surrounding villages. For many, these were hard things to believe.

There was already a dark feeling of inevitability in the air. The day before, around eighty Albanian refugees had arrived in Ćuška from the nearby village of Katundi I Ri. The Serbian police commander in the nearby village of Ozdrim had directed the refugees to Ćuška, explaining that the police would be sending the villagers there to Albania the next day. The commander of the Klicina police station, located about six to seven kilometres from Ćuška, had sent an officer named Mijo Brajović to Ćuška that same day to determine whether the Albanian townspeople were armed. Mr. Kelmendi spoke to Brajović when he arrived. Brajović told him that they shouldn't be afraid of the forces when they came, and that nothing would happen to the villagers.[3]

At around 7:00 a.m. on May 14, the townspeople began to hear automatic weapon fire. They watched as houses at the edge of the village were ignited in flames, thick black smoke darkening the morning sky. Some of the younger and middle-aged men quickly fled the village into the nearby woods, as they had on previous visits from Serb authorities. Some of them were shot and killed as they fled. Other men remained behind, unwilling or unable to flee, or reluctant to abandon their families.

A large group of Serbian forces quickly descended on the town, pushing from west to east. There were about eighty to one hundred in all, heavily armed. They wore a mixture of blue-camouflage police uniforms and solid green or green-camouflage army uniforms. Most wore black bandannas on their heads and many were wearing T-shirts. A number of them had also painted their faces. The villagers recognized some of the men. Kosovo is a small place.

The armed men asked the villagers repeatedly to identify the father of Agim Çeku. If there was ever a hated man amongst Serb forces it was Çeku, an ethnic Albanian born in Ćuška who had joined the Croatian army in 1991 and played key roles in a number of military operations against Serbia, including the alleged planning of Croatia's 1995 "Operation Storm" offensive, which violently expelled thousands of Serbs from the Serbian Krajina, a self-proclaimed Serb state within Croatian territory. In 1998, Çeku had returned to Kosovo to join the KLA, becoming their chief of staff and serving as their liaison with NATO.[4] When Hasan Çeku reluctantly identified himself as Agim's father and came forward, he was shot and then set on fire.

The Serbian forces systematically pushed the villagers to the town's centre, robbing some and killing others as they went. Some of the villagers went to the centre on their own; expecting to be forcibly deported to Albania, they felt it safer to assemble together than to resist or stand out. As the armed men moved through the village, Kelmendi managed to hide himself in a ditch, lying flat on the earth and peering up above the crest. He remained there, unseen. His friend and fellow villager Hazir Berisha was not so fortunate.


When I met Hazir Berisha in The Hague he was sitting silently in a room with one of my fellow prosecutors. Tall and thin, Berisha seemed to radiate a certain gentle calm — a perception that would remain throughout the time we spent together. I shook his hand as I entered and he smiled warmly, if somewhat tentatively. Without an interpreter it was impossible to say anything further, so the three of us sat and waited in silence, trying to convey with smiles and subtle body language what for the time being had to remain unsaid. The imposed silence seemed to emphasize our differences, though the mutual recognition of the absurdity of the situation and our shared desire to communicate seemed also to bring us together. I reread his statement while we waited.

The eventual appearance of an interpreter finally allowed us to exchange proper greetings. Mr. Berisha listened carefully and patiently as we explained who we were, when we expected he would testify, and what to expect.

"I just want to explain what happened," he said. "I just want to tell you what I saw."

Hazir Berisha was drinking coffee with some of his fellow villagers when the gunshots first rang out. They came from the upper part of the village. He ventured out and saw a large group of police and military men approaching, firing their weapons. He went to tell his neighbour first. When he returned home, his mother begged him to flee. As an able-bodied man, he was likely to be executed as a potential member of the KLA.

Mr. Berisha fled from his house, heading towards the centre of the village. He could see the forces setting things on fire and discharging their weapons into the air. As he neared the town centre, he met fellow villagers from the Lushi and Kelmendi families. They soon found themselves surrounded on all sides. The villagers now numbered about 200-250 people in all: men, women, and children. They were ordered to come out to the main road in the centre of town, near the cemetery.

The Serb forces were a motley group of men, unshaven and wearing mismatched fatigues. Two of the men ordered the villagers to divide into two groups, with the women and children on one side of the road and the men on the other. The groups reluctantly assembled, shuffling into place, terrified.

"Where is NATO now?" several of the armed men yelled. "Where is America?"

The villagers were ordered to throw down everything in their pockets. They tossed their money, cigarettes, and identity documents to the ground. The forces selected two children from the group to gather up the items, one to collect the money and another to gather the documents. As they spoke, the men made a show of firing their weapons into the air or at the feet of the villagers.

When the two children had finished gathering everything, one of the armed men grabbed a child by the hair, turned to the women, and threatened to cut the child's throat unless they threw everything they had to the ground. The women threw down their jewellery and everything else.

One of the armed men asked another how many male villagers they had gathered. The answer came back as more than forty.

"*Dobro*," he said. Good.


It was our second day and Mr. Kelmendi still hadn't had a chance to review his initial statement. But by 11:00 a.m. he still hadn't arrived. By sheer coincidence it was May 14, 2009 — the ten-year anniversary, to the day, of the Ćuška massacre. I'd been focused on the dates involved in the incident but was so lost in the routine of the trial that I hadn't made the connection until I was told by the Victim-Witness Office, who were taking care of Mr. Kelmendi during his stay in the Netherlands. There would be a memorial held in Ćuška today; the pain of that day ten years ago would be marked communally by the village. Mr. Kelmendi found himself in a hotel in an utterly foreign country, on this of all days.

I spent the rest of the morning in my office, catching up on other work and watching the clock. We were running out of time to prepare. I was growing increasingly worried that he wouldn't be able to testify.


As the villagers stood by, the Serb forces used an accelerant to ignite a nearby house. They ordered the women and children into the house's front yard, keeping them close as it burned. They were screaming in fear, unsure of what would come next.

Kelmendi looked on from about fifty metres away, now hiding behind a house as the forces began dividing the captive male villagers. Berisha watched as one of the senior soldiers pointed several of the officers towards a house behind him, then drew his hand across his throat. The armed men separated out twelve of the other captive men to form the first group. They took those men to a nearby house, which belonged to a villager named Syl Gashi.

The twelve captives were ordered into the empty house and stood up against the wall. One soldier pointed a machine gun mounted atop two legs at them. The others pointed normal machine guns. One of the men spoke into his walkie-talkie; there was an exchange of some sort. He stepped into the door, holding his machine gun, and announced that everyone would be shot. Then he opened fire.

At the announcement, and an instant before the shooting commenced, one of the captives — a man named Ibro Kelmendi — collapsed, falling on top of a man named Isa Gashi. The first round of firing thus missed Isa Gashi entirely. He lay on the ground, underneath the bodies of Ibro and his brother, pretending to be dead. After the first round of firing, the armed men moved through the fallen Albanians and continued shooting, making sure everyone was dead. When they'd finished, they pulled the stuffing out of a mattress, scattered it atop the bodies, and set it on fire. Isa Gashi was underneath the other bodies, shot in the leg but still alive. As the house burned, he struggled to his feet, then moved quickly to the window and jumped through.

From his hiding spot, Tahir Kelmendi watched the house burn.


When Mr. Kelmendi arrived I met his apology by reiterating our appreciation for his testimony. He was ready to proceed, he said. As he began to review his statement I sat quietly at his side.[5]

I would like, at this point, to describe the grief that I saw expressed by this man as a result of revisiting these events; to try to convey the very visible weight of what it meant to have to testify about them. Not to describe this in general terms — because I imagine it comes as no surprise to most people that grief can be a part of revisiting such memories — but to describe more directly what it looked like, and to explain what it was like to deal with this as part of the process. And yet it doesn't seem right, somehow, to write these details. What happens in the courtroom is by its nature public, and intended to be so. But the specific nature of someone's sadness, outside of court and yet still within the confines of the trial process, seems a different thing.

What I *can* describe is what I felt: that in this moment, in a very visceral way, I felt the divide between the detachment required of my professional role and a more basic impulse to comfort someone as a human being. I know that my few words sounded hollow — too formal and too tentative. I hoped, at least, that through the interpretation they might somehow seem more meaningful. I wanted to say that telling his story was the most he could do, and all he needed to do, and that maybe it would be worth the pain of revisiting these events in such detail, so far from home, on this of all days. I didn't, however. These things weren't for me to say, nor could I know if they were true.

We took a break. When we resumed, he was eager to press on.


Mr. Berisha could hear the gunshots from the first house as he waited amongst the other men gathered by the cemetery — first, loud bursts of automatic fire; then, single shots with space between them. The men standing around him went rigid. The armed men returned to their group, thick smoke and flames rising behind them. One of them drew his finger across his neck.

The armed men spoke amongst themselves. They took the watches off of the captive men's hands, making two piles — one for expensive watches, another for cheap. The richest person in the village was a man named Quash Lushi. The armed men told Lushi to bring them money, saying that if he did so they would spare his son. Lushi went to get the money, then returned and presented it to them. One of the men took the money and then led Lushi to an outhouse. He forced him inside and then the men opened fire, killing him instantly.

Srecko Popović, an apparent leader of the group, ordered the remaining captives to be divided into two. He directed Mr. Berisha's group towards the cemetery. He pointed the remaining men in the other direction.

There were twelve captives in Berisha's group, led by five armed soldiers and policemen. They were taken to the house of Sadik Gashi, then told to stop. They waited. One of the armed escorts announced, "Not here, there will be a stench," and urged them forward. Berisha thought they would be burned alive.

The captives were led to Sahik Gashi's house, the armed men firing their weapons in the air and at the ground as they walked. "Where is NATO now?" they taunted. "Where is Tony Blair?"

Berisha stood shoulder to shoulder with the other men as they were directed inside the house, forced into a small room containing two sofas, and ordered to sit down. Berisha was sitting at the corner. He knew the men sitting next to him — Arian Lushi on his left and Jusuf Shala to his right — Kosovo Albanians who had recently arrived in Ćuška from a neighbouring village. Four armed men stood at the entry to the room.

One man opened fire on Berisha's side of the room while another aimed towards the other side of the sofa. Looking straight on, Berisha could see the gunfire exploding from the barrels. Bullets tore through the gathered villagers and they collapsed downwards, almost in unison. Then the shooting stopped, the room suddenly silent. Berisha had not been hit. The pause didn't last long; moments later one of the men on the opposite side of the room opened fire again. This time bullets pierced Berisha's left leg and his right knee. When the firing stopped again, he found that he was still alive. The silence following the shooting was filled by the cries of his fellow villagers, several of whom were also still alive but riddled with bullets. The armed men moved through the bodies of the fallen Albanians to finish the job. They started on the left side. As they reached each man, Berisha could hear them firing a single bullet. They got as far as one or two men from Berisha and then stopped.


Both Kelmendi and Berisha would have precious little time in court to tell their stories. We would ask each of them to confirm that they had reviewed their statements, then ask whether those statements were accurate and whether they would testify to those same facts again. Assuming that these basic prerequisites were met, their statements would then be admitted directly into evidence — a convenience denied to prosecutors in Western legal systems, which with few exceptions exclude prior written accounts and require oral testimony to be given live in court.

Once their statements were admitted, we would only have about an hour for each witness, time we would use to highlight certain aspects of their evidence, flush out new details, or clarify anything confusing. Then the defence would have their turn to challenge the credibility and reliability of their evidence in cross-examination — likely challenging them on details or discrepancies with their statements or from other materials. The defence would also likely question whether they had any relationship to, involvement with, or knowledge of the KLA.

The ability to tender a witness's written statement directly into evidence makes sense, particularly in the context of such an enormous trial. It saves already limited court time and allows that time to be focused on what is likely to be in dispute. It doesn't prejudice the defence in any significant way because they are given free reign to cross-examine the witnesses on anything in their written statements, just as they could challenge anything said orally in court.

Given the scope of many international war crimes prosecutions, where the prosecutor is required to adduce evidence of a broad range of crimes committed on the ground, these small but significant tweaks of the rules of evidence have become essential to ensure that such trials don't collapse under their own weight. As I quickly discovered, however, the process of admitting statements directly into evidence sometimes presented an unexpected problem. For those who had travelled thousands of kilometres to tell their stories, who saw their accounts as representative of hundreds or thousands of other victims and who perceived their role as an ennobling and profoundly significant opportunity to tell their story to the world, the process of handing in a piece of paper and then only testifying live about a handful of potentially contentious but sometimes relatively obscure details could be alienating and confusing.

By the time Kelmendi and Berisha came to testify we had already seen these frustrations manifest themselves with other witnesses, despite our best efforts to explain the process beforehand. This was to be the first witness testimony in any courtroom addressing the Ćuška massacre. The responsibility of speaking on behalf of their village was clearly an important one for both men. It was clear that they would need the chance to tell the story of the massacre, as they observed it, and not merely confirm that they had described it previously in writing.

The day before they were expected to begin their testimonies — Berisha would be the first up, then Kelmendi — we took the men together to see the courtroom. We showed them where they would sit: in the single witness seat at the centre of the courtroom, directly facing the three judges who would hear their accounts. We showed them where the prosecutors would be sitting and the podium from which we would be asking our questions. Then we pointed to where the accused would be sitting when he was brought into court from the detention unit. We showed them the microphone that would amplify their voices and the headphones they would wear to receive live translation into Albanian. We pointed out the courtroom cameras and the video booth, and then watched as they studied the large gallery, now just row upon row of empty chairs.

We hoped that seeing the courtroom ahead of time would help to put them at ease. But it was difficult to tell.

Hazir Berisha cut a different figure from Mr. Kelmendi in the courtroom. He was quieter, more cautious, restrained. He told his story in short, clear sentences, though like Kelmendi he came directly to the point. Mr. Berisha did not need to be asked why the men had stopped shooting, or why he survived. It was something that had clearly weighed on him over the years, the sort of event about which very much could be said, or very little.

"I don't know the reason why they stopped," he said simply on the witness stand. "Maybe they ran out of bullets."[6]

With their firing squad execution over, the armed men had gone back outside. Berisha had survived. He described the situation he found himself in:

> I tried to open my eyes a little bit and have a look around in the room where I was. And on my left I saw them piled on top of each other, and I saw blankets on the upper part of the room to my left. I touched Arian Lushi. He was dead. I tried to move him. He wasn't moving. Jusuf Shala who was to my right was also dead. I was thinking of getting up. They were covered with sponge. I was thinking of getting up when I saw them piled like that, but in split of a second I decided to look through the window. The window was behind me, and instinctively I turned my head and saw five of them talking among each other. One of them broke away from that group and walked into the corridor of the house. He had kind of a bottle or something in his canister, a longish shape, and threw it in.[7]

The Serb forces had scattered a spongy material atop the bodies — likely the stuffing from a mattress — and then tossed in a canistered accelerant to burn the bodies and dispose of the evidence. Berisha found himself catching fire along with the bodies of his friends and fellow villagers, trapped in a room quickly filling with thick smoke. The men who had just shot him were still standing outside:

I started to catch fire very fast. The fire caught my face, and at that time I was — I didn't know where I was, whether on the ground or floating. For a moment I couldn't see anything. I thought I was buried deep in the ground. I was trying to stand on my foot. I couldn't, but I guess God helped me. I came next to the door. To tell you the truth, I tried to stand up not to survive that execution but to be killed by a bullet and not be burnt alive.[8]

Berisha had dragged himself to the door, where he could breathe again and where he could see. The men were gone now, though he didn't know where. Shot in both legs, Berisha leaned on the left leg and managed to move himself into the other room. He looked back and saw that the room where he had been, the room with the bodies of his fallen friends and neighbours, was now engulfed in flames.

Standing at the window, he couldn't see any of the armed men outside. He didn't have much choice and there wasn't much time. He pushed the window open, took his broken right leg in his hands, and used his left leg to push himself up through the window and outside. He landed in a heap and crawled to the corner of the house, where he lay on his back and listened to the events continuing in the village. He fastened his right leg with his belt, then tried to stem the flow of blood from his left leg. He waited and he listened.

The eight men in the final group were taken to a third house, this one belonging to Deme Gashi. The Serb forces directed the men inside, where they stood together. This time the armed men gave a lighter to one of the villagers — a man named Rexhe Isuf Kelmendi — and ordered him to burn the house down while they stood inside. As he bent down to light one of the curtains on fire, the men began shooting. In the hail of gunfire, and through the flames, Rexhe Isuf jumped through the window.

Tahir Kelmendi watched from about fifty metres away, lying on the ground.

When he was found later, after the events, Rexhe Isuf could scarcely speak. "What happened to us?" he said to a returning villager who had managed to escape into the hills. "What happened to us?"

Three houses, each full of Albanian fathers, grandfathers, brothers, and sons, shot and killed, then burned to destroy the evidence. And yet, for each of the three killing houses of Ćuška, one man had somehow survived. Some would call that a miracle. Some would point to the incredible strength of the human will to survive. Equally possible, however, is that the survival of these three men reflected the indifference of the executioners to the plight of their victims.

Over the course of the trial, we would hear a number of incredible stories of survival. From the time that Kelmendi and Berisha testified, I began to wonder about the weight of the guilt, pain, and relentless self-reflection that must come with the awareness that you survived while so many of your friends and relatives did not. I never asked either of them about it. What could one possibly say?

Mr. Berisha seemed to come across on the witness stand much as he did in person: a sincere, soft-spoken man who wanted to explain simply what had happened to him, without drama or embellishment.

Mr. Kelmendi stood through most of his testimony, holding his headphones in place with one hand as they sat awkwardly atop his qeleshe, speaking in a booming voice. Mr. Kelmendi's cross-examination was lengthy; at times he seemed angry when pushed by the defence. His anger was hardly surprising — it is one thing to know and understand objectively that defence counsel are playing a role within the criminal trial process (something I always try to explain), and quite another to remain calm and dispassionate when the obvious implication underlying the questioning is the denial or minimization of an unimaginable tragedy that you experienced first-hand. I do not envy the defence such cross-examinations.

In the end, some of his answers raised questions about how much he himself knew, or was prepared to acknowledge, about the activities of the KLA throughout the war. But the core of his evidence, with respect to the events in Ćuška, was unshaken.[9]

Satisfied that the killing was done, the executioners ordered the women and children out of the village, to be deported from Kosovo as part of the larger strategy of "cleansing" the territory of Albanians. The women and children were loaded onto tractors and escorted away by the Serb forces. Mr. Kelmendi's wife and two daughters were among them.

The Serb forces moved on from Ćuška to the nearby towns of Zahac and Pavljan, where they committed further killings.

Once the armed men were gone, Kelmendi emerged from hiding, as did the survivors. Some of the villagers who had escaped began to return, surveying the aftermath of their destroyed village. They began to gather the bodies of the men who had been executed, wrapping them crudely and then burying them together in a large grave. They sought to hide the bodies from the Serbian police, who they suspected would return. The villagers believed that the police wanted to cover up the evidence of their actions, and that they would seek to remove or destroy any evidence they could.

Days later, several Serb men returned to Ćuška in black Mercedes cars, asking about the whereabouts of the bodies.


When the Ćuška eyewitness testimony was complete, I joined Mr. Kelmendi in a small debriefing room, the air thick with cigarette smoke. Everyone from Kosovo smokes, or so it seemed at the Tribunal, where the stress of testifying all but guaranteed that our post-testimony meetings were held in smoke-filled rooms and that my robes always carried a faint odour of cigarettes. Mr. Kelmendi was relaxed now, and tired. For the first time since I'd met him, he was sitting back in his chair.

I went through the usual steps of debriefing — discussing his testimony in general terms, answering questions about the process, thanking him for the efforts he went through to testify. He thanked me in turn, an element of formality in our exchange, though the gratitude seemed deeply sincere and rather touching. We shook hands and said goodbye. Then he was led away by someone from the Victim-Witness unit, to be taken back to his hotel and then to the airport, where he would board a flight back to Kosovo.

# THE STORIES WE TELL

|

## The Stories We Tell

The international criminal trial begins when everything else has failed. A country has committed mass killings, rapes, deportations, genocide. The international community has failed to intervene quickly enough. The country in which the acts were committed has refused to bring the perpetrators to justice and in most cases has refused to acknowledge that what happened was wrong.

The trial process inserts itself into this space to identify what took place and to hold the perpetrators accountable. It is these two functions — truth finding and punishment — that draw the explicit focus of the legal system. The rather narrow focus of the trial, from a legal standpoint, is to determine whether the accused can be proven responsible for the crimes alleged. But there is a deeper level of meaning that unfolds in these prosecutions, which in many ways feels more important. This involves the identification of injustices through the telling of stories about what happened.

The international criminal justice system can hold specific individuals accountable for the acts they committed, punish them, and hopefully deter others from committing similar acts in the future. This we know. But it can also empower victims by giving them the opportunity to convey the injustices that were committed against them. Through these human accounts it can acknowledge and promote a broader understanding of the truth and an appreciation for the gravity of what took place. By exposing what happened it can provide a powerful corrective for the society that perpetrated the crimes — if they are willing to listen — and help to rewrite the narratives that led to the violence. It can even provide lessons to the rest of the world about the origins and nature of such violence, and how easily we can end up in this place.

To have this potential is one thing. To reach it is another.

## II

## Victims, Testimony, and the Trial Process

War crimes trials see victims and witnesses travel thousands of miles to recount the stories of the most devastating moments of their lives. They do so, in many cases, because they have survived and feel a responsibility to speak for those family members, friends, and fellow villagers who did not. They often find themselves speaking on behalf of the living as well — the others who lost their own relatives and friends, or who had similar experiences but may not themselves have a chance to speak out.

Testifying can be a highly varied experience. In the right context, it can give a voice to experiences of suffering and loss and at the same time convey the simple but vitally important message that the acts suffered were wrong — that they were transgressions of acceptable human behaviour. It is one thing — and still certainly a valuable one — to tell these stories of suffering, loss, and injustice in the course of ordinary life. It is another to tell them in the official setting of a courtroom, with the understanding that the events will be judged. For an international prosecution, the perception that the rest of the world is listening and can denounce what took place can be particularly meaningful. To have the person or people accused of orchestrating these acts sitting in the courtroom and forced to listen can add an even more powerful dimension, particularly where these perpetrators were functioning within a bureaucracy that shielded them from the humanity of their victims.

But the experience of testifying can, and often does, take a tremendous mental and emotional toll on witnesses. For victims who have endured such traumatic events, the memories often cast large and enduring shadows over their lives. The awareness that such suffering and loss was willfully caused by acts of human cruelty — the callous acts of others — can trigger a broad range of emotions: rage, despair, frustration, and hopelessness, to name just a few.

Testifying at the ICTY begins with the witness sitting in a closed room, an antechamber of sorts, waiting to be brought into the courtroom. Not knowing when the witness ahead of you will finish testifying — and this is virtually impossible to predict — means being left to ruminate on what you might be asked, what you plan to say, and how's it's all going to feel.[1]

Inside the courtroom, it's not uncommon for witnesses to break down. There can never be enough court breaks, or glasses of water, or tissues handed over by the court clerk, to provide any real measure of comfort through the experience. Witnesses can be supported through the process by an attentive and well-trained Victim-Witness staff, but when witnesses are on the stand they are very much on their own.

The cross-examination process tends to be particularly gruelling. It is hard enough to recount and relive the traumatic events you experienced when you testify in chief. But cross-examination means being openly and directly challenged on your account. Instead of being permitted to tell your story in your own way — difficult enough — cross-examination often intentionally breaks down any attempts at narrative cohesion and tries to sow confusion instead. Cross-examination can bring surprises, like being confronted with unexpected documents, photographs, or allegations, and having to respond in the moment. All of this, of course, is being conducted in support of the alleged perpetrator, sitting and watching mere feet away.

This is to speak only of the events inside the courtroom. Certain crimes, such as sexual assault, carry a terrible stigma for victims in many communities that can last far beyond the court proceedings. For witnesses who have to return to communities where the victims are still living alongside the perpetrators, testifying can be flat-out dangerous.

Re-awakening these memories, and requiring witnesses to relive them, is not something to be done lightly. But proving these cases requires witnesses to testify; the case *needs* them. Knowing that testifying may be traumatic — and worse, not knowing whether the witness will feel it was worth this trauma in the end — is one of the hardest things about being a prosecutor. This is true of any criminal prosecution; there were moments as a domestic prosecutor when I realized — too late, invariably — that the trauma of testifying had outweighed any possible benefit from the process. But in the case of war crimes trials, where the witnesses had so often suffered staggering devastation and loss, the experience could seem qualitatively different. The sheer weight of the events, and the strangeness of this foreign process, often made it something other.

Although witnesses were usually visibly relieved after they finished testifying, sometimes even elated, you could never assume that their longer-term reactions to the process were so positive. Some of the witnesses who had testified before told us as much, describing a rush of relief when they finished testifying for the first time and then an intense struggle with the reawakened memories in the months that followed — old wounds reopened, feeling themselves plunged once again into a more immediate state of sadness or despair.

This was to say nothing of those witnesses who faced particularly gruelling cross-examinations — witnesses to whom it was suggested, or outright declared, that the events that tore their lives apart had never happened at all. To face down such accusations and refute them could be redeeming, certainly, but to feel that you hadn't fared well, that you were confused, or that you were made to seem untruthful, could be deeply wounding — all the more so if you felt you had been there to speak not just for yourself but for an entire community.

In the end, of course, there also remained the very real possibility that the court might simply acquit the accused entirely.


III

## The Curious Theatre of the Courtroom

We often speak of bearing witness in the language of duty — both to the memory of events and to those who suffered. To strive for justice is to seek not only to punish but to declare that this is not the way things should be.[2]

Whether the legal system expressly recognizes it, and whether its day-to-day procedures indulge it, conducting international criminal trials means bearing the weight of broader expectations: to listen, to memorialize, and to denounce. The need for punishment is part of this, certainly — it's hard to imagine fulfilling any of these goals with the perpetrators walking out of the courtroom with the same impunity they walked in with. But the airing of the events that took place, in this context of judgment, is a crucial part of our hopes and expectations for the process.

The courtroom is a strangely sterile environment. The mood is invariably sombre, the air somehow heavy. Though we seldom speak of it, the look and atmosphere of every courtroom has a function. It conveys a sense of consequence, an impression that what happens inside is both official and purposive. It says that this is not mere pageantry or pantomime, that what happens here is consequential. This atmosphere is important to send the message, implicit but absolutely necessary, that the court has the authority to do what it does. Because if nobody believes that these courts have real authority, or that the words and pronouncements voiced there have real meaning, then they do not.

Those who play official roles in the courtroom tend to speak in halting, measured tones, and to carry themselves in a particular manner. You're never really taught this — how to pace your speech, frame your words, move slowly and purposefully — and I doubt that many lawyers have ever thought to inventory a checklist of essential mannerisms. It just happens. It happens the same way, I imagine, that TV reporters learn to speak in the halting cadence of TV news. It's how the role is supposed to sound.

This doesn't mean that the participants in criminal cases — the witnesses and accused persons it exists for — know to act and speak this way. They often address the court in the same casual manner that they, and the rest of the world, use in everyday life. But to hear a lawyer or judge speak in an everyday, nonchalant manner inside the courtroom would be jarring — the clear mark of an outsider.

Whether we intend it or not, the theatre of the courtroom — this curious pageantry of people in costumes, playing assigned roles, speaking in the only-for-court dialect of lawyer-speak, serves the purpose of reinforcing that the events in this room are official and that they matter.

The rigid structure of the courtroom also serves to reorder the chaos of the actual events being prosecuted. From the public gallery the Tribunal courtroom looks like a fishbowl, the space filled by robed lawyers and judges in assigned seats, everyone flanked by computer screens, wearing headphones, referring to binders. They take turns speaking — always addressing the court, never each other. The contrast between the slow and methodical procedures here and the chaos and surreality of the events being judged was seldom lost on the witnesses. Perpetrators who took the witness stand would often try to convey how different the circumstances were when the killings were committed — that those were times of upheaval, chaos, disruption; that murder was everywhere; that there wasn't time for sober thought or calculated reflection; that this was just how it was.

The careful and reasoned after-the-fact judgment of the courtroom, however, is precisely the point. In court, the events and allegations are laid bare, carefully — if laboriously — measured, and *then* judged. To recount the facts of what happened in this context is to purposefully situate them in a new and redefined structure. To judge, and perhaps punish, is to recast what happened and to reimpose some notion of balance. It is not to reverse the harm, which cannot be undone, but to seemingly restore the sense of order that was violated when the crimes were committed.

At the same time, however, the repackaging of these emotional events into the rigid procedures of the courtroom can undermine the impact and the very meaning of the proceedings. International criminal trials, at their core, are procedure-obsessed, heavily bureaucratic, and difficult to follow. The operations of the courtroom can often be dense, obscure, or flat-out incomprehensible, both to the witnesses who come to tell their stories and to the members of the public who watch and read about the proceedings.

The formal needs of the process — the baseline requirements of proof, relevance, and efficiency — would often clash with the ability of witnesses to tell the stories they wanted to tell. The focus of the adversarial criminal trial is proof: the prosecution files a comprehensive indictment setting out exactly what it will seek to prove, then goes about calling evidence to prove these points. This is the central, driving aim of the trial process and the focus of the prosecution, defence, and judiciary. What this means in practice is that the most relevant aspects of a witness's testimony in terms of proving the case are not necessarily the personal details of the tragedies they experienced.

It may not actually be contentious at trial, for example, that the killings being prosecuted took place. The defence can, and sometimes will, admit that people were massacred. What is more often at issue, and more difficult to prove, is *who* did the killing, and at whose direction. Witnesses who came to The Hague to testify about the murders of their family members or friends in Kosovo not infrequently found themselves spending much of their already very limited time answering questions that seemed unrelated to the killings. The colour of uniforms that various forces were wearing was a seemingly endless source of questions and disputes. Blue could mean police — but was it the blue camouflage worn by special police units or was it the blue worn by the regular officers? Were all of them or some of them wearing masks? Were they talking on radios? Were they wearing green, suggesting they were military, or might they have been members of paramilitary units?

The greatest evidentiary challenges in the Kosovo cases, as with most war crimes prosecutions of high-level offenders, tended to lie with the linkage evidence: establishing that the police, military, or political leaders stationed far away were aware of and directing what was happening. This meant that a significant portion of the prosecution case was invariably spent adducing, verifying, and confirming documentary evidence. It meant spending significant portions of valuable court time with insider witnesses to explain basic questions like how orders were issued or how the bureaucracy functioned. With victims and eyewitnesses who had been on the ground during military or police operations, it often meant trying to match up the places they remembered seeing armoured equipment and personnel with deployment orders that had been issued by the accused. Establishing that a tank was on a particular hill, on a particular day, could be highly significant if it allowed the prosecution to corroborate or distinguish that a particular accused had directed an operation.

These details could prompt more questions and consume more court time than the killings themselves. Even where witnesses grasped why such questions might be important — and we could not specifically explain this to them, because prosecutors are rightly proscribed from tainting or otherwise affecting a witness's testimony — these were not the things they thought they had come to describe. A number of these witnesses, in the debriefings following their testimony, expressed surprise and confusion about the number of questions that seemed utterly unrelated to what was important.

In an adversarial trial, the evidence called is in large part dictated by what the defendants admit to and what they challenge. In war crimes cases where the evidence that the events happened is overwhelming but the evidence *linking* those atrocities to the accused is more tenuous, it may well be a prudent strategy for the defence to simply admit that the crimes took place but dispute whether their client was aware of them and exercised control over what was unfolding. It is entirely possible, in other words, that in certain cases there would be little need for victim and eyewitness testimony at all. This did not happen in the Kosovo cases. But one could certainly question whether such a strategy might have benefitted some of the defendants.

There were, nonetheless, times in the trials at the ICTY when even an outsider could viscerally feel a sense of deeper meaning and purpose consonant with the weight and impact of the events: during the opening statements, when the allegations and evidence were painted in broad strokes; through segments of particularly moving and impactful eyewitness testimony; in those rare moments that an accused took the stand to testify and could be confronted directly; when the evidence was summarized into powerful and persuasive closing arguments; when a final judgment was pronounced.


Historically, the reliance on individual testimony from witnesses and survivors, as opposed to documentary evidence, has exerted a significant influence on the impact and legacy of international criminal trials. It bears keeping the historical perspective in mind.

Among the best examples, in a surprising way, were the Nuremberg Trials that saw the Nazis prosecuted for war crimes in the aftermath of World War II. Although "Nuremberg" tends to conjure images for many of stirring eyewitness testimony, exposing the inhumanity of the Holocaust, the central Nuremberg case relied primarily on documentary evidence — and was therefore not a particularly emotional, personal, or moving event. Part of a deliberate strategy pursued by the American chief prosecutor, Robert H. Jackson, the evidence focused on Nazi records, speeches, orders, and propaganda.[3] The aim was to convincingly show, based on the regime's own words and documents, that Nazi crimes were intentional and indisputable. The prosecution at Nuremberg called only thirty-three witnesses, as opposed to the eighty called by the defence,[4] and focused largely on crimes of war and aggression. Although Nuremberg left an important legal legacy, which would be taken up in earnest in the 1990s, the relative absence of personal eyewitness testimony meant that the proceedings never really communicated the immense human tragedy of the Holocaust.[5]

It is not a coincidence that a broader societal appreciation for the shocking inhumanity of the Holocaust didn't really percolate into the collective consciousness until the 1960s, when people began to speak more openly about what had taken place. The prosecution's case in the Adolf Eichmann trial, which captivated much of the world when it was conducted in Israel in 1961, was built chiefly from personal and moving eyewitness testimony. The trial of Mr. Eichmann, who was responsible for orchestrating the mass deportation of Jews to the extermination camps, was opened with a rather dramatic pronouncement from Israeli prosecutor Gideon Hausner: "As I stand here before you, Judges of Israel, to lead the prosecution of Adolf Eichmann, I do not stand alone. With me in this place and at this hour stand six million accusers."[6]

Hausner's opening set the stage for the personal and very human focus of the case to come. The one hundred representative eyewitnesses called by the prosecution, many of them survivors of the death camps, provided personal accounts of their experiences that were chilling and often emotionally charged. The trial had a significant and lasting impact on the collective consciousness.[7]

Two years later, in a case tried in Germany under ordinary German law, the Frankfurt Auschwitz Trial saw twenty-two defendants tried for murder for their roles at the Auschwitz death camp. Like the Israeli prosecution of Eichmann, the Auschwitz trial relied chiefly on live witness testimony, hearing evidence from over 350 witnesses. The testimony of the survivors was powerful, shocking, and often emotional, painting a vivid portrait of the inhumanity and cruelty of the camps.[8] The trial received extensive press coverage and forced the German populace to confront the brutality of the Holocaust, sparking discussions about the "inner resistance" ordinary Germans felt towards the acts their country had perpetrated.[9] The year after the trial concluded, Peter Weiss wrote the play *The Investigation*, which was fashioned entirely from portions of verbatim witness testimony and exchanges from the trial.[10] It made for powerful theatre.

An international criminal trial of course is not theatre. It is not for show and it is not designed to entertain. It is not a platform for preaching or sensationalist speech making and it is not television. The adversarial trial *is* a contest of sorts, in which the aim of the prosecution is to establish the guilt and responsibility of the accused. But the *law* is the set of rules, procedures, and customs that strictly govern how this process can and cannot be responsibly conducted. These rules balance the probity of any piece of evidence — oral testimony or physical exhibit — against its potential to prejudice, distort, or mislead the search for truth. They control who speaks when, and what can and cannot be said.

War crimes trials are real and they are consequential. Whether we like to acknowledge it or not, however, they also compete in the broader world of narrative and storytelling. These trials must necessarily answer to two taskmasters. On one hand, they must enable a meaningful human process, giving voice to the gravity of what unfolded. On the other hand, they must meet the needs of impartiality, rationality, and fairness. Striking balances between opposing interests is exactly what courts have always strived to do. This is a line that must be walked every day.

But there is a certain audacity in prosecuting the ethnic cleansing of a country — the organized murder of thousands, the displacement and deportation of entire cities and towns, the destruction of families and communities, trauma sustained across multiple generations. We take this and hand it to a small group of role-players assigned to act as prosecutors, defence lawyers, and judges; we try to convince or compel victims, witnesses, and even co-perpetrators to describe what happened; we tender documents into evidence, we make legal arguments, and then we purport to arrive at a final, definitive determination of what took place. Will people accept that this process, and the determination that comes out at the end of it, is official, legitimate, and sufficient?

If one man charged with one murder is convicted of that crime, the consequences are clear and direct: he goes to jail for life and society has condemned his actions. Where what is at stake is so much larger, however — when it is about thousands or even hundreds of thousands of people, victims and perpetrators alike, in the context of a conflict where people were divided by nationality or ethnicity — it can seem to be about much more than the fate of the person who stands accused. In these circumstances, such trials tend to become both symbolic and broadly representative, with the judgment of history seeming to hang in the balance.

# 6

# DISAPPEARING GRAVES: THE IZBICA MASSACRE

## I

## The Importance of Images

The video had the look of a home movie — grainy and unedited, one set of images abruptly ending and replaced by another.[1] A date is inscribed in the bottom corner of the screen: 31 March 1999. Men standing in a store with what looked like a body wrapped in a blanket, lifting and carrying it into a scene of destroyed houses, still smouldering fires, dead livestock rotting in the yard. A baby's cradle abandoned at the side of the road.

At the six-minute mark there are ethnic Albanian men digging graves, row upon row. A jump cut and we're somewhere else, piles of dead bodies lying crumpled on green grass. They are elderly men, recently killed, arrayed along a line. Dozens of men lumped unnaturally together, lying on their backs and sides, walking sticks and crutches strewn about them. Close-ups show heads still intact but with entire faces replaced by large gaping holes — clear indications of close-range gunshots to the face and head. Other bodies are lying in and around the undergrowth. Handwritten notes on little pieces of paper have been placed on some of their chests.

Then men digging graves again. Traditional ethnic Albanian garb. Exhausted. Some work, some sit, some stand and stare. One man seems to break down, he is yelling. Some of the other men surround him. Somewhere else an elderly man is talking to the camera from the bottom of a small hill. His gestures are wild; he's distraught. He starts to crawl.

A new date visible in the corner: 1 April 1999. Burned houses and dead animals. Now 9 April 1999. Men drinking tea, shots of a ruined village, household items strewn across a meadow. Another elderly man talking to the camera, recounting a story in Albanian. More men speaking to the camera. Then a funeral ceremony.

My first direct look at mass killings in Kosovo came with this video footage, shot in the municipality of Skenderaj in the immediate aftermath of what became known as the Izbica massacre.

The footage was captured by a man named Liri Loshi, who managed to sneak a tape out of the country while the war was still raging. One of my first tasks was to review and organize this footage, matching it to other evidence in the Đorđević case. I was given the coded electronic evidence numbers and after a couple of failed attempts to navigate the system I was able to pull the videos up and start watching them at my desk. From my work as a prosecutor in Canada I was used to seeing and dealing with the aftermath of violence, but the scale of this, the rawness of it, was something else altogether.

As was often the reality in a case that advanced rapidly and gave little time for context, when I started working with the video I was still learning about the events in Izbica. The video would be the centrepiece of our evidence of the Izbica massacre, raw corroboration that would tie together the eyewitness testimony of several men and of Loshi himself.

II

## "You know what you have to do"

Liri Loshi was a doctor. After a Serbian police offensive the previous year had burned his house in Padalishte to the ground, he relocated to the town of Leqina, joined a local medical team, and began travelling around the area treating patients. He moved his wife and three children out of the area.

Loshi also joined the KLA and was issued a firearm and a uniform. As the only doctor in the area he didn't see combat; instead, he spent his time travelling and treating sick or injured civilians and soldiers. When he had the time he did occasional volunteer reporting for Kosova Radio and Television, which had relocated to Albania, issuing bulletins from his cell phone.

On March 26, 1999, Serb forces were advancing rapidly across northwestern Kosovo. As they pushed through, Albanian villagers began flooding into the small town of Izbica from surrounding villages — Leqina, Vojnik, Gllareve, Jashanice, Likoc, Tejice, Kline, Kopiliq, Rakitnica, and Turiqevc, to name just a few. Loshi followed them, setting up in Izbica.

Fifty-two-year-old Milazim Thaqi, who lived in the nearby village of Broje with his wife and five children, also abandoned his home that day. He loaded the entire family onto his tractor and then climbed aboard himself. They pulled out onto the road, joining the rest of the village that was already massing, an exodus rolling slowly to Izbica. They had heard it would be safer there.

When Thaqi arrived in Izbica, he found thousands of other villagers gathered in a valley. Tucked between two hills, it seemed safe from the shelling. There were men, women, and children camped there in a large field near the centre of the village — some milling around, some sitting or lying on the grass, others trying to sleep on their tractors.

From the field it was impossible to see what was happening in the surrounding villages. But Thaqi could hear ominous noises, the creak and grind of heavy machinery. Tanks, he figured, and lorries. He and his family were among the lucky ones that first night, finding space inside someone's house. Some of the other villagers were telling troubling stories of Serbian actions in the surrounding villages.

On the morning of March 27, a rainy Saturday, the people clustered in Izbica decided it would be safest to gather outside. Thousands of people — Thaqi guessed there were ten to twelve thousand but couldn't be sure — came together in the open field and waited, huddling in the rain. The Serbian forces seemed to be on the outskirts of the village.

That night, as the forces drew closer, most people decided to leave. Thousands streamed out of the town, a mass of tractors, cars, and villagers, now heading to Tushile. Almost all of the younger men in the village left that night, heading for the mountains — fearing for their safety, surely, but perhaps also to gather with the KLA.[2]

Thaqi's sixteen-year-old son decided to leave as well. Thaqi tried to convince him to stay, thinking they would be safer together, reluctant to see his son go. But his son persisted. He eventually left with the others.

Thaqi and the rest of his family found themselves in the field with hundreds of women and children. The young and able-bodied men had fled but a number of elderly and disabled men had stayed behind — the journey to get there had been difficult enough. The men, women, and children who remained spent an uneasy night, waiting to see what the morning would bring.

The next day, shortly after Thaqi and his family had finished breakfast, they saw three Serbian policemen walking towards them in the field. The men lit a nearby pear tree on fire, then strode directly up to the gathered group. They demanded money to keep the town's houses and tractors safe. Thaqi had thirty Deutschmarks on him, which he handed over.

Only minutes later — so suddenly that Thaqi felt they had "cropped out from [the] earth" — a group of eighty-odd uniformed policemen and soldiers appeared in the field, armed with machine guns, grenades, and knives. Some wore scarves on their heads.

The men began taunting them. "Where is America?" they asked. "Where is Clinton?" They cursed Albanian leaders Ibrahim Rugova and Hashim Thaqi, then made the men remove their traditional hats. Wading into the group, several policemen pulled the men out, standing them apart from the women and children. Then they demanded that the women and children raise their thumb, index, and middle fingers in the air — a symbol that had come to connote Serbian identity. As the gathered men stood by, the Serbian forces told the women and children they were being sent to Albania. They sent them marching down the road, in the direction of the border.

As the women and children trudged into the distance, growing ever-smaller, about 160 disabled and elderly men stood rooted in the field, surrounded. The men, who ranged from around forty-five to eighty-six years old, were ordered to sit together in groups of four. As they waited, one of the armed men, who seemed to be in charge, addressed his colleagues.

"You know what you have to do," he said. "Let's start immediately."

The armed men separated the remaining ethnic Albanians into three groups. Thaqi found himself in the first group, along with about thirty-two other men. A single man, clad in a green uniform and carrying a large machine gun, directed them to walk two-by-two, up towards the mountain. They followed, straining with the effort, some of them leaning on canes and walking sticks as they were marched along the mountainside and by a creek. Abruptly, the armed man told them to stop — he spoke Serbian but they understood well enough. He told them to turn left, then he ordered them to kneel. The men obeyed, turning and facing the mountain and the creek, struggling to bend to the ground. Before they reached their knees the man opened fire. The bullets came in bursts. Thaqi fell immediately to the ground, with two bodies falling on top of him.

As the automatic fire rained over top of him, Thaqi lay prostrate underneath the bodies of two men he knew: Uke Uka Thaqi, who had been shot in the head, and Isuf Zezeqe Shala. He tried to stay completely still. He could hear the shooter talking to himself: "This one's still breathing," the man said. Thaqi thought he was referring to him. He stayed still. Then he heard a pistol shot, fired at someone else.

As Thaqi lay there, he heard the sounds of more shooting nearby. Then silence, then more shooting — from what he estimated was only twenty metres away. He lay there for what he thought was about forty minutes, until he felt it would be safe to move. The shooter was gone, and as he stood up he saw that two other men from his group, Sheqir Kotorri and Jetish Qallapeki, had also survived. The three of them crawled along the ground until they heard the Serb forces depart en masse. Then they fled into the mountains.

III

# Survival

Whereas Thaqi's group had been marched up towards the mountain, Mustafa Dragaj's group — maybe sixty to seventy men — was marched in the direction of the woods. When they neared the trees they were told to stop. As Mustafa described it: "And then they said to us, 'Turn in this direction,' and as soon as [we] turned, they opened gun-fire. Hajriz … was immediately caught by a bullet. He fell over me."[3]

He lay underneath Hajriz for about twenty minutes, not sure if it was safe to move. When he finally looked up, trying to survey the scene, he heard a voice calling to him from the woods. Musli Hajra was yelling at him to take shelter, saying that the Serb forces were in the village burning the houses down.

As Mustafa struggled out from underneath Hajriz, he realized the man was still alive. In a weak voice, Hajriz asked Mustafa for water. But he had none to give and there was none nearby. Mustafa crawled out into the woods, then turned and looked back. The bodies of the men he had been marched with lay piled in the field.

He had known many of these men, and would later name each of them in court. There were also men he had not known, to his regret, and some he feared he had forgotten. Hajriz Dragaj, who it seemed had taken the bullets that would otherwise have hit him, died from his wounds shortly thereafter.

Sadik Januzi's group was walked up the hill in two rows, the soldiers marching in behind and pushing the old men in the backs with their machine guns to hurry them up. In the midst of their walk, one of the soldiers told them to stop. As they stood waiting, some of the men turned to look and were told to turn back around. Then someone yelled "Fire!" and the soldiers began shooting, an execution squad standing three to four metres away. The men around Sadik collapsed together; he fell along with them, though he wasn't hit. He landed front-first and three men fell on top of him. He lay still as the soldiers moved quickly through the fallen bodies, looking for anyone alive and finishing them off with pistols. Then they left.

Januzi lay there for scarcely a minute before pulling himself along the ground to the woods. In the cover of the trees he sat down, pulled out his cigarettes, and tried to smoke. Then he saw a number of survivors emerging — some of them wounded, some unscathed.

IV

# The Evidence

Liri Loshi had gotten out of Izbica before the Serb forces rolled in, leaving for Tushile at around 4:00 a.m. When villagers began arriving from Izbica the next day, however, there was talk of a massacre. It sounded bad but was difficult to confirm — several of the women who had stayed behind said the men among them had been forced to stay. The women had heard gunshots as they were walking away but they hadn't dared to turn back.

On March 30, Loshi travelled back to Izbica to see for himself. When he arrived in town he headed out to the field, where he saw the bodies of men piled in the wet grass:

> When I returned to Izbica, I saw the bodies lying at the place where they were executed. I stayed there for a very short time. It was dark, but I could see that my fears came true, that there was a large number of people, which had been calculated as about a hundred or over a hundred, that had been killed.[4]

As he stood looking at the crumpled bodies, he realized he needed to get the evidence of what was unfolding to the outside world. He didn't have a camera but he asked around in the surrounding villages. He was put in touch with a local teacher named Sefedin Thaqi, who had hidden a camera and other valuables by burying them in a hole. When Loshi explained what he wanted to do, Thaqi dug the camera out of the earth and the two of them set out to the two fields where the bodies were lying.

Loshi directed and Thaqi filmed, wide shots revealing the number of people who had been killed, close-ups showing their injuries. The victims were almost all elderly, their canes and walking sticks lying alongside them in the grass. They had large wounds, suggesting they had been shot at close range. In the eastern field some of Loshi's own relatives were amongst the dead. Three generations of his family — a father, Selman, in his eighties; son, Jashar, about fifty-five; grandson,

Sami, about twenty-five — were killed together. They found the body of an eighty-year-old woman burnt alive in a tractor. Loshi decided not to film her, but the image stuck with him.

The two men continued to film as the villagers — survivors Mustafa Dragaj and Milazim Thaqi among them — gathered to bury the bodies. They were nervous, unsure if the Serb forces might return. Relatives identified the bodies wherever they could; where no relatives could be found, the villagers asked friends or acquaintances. The last person to be identified was a deaf man, no more than thirty.

With little time for ceremony, the villagers began digging shallow graves. The bodies were brought over from the massacre sites, though they were already starting to decompose and were difficult to carry. They were placed in the earth, the improvised graves marked by wooden planks bearing names and, if known, dates of birth. A quickly improvised burial council made a list of who was buried where. These were not proper burials, as Mustafa Dragaj later explained, but with the Serbian forces still in the area there simply wasn't time. The hope was that after the war, families could return to the village to give their loved ones a proper burial. The villagers buried about 135 bodies. It took two days.

Loshi filmed Milazim Thaqi telling the story of what had happened to him. The video is hard to watch. Thaqi, clearly still distraught, demonstrates how the men were marched, how they were shot, how he survived, and how he crawled along the ground and escaped.[5]

Video evidence of mass killings in Kosovo was rare and Loshi knew it. This was 1999 — the camera phone had not yet been invented, personal video cameras were not as ubiquitous as they would soon become, and none of this technology was widespread in Kosovo. The United Nations, the international media, and local human rights organizations had largely pulled out of Kosovo when the war began, taking their cameras with them. Few of the villagers who were targeted owned cameras and even fewer dared to risk using them. Traumatized refugees were already pouring out of Kosovo and into refugee camps along the borders; the world was aware that a crisis was unfolding. But there had been surprisingly little visual evidence to support the personal accounts of what was happening. Both NATO and the Serbian government were well aware of the potential impact such evidence could have.

The problem for Loshi was how to get the videotape out of the country so the world could see it. Sefedin Thaqi had decided to join the convoys and flee to Albania. Before he left he had plugged his camera into a generator — electrical power was hard to come by — and transferred the recordings to a large VHS cassette. Then he dug another hole in the ground and buried the camera for safekeeping, with the original videocassette still inside. Loshi took the VHS tape in the hope he could get a copy across the border.

As a middle-aged man, not to mention a member of the KLA, being caught was already dangerous. Moving with the convoys meant being searched and possibly robbed — if not worse — and to be found carrying a videotape seemed extremely risky. Loshi thus set out by himself, avoiding the roads, travelling by night, and hiding in valleys during the day. He soon discovered that the Serbian forces had the area surrounded. He simply couldn't find a way through. After four or five days he gave up and returned to Izbica. He stayed in the village for another month.

In early May he decided to try again. He dug up Thaqi's original tape, this one smaller in size, and left Izbica with both tapes on May 3. He headed towards Montenegro, staying in the Istok Mountains for four days. Afraid of being caught with the larger videotape, he left it with a man he stayed with in the mountains, keeping the smaller tape hidden on his body. On May 7, Loshi made it to a refugee camp in Montenegro. He bought a fake ID card and took a bus across the border to Albania. From there he headed to the capital.

Once in Tirana, Loshi reached out to the global media. Copies of the tape were provided to CNN and the BBC and sent to the White House and NATO. The graphic footage immediately provoked a response. Portions of the video were broadcast on television and striking still photos of the bodies lying together in the fields were printed in newspapers. Loshi was interviewed and talked about what he had seen. Reporters like CNN's Amanda Kibel found other refugees who had escaped from Izbica, who provided similar accounts. The U.S. State Department held a special briefing in which it announced that the contents of the video had been confirmed by overhead imagery. On May 19, Loshi turned over the original tape to the ICTY.[6]

The Serbian government, of course, was watching CNN as well.

## V
# The Cover-Up

After the war ended on June 11, expelled and internally displaced ethnic Albanians began to return to their homes. Dr. Loshi took a camera and went back to Kosovo, returning to the location of the burials he had filmed on March 31 and April 1. Milazim Thaqi returned as well, with two BBC journalists in tow.

When the men arrived at the site where the bodies had been buried, however, they found that the grave markers had vanished and the ground had been levelled. There was no sign of the bodies. Some of the wooden markers bearing the names of the dead were still scattered on the ground. Prodding through the earth, Thaqi found only a single arm and a leg.

Some of the villagers told them that Serb forces had entered the area, dug up the bodies, and taken them away. Satellite photographs released by the U.S. State Department would soon confirm this: the images of long rows of graves visible in mid-May contrasted sharply with the very distinct tract of flattened earth apparent in June.

It smacked of a cover-up. As NATO general Wesley Clark put it: "Not only had the Serbs killed civilians and were trying to hide them, but there was a system behind this, where they were responding to discoveries. This was an important finding for us. It deepened the recognition that the Serb high command in some way was involved in this."[7]

Between June 28 and June 30, a French forensic team investigated the Izbica burial site. They identified 139 grave plots that had been dug and confirmed that there wasn't a single body left in the graves. They did find signs of what had once been buried there: bone fragments, pieces of hair and skin, and items of clothing riddled with bullet holes, mostly in the areas of the back and neck. They found latex gloves and saw obvious tire-track marks on the ground, along with teeth marks from the digging bucket of an excavator. The forensic team also investigated the areas where the executions had taken place. They found three clear sites, each of which was marked by large numbers of spent cartridge cases that the killers had left behind.

It was obvious that these bodies had been made to disappear. The question for the surviving relatives, friends, and fellow villagers was where they had been taken.

# 7

# NARRATIVES OF INJUSTICE

I

## "No one will beat you again"

In April of 1987 the president of the Serbian Communist Party, Ivan Stambolić, asked his trusted associate, a then relatively unknown man named Slobodan Milošević, to travel to Kosovo in his stead.

It was a delicate time in the history of Yugoslavia. Josip Broz Tito, the only leader the Socialist Federal Republic of Yugoslavia had known since it was founded after World War II, had died in 1980. Under Tito's leadership, the federation of Slovenia, Croatia, Bosnia-Hercegovina, Montenegro, Serbia, and Macedonia, along with the autonomous territories of Vojvodina and Kosovo, had not only held solidly together, it had become the poster child for the non-aligned movement during the Cold War. Tito's Yugoslavia was a tightly controlled police state, but its brand of Communism-light, which had managed to remain independent from the Stalinist empire next-door, made it in many ways the envy of Eastern Europe. By the 1960s its economy was booming and its citizens enjoyed the freedom — unusual at the time — to work abroad. What was not tolerated was ethnic nationalism, or the politics of ethnic identity, in any form. Throughout his reign, Tito had aggressively cracked down on any signs of emergent nationalism within Yugoslavia, snuffing out movements before they had a chance to ignite.

The Yugoslav federation held together after Tito's death. But by 1987 the social and political landscape was shifting underfoot. Yugoslavia had lived very much in the shadow of the Soviet Union since being founded as a modern state, and by 1987 both the Cold War and the Soviet Union itself were unwinding. At the same time, the Yugoslav economy began to worsen, and as the willingness and ability of the state to crack down became increasingly unclear, nationalist stirrings were beginning to emerge from the republics.

Kosovo held a strong symbolic importance for the Serbs. It was the seat of the early Serbian Orthodox Church, home to the community's most sacred churches, and the site of the legendary Battle of Kosovo Polje, where the Serb army was defeated by the invading Ottomans in 1389 — a battle that would become an increasingly invoked piece of the Serbian self-narrative. By the 1980s, however, Kosovo's now 90 percent Albanian population was showing increasingly nationalist tendencies, responding to what they saw as the Serbian domination of politics and governance and the heavy presence of Serbian soldiers and police.[1]

In 1981 there were protests and then rioting amongst Kosovo Albanian students at the University of Pristina. What reportedly began with a disgusted student throwing his lunch tray to the floor — a reaction, some say, to finding a cockroach in his soup — grew into a demonstration against conditions at the university and then riots involving thousands of people. Within a month, demands had grown from more localized calls for better treatment for Kosovo Albanians to multi-city protests calling for a "Kosovo Republic" distinct from Serbia. In a country where open protests had been essentially unheard of, the events were shocking. The state's response was correspondingly harsh: they brought in tanks, declared a state of emergency, and arrested (and later convicted) hundreds of people. The number of people killed in the riots and the subsequent response was never clearly established.[2]

Following the riots, significant portions of the Serbian media, realizing that they were no longer constrained as they had been under Tito, began to promote the narrative that Kosovo Serbs were being victimized by Albanians. There were, undoubtedly, genuine cases in which Serbs were being subjected to abuse and intimidation. But the media painted an exaggerated and caricatured picture of crime and injustice, which many members of the public were all too enthusiastic to hear.

In 1985, the Belgrade magazine *NIN* made national news of a brutal assault in which a Serb farmer named Đorđe Martinović was allegedly attacked by two masked Albanians and tied up in a field near his house. When he was treated in the hospital, doctors had to remove a broken beer bottle from his anus. The case was invoked by the Yugoslav Assembly that year, and the following year it was made the subject of a lengthy book with a reported initial print run of fifty thousand copies.[3] The actual facts of the assault were unclear; there were reports that Martinović had confessed to impaling himself on the bottle, and while neither the Belgrade Military Medical Academy nor the Federal Ministry of Justice could find sufficient evidence to determine the wound's origin, the Yugoslav secret police and military intelligence subsequently concluded that the injuries were self-inflicted. Regardless of what actually happened, the enthusiastically graphic coverage of the alleged incident willingly fed a perception throughout Serbia that the Kosovo Serbs were being brutally victimized.[4]

During this same period, the Serbian media also trumpeted salacious allegations of epidemics of rape being perpetrated by Kosovo Albanian men against Kosovo Serb women, prompting local movements and complaint campaigns. In contrast to these media depictions, however, an independent committee of Serbian lawyers and human rights experts found that the incidence of rape in Kosovo was in fact markedly lower than in other regions of Yugoslavia. The committee found that there were only a total of thirty-one reported rapes in Kosovo, either committed or attempted, from 1982 to 1989.[5] At the time, Kosovo also had the lowest murder rate in Yugoslavia. The period from 1981 to 1987 saw only five inter-ethnic murders in total: two Serbs killed by Albanians and three Albanians killed by Serbs.[6]

In 1986, an inflammatory "Memorandum" produced by the Serbian Academy of Sciences and Arts was leaked to the press, painting the Serbs as victims of the Yugoslavian Communist regime and claiming that Tito — whose parents were a Croat and a Slovene — had been biased against the Serbs, particularly in the granting of autonomous status to the Serbian territories of Kosovo and Vojvodina. With particularly inflammatory aplomb, the Memorandum described expulsions of Kosovo Serbs by the Albanians as a "genocide." The Martinović bottle case was described as "reminiscent of the blackest periods of Turkish impalings." The Memorandum urged Serbia not to "take a passive stand in all this, waiting to hear what others will say, as she has done so often in the past." It was received by many as a call for the expansion of Greater Serbia.[7]

It was against this backdrop that President Stambolić sent Slobodan Milošević to Kosovo. There was news that a large protest was being planned and a request had been made for Stambolić to address a group of Kosovo Serb nationalists in Kosovo Polje. Stambolić had already made several speeches cautioning against the dangers of Serb nationalism and it was clear that some sort of steady-handed appearance by the leadership was called for to quell nationalist sentiments.[8] Fearing a potentially volatile political situation, Stambolić chose to send Milošević in his stead. It would prove a fatal political mistake.

On April 20, Milošević spoke to a crowd of Kosovo Serbs, cautioning them generally against the dangers of "exclusive nationalism based on national hatreds," repeating the Communist Party position. But in a controversial move, breaking with party and government policy that had always cautiously restricted nationalist expression, Milošević agreed to meet with a group of Kosovo Serb nationalists several days later.[9]

On Friday, April 24, 1987, Milošević sat in a town hall in Kosovo Polje, where a large gathering of local Serbs described a litany of injustices committed against them by the Kosovo Albanians, the local police, and the local government. The events were well orchestrated: outside the hall the Kosovo Serb nationalists had organized an unwieldy mob of protestors who were shouting at the police and pelting them with large rocks — rocks that the organizers had arranged to have brought in on flatbed trucks. The media had been alerted and were on hand to broadcast the spectacle. As the events grew increasingly out of hand, Milošević strode out of the town hall and onto the street. He was flanked by bureaucrats, the chants around him deafening. He took a calculated pause and then waded into the crowd, cameras rolling, men pressing in all around him. It was a bold piece of political theatre.

"Comrades," he said firmly, "speak up!"

One of the men pressed in towards him, just inches from his face, media microphones and notepads encircling them.

"The police attacked us, they hit women and children," the man said. "The Albanians got in among us, we were beaten up."

"They're beating us!" someone yelled.

Milošević's response, spoken in front of the cameras and instantly lionized by the Serbian media back in Belgrade, changed the course of Yugoslavian politics.

"*Niko ne sme da vas bije*," he said. "No one will dare beat you again."[10]

Casting the Serbs as the victims of injustice, Milošević's words galvanized the Serbian public, stoked pride, and puffed chests. Repeatedly rebroadcast by Radio Television Belgrade, they instantly inflamed divisions between Serbs and Albanians in Kosovo and caused deep concerns amongst the other Yugoslav republics — most notably Croatia — who were wary of Serbian expansion into other territories.

Milošević returned to Belgrade as a heroic figure. As hardline Serb activists organized corresponding protests involving thousands of people, he capitalized on his new-found popularity. He continued to emphasize the injustices perpetrated against the threatened Serbian people, riding this populist drama and the spectre of threatened and victimized Kosovo Serbs into power. By September of 1987 he had ousted Stambolić and gained control of the Communist Central Committee. From there his divisive nationalist agenda spread quickly, and the flames of nationalism and ethnic tension were soon fueled from many sides. What unfolded was a frighteningly rapid descent into war and ethnic cleansing, amongst people who had lived comfortably together as neighbours since the founding of the modern Yugoslavian republic.

Interviewed later about the events in Kosovo that spurred his rise to power, Milošević would say that it was the Albanians who had wanted an ethnically pure Kosovo, not the Serbs. "They murdered Serbs, defiled our graves, burned monasteries," he said. "The exodus of Serbs began."

These words would serve as a remarkably succinct summary, if not a blueprint, for the actions *Serb* forces would ultimately take against the Kosovo Albanians in 1999, actions that many saw as the culmination of what had begun when Milošević first came to power. It would perhaps be ironic — the almost perfect inversion between the injustices that Milošević described the Serbs suffering and the injustices the Serb forces would subsequently commit against the Albanians — if the causal link between this rhetoric, and the atrocities that followed, were not so clear.

II

## Reclaiming the Field of Blackbirds

It was surely no accident that the moment that transformed Milošević's career, and that set the former Yugoslavia on the path to ethnic bloodshed, took place in the town of Kosovo Polje, where six hundred years earlier the Serbs had fought and lost the fateful battle for their homeland with the Ottoman Turks.

Serbian legend told that prior to the monumental battle with the sultan's army on the "Field of Blackbirds," a grey falcon alighted from Jerusalem and came to Serbian Prince Lazar in a dream. The hawk presented him with a choice: a victory over the sultan's men and a kingdom on earth, or a loss on the battlefield and the promise of an eternal kingdom in heaven. Lazar, of course, chose the heavenly kingdom. The Serbs thus lost the pivotal battle for their homeland and became martyrs instead.[11]

Historians have disputed the details of the battle, its ultimate significance, and even whether the Serbian army (really a Serb-dominated Western coalition with Bosnians, Albanians, Bulgarians, and some Hungarians) actually won or lost. What is relatively clear is that the battle saw the Serbian army kill Ottoman Sultan Murad I, the Ottomans kill Prince Lazar, and both sides sustain massive casualties. The battle ended with the Serbian army fleeing, and although both armies declared themselves victorious afterward, the Ottomans held on to the field.[12] Although the Ottomans lost their sultan, he was quickly replaced by his son Bayezid. For Serbia, the defeat marked the end of the independent Serbian kingdom and entrenched the Ottoman Empire in the Balkans.[13]

The narrative of the Field of Blackbirds stoked powerful feelings of nationalism. Though Serbs and Albanians were living in Kosovo together in the late 1980s — as they had done for decades under Tito — the myth defined and divided its stakeholders based on ethnicity, seemingly aligning the Muslim Kosovo Albanians with the Ottomans and the Serbs with … well, the Serbs. It was a historical narrative of war and conquest that seemed to cry out for redemption.

The story also dovetailed well with claims that Kosovo's Serbs had been the victims of ongoing injustices at the hands of the Albanians. Propaganda claimed that the Albanians had been killing and deporting Kosovo Serbs since the Ottoman conquest in 1389, often referring to the flight of Serbs and the settlement and growth of the Albanian population as a genocide. A number of Serbian historians similarly claimed that under Communism in Yugoslavia, Kosovo's Albanians had instituted policies of "ethnic cleansing" in order to create an ethnically pure Kosovo. They described ongoing persecution, rape, and murder, and the desecration and destruction of Serbian religious institutions.[14] The creation of this widely held perception that the Serbs were the victims of ongoing atrocities meant that oppressive Serbian actions, dictated from Belgrade, could be cast as a justified response to an ongoing injustice.

The six-hundred-year anniversary of the Battle of Kosovo Polje came in 1989, less than two years from Milošević's ascendance to power. The event was marked with great pomp and circumstance: Prince Lazar's remains were marched around Serbia, hundreds of thousands of pilgrims journeyed to the field, and Milošević made a well-timed appearance in a helicopter to greet them.[15] The battle was recreated in a popular film that year, with Kosovo Albanian extras playing hordes of Ottoman Turks.

That same year, the Serbian assembly tabled amendments to the constitution that would strip Kosovo of its autonomy. Though Kosovo had been an equal subject within the Yugoslav federation pursuant to the 1974 constitution, these amendments transferred control of the local police, courts, and civil defence to Serbia. They also empowered the Serbs to dictate social policy and deem an official language. For the amendments to take effect, they would need to be formally accepted by the Kosovo Assembly. In advance of the vote, Serbian forces brought heavy pressure to bear on the members of the Assembly to support the amendments. On the day of the vote, Serbian military and police vehicles were brought in to surround the Assembly and reinforce the message. In this climate of fear, and with people who were not members of the Assembly casting votes, the amendments passed. When they were subsequently ratified by the Serbian Assembly, "Serbia at last had become one."[16] With its autonomous status now revoked, Kosovo's political future was dictated from Belgrade.

In response, ethnic Albanian protests raged across Kosovo. Another state of emergency was declared and troops were brought in to control the population. With the territory now an "effective police state," overt discrimination against Kosovo's ethnic Albanians began in earnest. Albanians were harassed, stopped at checkpoints, and often detained in prisons, where they could be held for sixty days at a time. Prominent Kosovo institutions, including radio, television, and newspapers, were shut down. Throughout 1990 and 1991, ethnic Albanians were asked to sign declarations of loyalty to Serbia or face termination from their jobs. They were removed from prominent positions across the public sector and from the police force. Serbian was declared the official language and the entire Albanian school system was shut down, up to and including the University of Pristina, replaced with an overhauled Serbian curriculum to be taught by non-Albanians.

The Kosovo Albanians, in turn, boycotted Serbian institutions and initiated a non-violent campaign led by Ibrahim Rugova. They created a parallel education system for Albanians that took place in improvised classrooms, often in people's homes. They created their own municipal government structures and separate health care centres. The ethnic divisions in Kosovo grew increasingly more entrenched.

Events in Kosovo would serve to bracket the beginning and the end of the most brutal ethnic violence that unfolded in the former Yugoslavia.


III

# Violence and Justification

*Justified* is a powerful word, which seems to receive too little of our attention. It conveys that an act that would otherwise have been unacceptable is considered — for some particular reason — to be morally and ethically permissible. To feel that we were justified is to feel that we were morally and ethically *right* to act as we did.

Where wrongful acts have been committed, various claims to some sort of righteous justification always seem to follow. Children invoke these justifications intuitively, trying to evade blame: he hit me first, he took my toy from me, he started it. Adults do the same, although they tend to be somewhat more sophisticated in their delivery. We are all intimately familiar, through personal experience, with the ready resort to justifications for violence after the fact. What we too often ignore is the way in which the language and emotion of justification can impel us to commit acts of violence in the first place, and then to continue to perpetuate those acts in the face of any otherwise objective notion of immorality or inhumanity. Where hearts and minds must be recruited to a cause — both to initiate violence and to maintain it — the groundwork of righteous justification must be laid in advance.[17]

What goes too often unnoticed, then, and in fact constitutes an important and fundamental inversion of the traditional lens through which we see international justice, is that collective violence is almost always motivated by the perpetrators and their base of supporters responding to what *they* see as injustice, and pursuing a form of justice for themselves. It is perpetuated, in much the same way, by the perception that what they are doing, while it might otherwise have been immoral, is justified. Such violence is not typically caused by an *absence* of, or lack of attention to, justice and morality. It is, instead, caused by the direct and overriding pursuit of a *misdirected* view of morality and justice, constructed as justification in the minds of the perpetrators.

American sociologist Donald Black was one of the first to reinterpret crime and violence in this way — as a form of justification. Black understood crime not as the intentional violation of a prohibition but instead as a moralistic pursuit of justice. Crime is not about breaking the law, in other words, but about seeking a sort of "self-help" justice. He observed that murder is less often committed to gain something and more often "related to a grievance or quarrel of some kind."[18] This is not to say that murders are never committed for the mere purpose of gaining some benefit, like money, but that those instances are surprisingly rare. Murders are more often committed in response to adultery, affronts to honour, and *disputes* over money.[19]

Black observed that when we deal with an event in court, we may completely redefine that event from the way it was originally conceived by the perpetrator. As he put it:

In the case of a husband who shoots his wife's lover, for example, the definition of who is the offender and who is the victim is reversed: The wife's lover is defined as the victim, even though he was shot because of an offence he committed against the woman's husband. Moreover, the lover's offense is precisely the kind for which violent social control — by the husband — is viewed as acceptable and appropriate, if not obligatory, in numerous tribal and other traditional societies.[20]

This may be just how we want it, of course — to use the courtroom to redefine the just and the unjust, to reassert a more appropriate societal view of right and wrong.[21] But recognizing the potential power of our reaction to injustice to *motivate* crime has particularly profound implications in the context of mass violence, where the forces of the state are collectively mobilized, where participants must be rallied to the cause, and where questions of national identity, history, and collective pride are easily brought into play. These are the circumstances in which the potential to warp and distort a collective sense of injustice and victimhood are particularly dangerous.

Our notions of justice, injustice, and victimhood are conveyed — and take hold of us — through the stories that we tell, and the stories that we choose to listen to.

IV

# Narratives of Injustice

For the Serbs, the bloodshed and ethnic violence that would spread across Yugoslavia in the 1990s was propelled by narratives of injustice that cast them as the long-oppressed victims of ethnic enemies striving to destroy them. These beliefs were self-perpetuating and became self-fulfilling. Though Milošević climbed to power on the back of events in Kosovo, the rhetoric of victimhood and injustice, and the marshalling of history, was perhaps most vociferous in relation to Croatia.

As David Bruce MacDonald has traced persuasively in *Balkan Holocausts: Serbian and Croatian Victim-Centred Propaganda and the War in Yugoslavia*,the run-up to the inter-ethnic bloodshed in the former Yugoslavia involved a sweeping "tragedizing of history" in which "every aspect of Serbian history was seen to be another example of persecution and victimisation at the hands of external negative forces."[22] The past became a tool fashioned for the present, with ancient battles, the very real brutality of World War II, and the years of federation within Tito's Yugoslavia all marshalled into narratives of injustice and victimhood at the hands of other ethnic groups. The result was a repositioning of the present along a narrative arc in which ethnic conflict was made to seem inevitable, and "pre-emptive" violence somehow justified. Casting themselves as threatened victims in the long and short arcs of history, violent acts could be repurposed as defensive actions.

It was not just the Serbs. Responding to what they perceived as an inevitable Serbian ideology of aggressive expansion, other nationalities within the now-precarious Yugoslav federation — Croatia chief among them — kicked their own corresponding national narratives into overdrive. History was recast and contemporary events were viewed through this narrowing prism, with individuals and territories increasingly defined along ethnic lines. As the republics sought their independence from the Yugoslav federation following Milošević's rise to power, events soon turned catastrophically violent.

The secessionist movements began with Slovenia, which voted for independence on December 23, 1990. On June 27, 1991, two days after its independence was formally declared, the Yugoslav army was dispatched to Slovenia. The fighting that followed — later dubbed the Ten Day War — was brief and relatively uneventful, resulting in forty deaths, most of them members of the Yugoslav Army, before the European Community brokered a ceasefire on July 7, 1991.

But more violent fissures had been forming in Croatia, which had declared its independence on the same day as Slovenia. Croatia's ethnic Serb minority rebelled and the Yugoslav National Army and Serb paramilitaries commenced attacks to support them. Intense fighting in the second half of 1991 saw the historic city of Dubrovnik shelled, the town of Vukovar levelled, and almost one third of Croatia become Serb territory, violently "cleansed" of Croats and other non-Serbs. Early 1992 saw a U.N.-monitored ceasefire imposed, which Croatia used to arm and reinforce its military. In 1995, the Croatian army mounted two major offensives and drove out tens of thousands of Serbs. The events in Croatia, which came to an end later that year, saw extensive inter-ethnic violence between men and women who had been living and working side by side for their entire lives. It resulted in the indictment and subsequent prosecution of both Serbs and Croats at the ICTY.

The events in Bosnia would turn out to be the deadliest, however, marking one of the darkest chapters of the twentieth century. Following the declarations of independence in Slovenia and Croatia, a majority of Bosnians voted for independence in March of 1992. With an ethnically diverse population that was approximately 45 percent Bosnian Muslim, 30 percent Bosnian Serb, and 15 percent Bosnian Croat, there soon developed a protracted and shockingly violent three-sided fight for territory.

The Bosnian Serbs, supported by the Yugoslav National Army and forces from Serbia, waged a brutal campaign of ethnic cleansing and took control of 60 percent of Bosnia, declaring it a Serb republic. Bosnian Croats followed suit, declaring a republic of their own. Violence from all sides claimed an estimated one hundred thousand lives and saw an epidemic of systematic rape, the extended and ruthless shelling of Sarajevo, brutal civilian detention centres established throughout the country, and the organized slaughter of eight thousand Bosnian Muslim men and boys who had been sheltering in Srebrenica, a supposed "safe area" under United Nations protection. When international pressure by a global community that had been too slow to act finally forced an end to the violence with the signing of the Dayton Accords in November 1995, an estimated two million people had been forced from their homes and the Serbs had consolidated their hold over Bosnian territory, now dubbed Republica Srpska.

The final stage of the conflict would unfold in Kosovo, which had been slow-warming on the back burner as the brutal violence in Croatia and Bosnia played out.

# 8

# SUVA REKA

|

## The Berisha Family Tree

Exhibit P272 was a multicoloured family tree, its connected circles and rectangles showing three generations of the Berisha family in the Kosovo town of Suva Reka. The names inside the respective shapes — parents and grandparents, sons and daughters, aunts, uncles, and cousins — appeared in three colours. Those in blue were family members who had been murdered together as they hid inside a pizzeria. Those in red were family members who had been killed elsewhere in Suva Reka. The handful of remaining names, dotted sparsely across the chart in black, were the family members who were still alive.[1]

Shyrete Berisha was alive but her name appeared in blue. She had been inside that small pizzeria, through gunshots and two grenades, and had somehow managed to survive. Her husband and her four children were not so fortunate.

The family tree told a story of unimaginable loss. On a practical level, it served to identify the many members of her family who had been killed, showing how they had been related and how they had died. These bonds of family would end up being more than just illustrative, however — they became a crucial tool to answer the question of who had organized these killings and what they had done with the evidence. Because family members also share a common code, expressed at the level of their DNA.

In 1999, Shyrete lived in the town of Suva Reka with her husband Nexhat, their teenaged daughters Majlinda and Heroldina, and their sons Altin and Redon. Their house was one of the largest in the town and they shared it with their extended family; they lived on the left side of the house while the right was home to her husband's nephew Faton, his wife, their two young sons, and his mother and sister.

When the Organization for Security and Cooperation in Europe (OSCE) moved into Suva Reka, they arranged to rent the Berisha house for their own use, preferring it to their previous location of a hotel in a neighbouring village. Shyrete and her family went to live with her parents in the village of Mushtisht, where she was born, and Faton's family went to stay with his grandfather. The OSCE used Faton's side of the house as their sleeping quarters and Shyrete's side as their office. That office became a repository of the evidence they had collected showing the violence and destruction Serbian forces were causing in the surrounding area. When the OSCE moved out on March 20, Shyrete and her family moved back into the house, now sleeping on Faton's side. The NATO bombing began four days later.

The following morning, March 25, Shyrete and her family were awoken at 5:00 a.m. by a knock at the door. Shyrete opened it to find three uniformed Serb policemen. They pointed automatic weapons at her and asked, "Where are your guests, the Americans?" Their house's affiliation with the OSCE had marked them as an early target for retribution.

The police demanded that she tell her husband to come down. When he did, they took him to the other side of the house, where the OSCE had kept its office.

Shyrete watched as another police officer came inside and started searching the house. He turned to her and made "the sign with his fingers, the money sign," and told her that her husband's life was in danger. She understood, heading upstairs and then returning with one thousand Deutschmarks. The man took it but demanded more. There were fifteen to twenty police officers now swarming around the house. They helped themselves to the family's valuables, even loading their furniture into a truck.

On the other side of the house, with Nexhat standing by, the police were searching through the former OSCE offices. When they found photographs showing burnt Kosovo Albanian villages they became violent, swearing at Nexhat about America while they beat him.

They brought him back to the other side of the house and Shyrete stood watching as they hit her husband with their automatic rifles. The men demanded money, insisting that Nexhat had more because he had rented his house to the OSCE. They pointed outside, where a tank was now sitting. "You see this tank?" they said, "We'll blow up your house with all the children in it." Shyrete produced their remaining money, three thousand Deutschmarks.

The police eventually left, but Serb forces had moved into the town. Some wore blue camouflage uniforms: police. Some wore green camouflage: probably army. Others wore black, and many of the men wore bandanas on their heads. They were armed with AK-47s.

Shyrete and her family left their house and went to stay with Shyrete's uncle. They gathered there with Faton's family and a number of others, about twenty to twenty-five people in all.

They awoke the next morning, March 26, to find two tanks sitting on a nearby hill, their cannons pointing at the house. By around noon a large group of Serb policemen and civilians had gathered outside. A man they recognized as Zoran, a Serb who lived and worked in Suva Reka and spoke fluent Albanian, stood in the yard. "Call on the Americans, your friends, to help you now," he yelled.

Zoran yelled for Bujar, one of the men hiding inside, to come out to join him. The family huddled together, terrified, unsure of what to do. At first there was no response. Then Bujar's mother walked out alone, hoping to dissuade him. "Let Bujar come outside," Zoran yelled, "not you."

There seemed little choice. Bujar walked outside, alone. As the family listened from inside they heard a sudden burst of gunshots. In a panic, they ran. Shyrete saw Bujar as she passed, now a body lying on the ground. She could hear his wife screaming.

They ran towards Shyrete's house. When they arrived there were armed men waiting, some of them clad all in black. They quickly selected four of the men — Shyrete's husband Nexhat, his nephew Faton, and his cousins Sedat and Nexhmedin — and took them off to the side. Faton's mother, Fatime Berisha, pleaded with them to let her son go, to take her instead. Sedat Berisha started to run. Shyrete never saw him again.

Shyrete stood holding her son Altin by the hand. Her sixteen-year-old daughter Majlinda held their youngest, and her thirteen-year-old daughter Herolinda stood alongside them. The children refused to leave their father behind. They watched as one of the officers grabbed him by the arm. "Now the Americans should come and rescue you," he said. With his family looking on, Nexhat was shot twice in the back. He collapsed to the ground.

Other shots rang out around them and Shyrete heard voices in Serbian imploring others to fire. "Shoot!" they yelled, "What are you waiting for?" Gunshots and shouting erupted all around them and Shyrete and her family ran. In the chaos, she and Herolinda headed in one direction, Majlinda and the two boys in another. As she ran, she saw Faton and his mother Fatime fall to the ground.

Shyrete and Herolinda ran until they reached the vicinity of the town's shopping centre, where they encountered two other Berisha families standing rooted in place. "Why are we stopped here?" she asked. One of the men, her husband's cousin and closest friend, told Shyrete that the police had told them to stop at the pizzeria.

When Shyrete's children arrived at that same spot, she saw that her son Altin was pale and bleeding from the arm. "The police were shooting in my direction," he said, "but they didn't quite hit me."

A group of policemen, Zoran among them, saw the families and walked towards them. They pointed them to the nearby pizzeria and directed them inside. The entire group, Shyrete and her four children among them, obeyed. They were told to sit down at the tables. Thirty-five members of the Berisha family sat huddled inside the pizzeria, waiting and terrified.

Shortly thereafter, with the families inside, the police opened fire into the pizzeria. Shyrete described it:

First, as I said, they opened fire, bursts of fire. Then they stopped. And as soon as they would notice that there were voices inside, people alive, then they were throwing things in and children, women, were just dying afterwards. It was sort of a grenade. As I said, I couldn't see. I was lying on the ground. I just could hear people crying, moaning, and after these things were thrown inside, it was just calm. They would not speak anymore.[2]

Shyrete had sustained injuries to her leg, chest, and stomach, but had somehow survived both grenades and gunfire. In a lull between bursts of fire, police had noticed she was still alive. They turned their weapons and fired on her directly. A bullet passed through her arm. She pretended she was dead and the police stopped firing. "God saved me to come here and tell the truth," she would later say.[3]

As she lay there, she heard the men speaking to each other in Serbian. "What life is this?" one man said. "Why are they killing women and children?" They discussed the need to clean up, then spoke about a truck.

The men moved into the pizzeria, loading the bodies of the dead onto stretchers and carrying them out. As they began to disturb the bodies, they were surprised to find some signs of life. Shyrete listened, eyes pressed shut, as survivors around her were identified and then shot and killed, one by one.

Her son Altin was lying next to her and she could feel he was still alive. She urged him quietly to pretend he was dead. He lay there silently, but when the men lifted his body to take it away, they noticed he was alive. She heard the men fire and she heard her son moan. Then they were standing above her, looking down. She felt hands around her neck, then a sharp tug as they took her two gold chains. She felt herself being hoisted up and carried, then she was dropped down roughly. Something cushioned her landing. When it grew momentarily quiet she took a look around. She was lying amidst a pile of bodies, covered by a tarpaulin. The back of a truck.

After some time, the truck began to move. She raised her head and looked at the lifeless body of her son Altin beside her. She tried to speak to him but he didn't respond.

Then she heard another voice, quiet, from somewhere amongst the bodies.

"Are you still alive?"

It was Vjollca, Sedat's wife. Her son, eight-year-old Gramoz, had somehow survived as well. They looked at each other as the truck rumbled down the road.

It stopped some distance later. Shyrete could hear a woman's voice outside, speaking Serbian.

"My son, are you finished?" the woman asked.

"Yes, we are finished."

"Have a good trip," the woman said. Shyrete thought she recognized the voice as Zoran's mother.

As the truck sped off, Shyrete told Vjollca that they needed to jump. Vjollca was afraid; they were going quickly, she pointed out, and they'd been lucky to survive thus far. She suggested that they wait until they were buried and then "try and come out of the earth."

Shyrete persisted. She looked out through a hole in the tarpaulin, not sure where they were. Seeing Vjollca moving to the side of the truck, Shyrete pulled her back. The drivers would see them in the side mirrors if they jumped that way. It had to be from the back.

The truck was moving fast but Shyrete climbed to the rear and jumped. She hit the road hard, tumbling and hitting her forehead. Further down, both Vjollca and Gramoz jumped to the pavement as well.

The three of them lay on the road, watching as the truck rumbled into the distance. They were found by a local Kosovo Albanian girl, who went to get help.


Halit Berisha had been in The Hague before. He had testified first in the prosecution of Slobodan Milošević, and in moments that must certainly have felt surreal, he was cross-examined by Milošević himself. He would also testify, years later, against the Kosovo 6. But trying to figure out what had happened to the disappeared bodies of his fellow villagers would come to consume his life in the years after the war, and the operation that had concealed those bodies lay at the core of the Đorđević trial. It would end up being a particular detail of Halit

Berisha's testimony, involving his brother Jashar, that became a crucial piece of the puzzle.

Halit Berisha was born in Suva Reka in 1940. He spent most of his life there, even serving as the town's mayor for two years, starting in 1989. His term ended abruptly when on April 5, 1991, five Serbian men, including three members of the state security, came into his office and told him he was being removed. One of them was a local doctor named Boban Vuksanović, who was appointed head of Suva Reka's Executive Council in Halit's stead. "Bobek," as he was known, had an Albanian father and a Serbian mother but was regarded by the townspeople of Suva Reka as a Serb.

Halit's brother Jashar Berisha was the manager of the Beopetrol gas station in the centre of Suva Reka. He had worked there for thirty years. But on the morning of March 26, 1999, Halit told Jashar to stay home. There was a war going on, and he was concerned that something bad would happen.

Jashar didn't listen. He pulled on a pair of long underwear, then red track pants, then a pair of blue jeans on top of that, layering to keep warm. Then he packed up his lunch and took a bottle of milk. He grabbed his blue Beopetrol jacket on the way out the door.

Just after noon, Jashar called home to tell Halit there was a massacre taking place at the shopping centre. Halit urged his brother to leave the station right away but Jashar insisted he would be home by 5:00 p.m. When he got off the phone, Halit gathered his family and neighbours, about two hundred people, and they went to the river and hid.

At around 2:30 p.m., Halit snuck away and called his brother again — both to see what was happening in town and to make sure he was okay. Jashar told him he'd heard shooting, explosions, and screaming near the shopping centre. Still, Jashar refused to leave.

Halit's family and their neighbours spent that night in two houses — the men in one, the women in the other. Halit snuck away again, this time risking a trip home to look for Jashar. But his brother hadn't returned from the petrol station.

The next day, Serbian forces exploded the minaret of the local mosque. Halit's neighbour, a local policeman named Djura Nojić, tipped him off that the police and military were on their way back to town.

"The army and the police will come and are going to kill you all," he told him. "They're going to slit your throats."[4] He told Halit to get ready to go to Albania.

Halit and his family quickly left town. After a harrowing journey, they were forced out of Kosovo on May 21, 1999.

Halit never saw Jashar again. His final memory of their last morning together, when he had tried to persuade his brother to stay and then watched him walk out the door, remained fixed in his mind. That image would end up being important, for reasons he had never imagined.

II

# The Men on the Ground

*Prosecutor:*
Does the witness believe
it is possible that the Chief officer
was not informed of the proceedings
in the crematoria

*Witness 3:*
I believe it is impossible
These proceedings were known
to every one of the 6,000 members
of the camp personnel
and everyone carried out in his own job
what had to be carried out
for the functioning of the whole
Furthermore every train engineer
every linesman
every railway employee
who had dealt with the transport of men
knew what was happening in the camp
Every telegraph girl and every stenographer

who passed on the deportation orders
knew about it
Every single one
of the hundreds of thousands
of office workers
who were concerned with the actions
knew
what they were about.

— Peter Weiss, from *The Investigation*, a dramatic
reconstruction of the Frankfurt Auschwitz
War Crimes Trials of 1963–1965[5]

It's a question worth contemplating: What would you say, years later, if you had been complicit in a mass killing? Would your conscience implore you to tell the truth? What if you faced potential prosecution yourself? What if someone you knew — your friend, your former boss, or the entire senior leadership of your home country — faced condemnation and a prison sentence as a result of your testimony? What if some saw the courtroom as a battleground between ethnicities and your testimony could be seen as traitorous? What if someone had gotten to you, and you or your family had been threatened with death — or what if you knew those dangers without being spoken to at all? What if you just didn't want to remember?

When such men testified as prosecution witnesses, their motivations were often opaque. In many cases, the prosecution had obtained one or more previous statements from these witnesses, taken years earlier, typically on the ground in Kosovo or in Serbia. Sometimes they were provided to local Serbian investigators in relation to separate internal investigations of specific incidents — some of which seemed legitimate, some of which were dubious, and some of which, for reasons often difficult to discern, simply proved inconsequential. The witnesses we ended up calling had typically described something of crucial importance to our case, somewhere along the line, perhaps without knowing its value at the time.

These admissions could be buried within a broader context of denial — denial that the witness himself had been involved in committing atrocities, denial that the accused before the court was in any way culpable, or denial that the killings, even if acknowledged, were orchestrated, planned, or anything more than some unfortunate acts during a difficult war.


Velibor Veljković had started as a beat officer. He soon found himself working traffic misdemeanors, spending his days entering information into a computer. The desk work suited him, or so he said. From 1997 to the end of the war, he managed the police station's records, organizing the schedules of the officers on patrol. By March of 1999, when the killings in Suva Reka began, he had been a member of the Suva Reka police for five years.

With respect to the events of March 26, Veljković testified that at around noon he had encountered several of his colleagues standing at the entrance to the duty station: Sladjan Cukarić, Radovan Tanović, Miroslav Petković, and their commander, Radojko Repanović. The men were holding automatic rifles and wearing flak jackets.

He testified that Commander Repanović gave the men a direct order. But he said he couldn't remember what the order was. He remembered only that he refused to carry it out:

> Just as I was getting ready to enter the Suva Reka OUP building, Commander Repanović told me, I can't recall the exact words, but I figured that what he had told me was, in fact, a criminal offence. He told me to go to with the colleagues that I — whose names I mentioned, somewhere. I don't recall what I replied, but I just refused. I simply refused to go with him and entered the premises of the duty operations room.[6]

In his previous statements, Veljković had remembered the order well enough. He was provided with these statements in open court in the hope that "refreshing his memory" might help. Three years prior, he had described Commander Repanović directing he, Cukarić, Tanović, and Petković to go from house to house killing Albanians. "He did not say why this was to be done," Veljković had added, "and he did not specify any particular individuals. He just said that they were all to be killed."[7]

Veljković claimed first that his prior statement had been forced. Then he claimed he had repeated what other people had told him. He tried to maintain both that he couldn't remember what order had been given and that he knew the order was illegal.[8]

His position became more untenable when he was shown a transcript of evidence he gave to an investigative judge in Belgrade in 2004. There he had confirmed the order, and clarified it:

> Q. Tell me, you said in this report that you know that there was an order to go from door to door and kill Albanians in Suva Reka. Who gave that order?
>
> A. The order was given first by superior officers so I got it from them. From — from — the order was from the station commander, Radojko Repanović, and he said he probably — and he did not make decisions or the station commander only and the rest.
>
> Q. How did he tell you this?
>
> A. You see that day when there were killings, I mean, he said "Go there, load, and kill." And even a few days before that there were killings. But I do not know how he had said that, he must have said, "Go from house to house and kill," probably something to that effect.[9]

Veljković claimed that he couldn't remember this anymore.

After his commander gave the order that he couldn't seem to recall, he went inside the police station. There he encountered an older Kosovo Albanian man, Petrit Elshani, who was being detained. He described what happened next:

> … he was eventually taken out of the station building. I don't remember who took him out. In any case, they took him out and brought him to the courtyard. Less than half a minute later, I heard shots from a firearm, although I don't know which firearm it was. I don't know

if it was an automatic rifle or the CZ-99 handgun. I heard several shots, I believe.

When I came out of the building, I saw him dead in the courtyard. Next to him in the courtyard was Sladjan Cukarić, Radovan Tanović, and Miroslav Petković; they were all there. Which one of them shot him dead, is something I cannot say.[10]

Ten minutes after Cukarić, Tanović and Petković left the station, Veljković heard automatic weapon fire coming from outside. He came out to find a nearby house on fire, with people running away and "falling dead." He saw five or six dead bodies lying in the yard and watched the survivors run across the grounds of the bus station, continuing to the shopping centre. He insisted he couldn't see who was firing the shots.

This was not what he had said before. In 2004, he had described a group of police officers standing and shooting outside of the house.[11] He had identified Tanović, Cukarić, and Petković among them, and he was clear that the police were shooting the civilians in the back as they ran. Now he denied seeing the shooters. He claimed that you could never actually "see" someone shooting:

> This was, as I've already said, audio recorded, and I was rather scared. And now as you read this, it seems funny to me how I spoke about some things. Well, first of all, you cannot see someone shooting. You can hear a shot. You can't see it. You can see a murder. And I said I saw a shot. So I really did not say it properly. I heard the shots. So those people that I mentioned, now I have some doubts.[12]

He did testify, however, that he was specifically ordered to collect the bodies of Albanians who had been killed. He described taking his rifle from the administrative office and setting out with two reservists to start collecting bodies. A truck arrived from Prizren and they were asked to load the bodies inside. They started with the body of Petrit Elshani.

Then they headed to the Berisha house, with the truck driving ahead and Veljković and the two reservists following behind on foot. They loaded the bodies from the yard.

Veljković said he couldn't remember who was driving the truck. Nor would he say who arranged the truck, or pursuant to what orders. "I can't remember that," he said. "Actually, I don't know. The true answer is that I don't know."[13]

He testified that the truck headed towards the town of Studencani, continuing to look for bodies. As he walked behind, he heard a grenade explode. This was, he presumed, the grenade that had been thrown into the pizzeria and had killed so many women and children. He continued: "I also heard automatic rifle gunshots. After that, I went in the direction of the gunshots because I was — I presumed that the people who had fled the house wanted to hide in a shop. They did so, but that presented them with no refuge."[14]

Veljković then "went to see where they were killed." When he arrived at the pizzeria he saw people congregated outside — again identifying Cukarić, Tanović, and Petković. He approached the door and saw that the pizzeria was full of the bodies of Albanian civilians. He estimated there were ninety to one hundred bodies. They were predominantly women and children.[15]

He initially described that the bodies were all dead when he arrived, and that the Serb forces on scene had "simply started loading them.... Nobody said a word."[16] Shyrete Berisha, of course, had stated that there were survivors after the initial killings, and that Serb forces had shot and killed the survivors one by one.

Veljković was asked again whether any of the bodies "spoke or moved" after he arrived. This time he described that after he had loaded a few of the bodies onto the truck, an elderly woman near the door reached out her arm and said something to him. According to Veljković, he picked up his rifle, which he had left by the door: "I think I said, 'Oh, she is alive'; when one of my colleagues entered the pizzeria, fired a shot, and killed the woman.... I cannot say who fired and who shot her execution style in the pizzeria, but then I just continued loading the bodies."[17]

When he was asked to clarify this, he said, "I can't really say," and then, "I simply cannot recall."[18]

When he was asked yet again about the bodies in the pizzeria, Veljković described recognizing a bus driver he knew: "He just said — I saw him actually getting up to his feet and he said, 'You've shot my entire family dead. Spare me at least.' I left the room again and again somebody entered the pizzeria, fired a shot, and killed the man. And I can't recall who it was who shot him."[19]

Veljković explained that the loading of the bodies was supervised by Dr. Boban Vuksanović — the director of the medical centre and also the man who had ousted Halit Berisha from his position as mayor in 1991. With "Bobek" directing them, workers from the Suva Reka public utilities company helped to load the bodies into the truck so they could be driven away.

Veljković described returning to the police station on his own, leaving the workers to continue the job.

Back at the station, he testified, he "heard from someone that the order was that those competent within the Ministry from Belgrade ordered that the killing should cease, and that the Albanians were to be told that they had to leave the territory of Suva Reka within half an hour, otherwise they would meet the fate of the Berisha family."[20]

Veljković described receiving a phone call at the station from an Albanian woman, who asked him what this meant and why the Albanians had been told to leave:

> I told her that, indeed, they had to leave. She asked me where to, and I told her to Albania. She asked me, "What are we going to do in Albania?" I didn't want to continue this conversation. I simply said, "Go to Albania; you have to leave otherwise you will suffer the fate of the other ones." People who were nearby heard the firing in the Berisha compound and everyone knew what had taken place. I hung up and within half an hour there was an en masse departure of the members of the Albanian community by vehicles. They all went towards Prizren and Albania. As of that moment, there was no more killing. People simply left. We resumed our work.[21]

The Trial Chamber, in its final judgment, did rely on Veljković's testimony. But it did so only to the degree that it was corroborated by other evidence. His very particular failures of observation and memory, and his attempts to limit his own involvement, put his credibility into question.[22] It was a reasonable result.

K83 was a codename, one of the protective measures the Tribunal makes available to its witnesses. He testified behind a screen and his personal details were not provided to the public, either in the gallery or via broadcast. As was always the case with such protected witnesses, his identity was disclosed to the accused so his lawyers could prepare for cross-examination. The contents of K83's evidence, however, were public.[23]

K83 testified that at around 11:00 a.m. he stopped outside of the police station with his fellow officers and watched as two camouflage military trucks full of police pulled in. Their commander Rado Mitrović, better known by his "secret identity code" and radio handle *Cegar 1*, arrived in a Jeep. He walked up to Nenad Jovanović, the assistant commander of the Suva Reka police. As Jovanović moved to salute him, Cegar turned and yelled at him instead: "What are you staring at? What are you waiting for?" he shouted. "Go after these men." Jovanović turned to his officers and told them to move.

K83 testified that the men went straight to the house that had served as the OSCE's headquarters — Shyrete Berisha's house, in other words. Tanović and Cukarić ordered K83 and Petković to provide cover from the back of the house and the two of them spread out to opposite sides. Tanović and Cukarić took four Kosovo Albanian men aside — we now know these were Shyrete's husband, Nexhat, his cousin Faton, and Sedat and Nexhmedin Berisha. The men were lined face-first against the wall of the house and shot and killed on the spot. The police officers who had arrived in the trucks began firing at the house next door.

K83 said it seemed like a movie. He saw thirty or thirty-five people — women, children, the elderly — spill out of the house, running together towards the shopping centre. Tanović and Cukarić ordered K83 and Petković to follow the group to see where they were going.

He testified that he and Petković followed the group towards the mall. Then they returned to the house and told Tanović and Cukarić that the group had taken shelter inside a pizzeria.

He described that as he was following the group, he and Petković had passed an elderly man and woman who had been shot in the legs and were lying on the pavement. He said that somehow the man and woman were killed: "I didn't see anything, but I just heard a shot or shots, and when I came back I saw that Cukarić had a rifle in his hands, and then we sat down to have a drink, the drink that I had fetched."[24]

He said that Cukarić had told him to go to a nearby cafe and "to have a drink and sort of relax and come to, to relax and feel better." He said he was frightened and couldn't calm down. He said that after the four officers finished their drinks, Tanović broke the window of the pizzeria with the butt of his rifle and threw a hand-grenade inside:

> … all you could hear were cries and screams and moans and crying, and after several minutes, a couple of minutes later — not even that much, maybe — a second bomb was thrown in, hand-grenade was thrown in. And when things had calmed down a bit, then they started shooting, Cukarić and Tanović, with a burst of gun-fire, through the shop window, the window to the pizzeria. So they took turns in shooting until all went quiet and none of the cries could be heard anymore.[25]

He said that Cukarić and Tanović asked him to take part in the shooting, but that he didn't. "I had known these people," he said, "and I couldn't do it."[26]

He described that Cukarić had two Motorola radios with him, which he used after the killings. Fifteen to twenty minutes later, Dr. Vuksanović arrived at the scene. He moved through the pizzeria, examining the bodies and confirming that they were dead. Then an empty truck arrived, pulling right to the front of the pizzeria. Another truck pulled up shortly thereafter, this one carrying an oddly mismatched group of elderly men and adolescent boys. Known as the "civilian defence," they had been driving around collecting livestock, primarily sheep, cows, and pigs. Vuksanović gestured inside and told them to load the human carnage into the first truck. They stood rooted on the spot, refusing to move. Cukarić intervened, threatening them directly: "Load up the bodies or you'll end up like them," he said. They obeyed, loading the bodies. When the first truck drove off, towards Prizren, a new truck showed up and the loading began again. When it was full it drove off in the same direction.

K83 said that he stayed at the scene for about two hours. Then he was taken to the health centre. He was asked how he felt:

> A. I was shattered. I felt sick, that kind of thing. I wasn't feeling well. I had a difficult time of it.
>
> Q. To this day, have you recovered from the illness, the feeling of being shattered, having regard to what you witnessed?
>
> A. You know how it is. Well, the film I saw is never interrupted. Everything goes normally during the day, but when I go to sleep I can't — actually, I can't sleep. I don't sleep well, and I have nightmares, and when I get up in the morning, I feel tired, as if I hadn't slept the whole night. So that's what happens.[27]

K83 had also witnessed the fate of Jashar Berisha, the manager of the local gas station. He explained that Jashar had been detained at the police station while the shootings were taking place. After the killings at the pizzeria, police crime technician Todor Jovanović drove Jashar to the pizzeria in a squad car. Jovanović walked him right up to the building. As he neared the entrance, Jashar resisted. Jovanović forced him ahead. K83 watched as Dr. Vuksanović called Jashar closer, as if to show him something.

"I don't deserve to be here," Jashar said.

Cukarić grabbed him by the arm, pushed him inside, and shot him in the back.

# Aftermath

Hysni Berisha was born in Suva Reka and had spent his entire life there. He and his family had survived the first part of the campaign, in late March, by moving from house to house, on one occasion hiding in a neighbour's basement with seventy to one hundred other people.

In early April, the house they were hiding in was advanced on by a ragtag group of Serbian forces, wearing a combination of uniforms and sporting bandannas. They were armed with AK-47s and torching houses with flamethrowers as they walked. Everyone in the house ran, but there seemed nowhere to go. They soon found themselves in an open field, surrounded. The Serb forces demanded money. One of them grabbed Hysni's daughter and threatened to shoot her unless he paid. The man's commander saw the attempted extortion and ordered the girl released. He told the group to go to Albania.

Thus commenced a harrowing journey, moving in convoys alongside hundreds of thousands of other Kosovo Albanian civilians who had been displaced from their homes and were being clumsily shepherded out of the country. As they moved, Hysni saw Serb forces throw a knife from a passing truck, presumably for sport, hitting an old woman in the head. He saw a passing vehicle fire shots at a thirteen-year-old girl, hitting her in the arm. His group was robbed multiple times.

The war ended on June 11, and on June 13 he followed members of the NATO-led peacekeeping force KFOR (Kosovo Force) from Prizren back to Suva Reka. What he encountered there was to set the stage for the rest of his life.

On the day he returned, with the town now free of Serb policemen and army troops, Berisha set out to the pizzeria to see what remained. He found a walking stick on the grass outside the front door. The building itself was covered in burn marks and had blown-out windows. There were blue-red stains on the door, the window frames, and the freezer, and there were bloodstains and blue-red footprints on the ground. The walls were pockmarked with bullet holes and the floor was littered with cartridge and magazine cases. There were piles of partially burnt clothing and two different children's sandals, both of them burnt.

He traced a path back to the Berisha neighbourhood and found a puddle of dried blood in front of Shyrete's house, with a white-striped cardigan sweater lying next to it. Behind the house he found ashes, burnt clothing, Yugoslav coins, a watch, and a burnt piece of bone. There were bullet marks and blood stains on the house's rear wall.

He continued walking amongst the neighbourhood's quiet, abandoned houses. One yard had family photographs scattered across the lawn. Another was strewn with cans of food, both empty and full. Some of it was pork, which the predominantly Muslim ethnic Albanians didn't eat.

He went to the local cemetery, where he counted thirty-four new graves, each with a small board marking the plot. Some bore a last name and a first initial, others were marked "NN" for unknown.

He spent days wandering through the scattered remains of his village's destruction, piecing together what had happened and identifying who was missing. He began speaking to surviving family members as they returned to Suva Reka, gathering information about what they had seen and the people they still couldn't find. He examined the houses in which killings had been committed. It became clear that a great many people were unaccounted for.

At the local cemetery he saw that desperate family members were starting to dig up some of the grave sites, looking for the bodies of their loved ones. He contacted the ICTY's office in Prizren and enlisted KFOR's help to ensure the areas weren't mined or otherwise booby-trapped, and to arrange for a proper examination of the graves.

Hysni had been an administrative worker — a legal officer for a construction company — and he had no formal investigative training. But the forty-eight people he had lost from his extended family seemed to compel him to continue. What began as a one-man crusade turned into the Commission for Missing Persons in Suva Reka, which he chaired. In Albanian, the organization was called *Shpresimi*: "hope."

In 2001 he provided the ICTY with the information he had gathered and gave a statement to one of the Tribunal's investigators, describing the extent of the destruction: 9,895 of 11,955 houses destroyed; four mosques levelled and eleven partially destroyed; and a list of more than five hundred people who had been killed.

On July 4, 2002, he was called as a prosecution witness in the Milošević trial. His testimony was brief, with the prosecutor introducing his statement directly into evidence, not asking any substantive questions in the courtroom. But Mr. Milošević, representing himself, took full advantage of his opportunity to cross-examine. At the conclusion of the cross-examination, when Mr. Milošević pressed him with respect to what he had seen on his return to the pizzeria and who committed the massacre, Berisha snapped:

> It was the Yugoslav police. You were their commander. All the Berisha family was in there, forty-eight members of which eighteen [were] children and old people and women. They were all forced into there, that cafe, and they were executed by firearms. And then the building was burnt to cover up the traces of the crime.[28]

As evidence, this declaration would have no real value. It was not for Berisha to reach the conclusions he was describing; the value in his evidence lay in the confirmatory observations he made after the events had taken place, while it would be for the court to draw the ultimate conclusions about what had actually happened. But he had confronted Milošević himself, the man most responsible for the conflict and who had overseen the war campaign from the top.

In August and September of 1999, the British Forensic Team had conducted autopsies in Suva Reka. At the Suva Reka cemetery they identified a minimum of eighteen bodies, the commingled and skeletonized body parts making it hard to establish the total number with absolute certainty. Amongst the bodies were three members of the Berisha family who had been killed behind Shyrete's house. Autopsy showed that Faton Berisha had been killed by gunshot wounds to the torso. His mother, Fatime, died from gunshot wounds to the brain. Fatime's cousin Sedat was identified by his shoes, which were recovered along with his body.[29]

Hysni also accompanied the British Forensic Team to a location in Korisha known as Kroj-i-Popit, an isolated field about thirteen kilometres outside of Suva Reka, on the way to Prizren. Once used as a firing range by the Yugoslav National Army, there was little to mark the location besides a solitary white shack sitting by a scattered dirt road. But the earth nearby had been disturbed. The ground was peppered with small hills of brown dirt and a number of gaping black pits.

Here the British Forensic Team exhumed two large graves, in which they found a range of personal items and pieces of clothing. On September 24, after being photographed and analyzed, all of the items were cleaned and laid out to be identified. Surviving family members, looking for any signs of their loved ones, shuffled uneasily through the scene. They recognized torn and blackened jackets, mud-caked shoes, wallets and keys, tattered handbags, slippers and walking sticks.

Dashurije Berisha recognized her father's black leather shoe from the brown thread she had once sown in so he could find them. Tagged by the team as KRA-1097 was a child's pencil-case and coloured pencils. Tagged as KO-01/13 was a picture of two objects. The first was a Polaroid photograph, dirtied around the edges and dog-eared in the top-right corner; the photo showed a young Kosovo Albanian woman, her arm resting proudly on the shoulder of a cherubic young boy. The second object, to the right of the Polaroid, was a child's notebook — blue beneath the soot stains, with ABC stenciled across the front in orange. On the label, still faintly legible, was a hand-written name: Mirat.[30]

The photographs were shown to Hysni Berisha in court:

> This picture reminds me of the worst moment I experienced in September — on September 1st, 1999. In that mass grave this photograph was found. This is Zelihe Berisha, my cousin's wife, Hamdi's wife, and her son Mirat. Maybe you cannot see it here or discern what it is, but this is the pencil box, Mirat's pencil box, who was in first grade. And that day, it was the first day of school, and on that day he was not amongst us anymore.[31]

Mirat and his family were included in Shyrete Berisha's family tree. As Hysni explained in court, Mirat's father and four sisters had been killed as well. Not a single member of the family had survived.

Amongst the family members gathered at Kroj-i-Popit was Halit Berisha, who had come looking for any trace of his missing brother, Jashar, unseen since he left for the petrol station on March 26. Amongst the individually numbered objects was KRA-1072, an oblong object partially wrapped in red cloth. Halit recognized it: his brother's telltale red track pants, worn beneath his jeans, over top of his severed leg. Exhibit KRA-1091 was a piece of paper, on which was handwritten "Jashar Berisha." But the rest of his body was nowhere to be found.

It wasn't just Jashar Berisha's body that was missing. A great many of the other bodies of people killed in Suva Reka were missing as well. They appeared to have been unearthed and moved again. The question, for everyone, was where these bodies had ultimately been taken.

Halit, along with his brother Eqrim and his sister Aziza, provided blood samples to the forensic team at the site. The hope was that the common markers of blood and family, in the form of DNA, might help to identify what had happened to the rest of his brother's body. Shyrete Berisha provided a DNA sample to international authorities as well, hoping that they might one day discover what had happened to the missing bodies of her family members.

# 9

# HOW WE GOT HERE

I

## Kosovo and the Path to War

The implementation of the Dayton Accords in 1995 ended the brutal war in Bosnia and marked the beginning of a slow return to normal life for its traumatized citizens. The peace was enforced by an unprecedented sixty thousand NATO peacekeeping troops patrolling the country.

As the fog of war began to lift in Serbia, the weakened state of the domestic economy — stretched to the breaking point by the war and ravaged by economic sanctions — came more sharply into focus. Frustrated with a diminishing quality of life at home, Serbian citizens staged widespread protests against Milošević. He responded to his newfound disfavour by silencing dissent in the media, tampering with elections, and cracking down on his opponents.[1] Then he turned his attention back to Kosovo, where his populist appeal had been born.

When NATO had negotiated the Dayton Accords, many Kosovo Albanians hoped that the terms of the settlement would recognize the precariousness of their situation and restore Kosovo's pre-existing autonomous status, rolling back the oppressive measures Milošević had imposed on them. But the Accords left the situation in Kosovo unresolved, in fact acknowledging the territory as an integral part of Serbia.

The approach of peaceful non-resistance that leader Ibrahim Rugova had long advocated seemed not to have borne fruit, and more radical Kosovo Albanian voices started to gain traction. The frustration saw the emergence of a group of guerrilla fighters who sought to take matters into their own hands: the Kosovo Liberation Army (KLA).

The KLA's rapid rise to prominence owed much to some remarkable moments of serendipity. Coinciding with the group's emergence in the spring of 1997 were transformative events in the country of Albania next door. As Albania's economy collapsed, sparked by corrupt business practices and the unwinding of extensive pyramid schemes, riots and protests saw the Albanian police flee and the army dissolve. In the chaos, Albanian civilians began to raid local arms depots, emptying them of hundreds of thousands of weapons. With their ethnic brothers selling Kalashnikovs for $10 each, the KLA had a seemingly endless source of weaponry.[2]

Despite this easy access to weapons, in 1997 the KLA was a small group of about two hundred members that had trouble attracting recruits.[3] Ironically, it was Serbia's response to the KLA, characterized by brutal and over-reaching retaliatory attacks, that saw its popularity and recruiting base surge.

In February of 1998, after the KLA ambushed a police patrol in Drenica, Serbian police and special anti-terrorist (SAJ) units launched attacks against the towns of Likosane and Cirez, firing indiscriminately at non-combatants and killing twenty-five people. Days later, the police and army launched a joint attack on the family compound of Adem Jashari, one of the KLA's founders, in the village of Prekaz. The attack, which was coordinated by Đorđević and Jovica Stanisić, killed an estimated fifty-eight people, including eighteen women and ten children.[4] Police arranged for the bodies of those killed to be put on display in a "warehouse without walls" on the outskirts of town. Then they buried the bodies in a large grave before they could be autopsied. The following day the family members had to dig their relatives out to bury them in accordance with Islamic law.[5]

The attacks outraged the Kosovo Albanian community and a combination of fear, anger, and indignation swelled the ranks of the KLA. The spiralling events also provoked international condemnation, with the international community fearful of another Bosnia. The United Nations Security Council passed Resolution 1160 on March 31, condemning the Serbian police for using excessive force against civilians and censuring "all acts of terrorism by the Kosovo Liberation Army."

Serbia dramatically escalated the build-up of police and military forces in the weeks and months that followed, launching violent retaliatory attacks against the KLA and using "scorched earth" tactics against entire communities. At the same time, the KLA continued to grow and expand its reach, spreading across significant portions of Kosovo. Although they didn't have artillery, KLA gunmen launched attacks on the police and army, including attacks on police stations in Suva Reka and Rudnik. They directed attacks and kidnappings at ethnic Serbs and at ethnic Albanians perceived to be collaborators.[6]

The summer of 1998 saw the unfolding of a three-way chess match played by the newly emboldened KLA, Serbian authorities, and an increasingly nervous international community. Following a meeting with Russian president Boris Yeltsin, Milošević agreed to the establishment of the Kosovo Diplomatic Observer Mission (KDOM), an international mission that began monitoring the situation on the ground in early July. Just weeks later, however, the most senior members of the Serbian political, military, and police leadership (including Milošević, Milutinović, Sainović, Pavković, and Đorđević) met to implement the "Plan for Suppressing Terrorism in Kosovo," a large-scale offensive aimed at both the KLA and at Kosovo Albanian civilians more generally. The coordinated operations that followed, in which the military would shell towns and villages and then the police would advance through on foot, would become a sort of dry run for what followed in 1999. The campaign, which ran from the end of July to the end of September 1998, destroyed countless villages, resulted in several thousand deaths, and displaced between 100,000 and 400,000 people from their homes.[7]

As the humanitarian crisis intensified, the international community sought to stop the worsening violence. U.N. Security Council Resolution 1199 called out the "excessive and indiscriminate force" being used by

Serbian forces.[8] In its wake, October of 1998 saw several agreements reached — known as the "October Agreements" — in which Serbia agreed to withdraw forces from Kosovo, reduce police and troop levels, and accept the establishment of the OSCE-led Kosovo Verification Mission (KVM) to ensure their compliance. Sainović led the negotiations for the Yugoslavian government and Đorđević represented the police.

The Serbian regime, however, had no intention of honouring the agreements. Instead of reducing troop levels, they increased their numbers. They stepped up efforts to arm Serb civilians, ultimately arming somewhere in the range of fifty thousand Serbs so they could participate in joint operations. They continued their coordinated operations on the ground, stonewalling the Kosovo Verification Mission and then ultimately ignoring it.

January 15, 1999 was a significant day on the path to NATO's military intervention in Kosovo. In response to two KLA attacks that had killed policemen several days earlier — an attack on a patrol between Suva Reka and Stimlje that killed three officers and an attack between Stimlje and Urosevac that killed one — Serbia began massing its forces in the area of Racak. A platoon of special police and a number of elite SAJ[9] anti-terrorist commandos were deployed. Rather unusually, a number of senior police officials arrived at the local police station, including Đorđević, who was seen taking phone calls on site from Deputy Prime Minister Nikola Sainović.[10]

When KDOM and KVM observers tried to position themselves between the massing Serb forces and the villages they surrounded, the Serb forces advanced directly past them. Pragas and T-55 tanks fired heavy artillery directly into the village, pinning the villagers in the town. Then police swept through the village and were seen moving from house to house.

The next day, KVM and KDOM observers found twenty bodies lying in a line along a gully — mostly older men in their fifties and sixties, but younger men in their twenties and thirties as well. Their bullet wounds were to the head and most had visible powder burns, indicating short-range gunshots — telltale signs of execution. Observers counted forty-five bodies in the village, including three women and a twelve-year-old boy.[11]

Ambassador William Walker condemned the massacre in a press conference later that day. The ICTY, including Prosecutor Louise Arbour, were denied visas and prevented from visiting the site. Serbia instead sent its own representatives, led by Investigative Judge Danica Marinković, who the police escorted to the site several days later. Marinković was presented with a staged scene — the only bodies her team inspected had been moved to a mosque and showed no sign of being shot in the head, and no one on her team visited or even apparently located the gully where the twenty bodies had been found.[12] The purported investigation bore all the signs of an institutional whitewashing. Indeed, as the autopsies were beginning, Marinković was quoted in the newspaper declaring, "The terrorist corpses have not been massacred, as the more than biased head of Kosovo Verification Mission William Walker has claimed."[13]

After the Racak killings, the pretense of a ceasefire was clearly gone.

II

# Metaphors of Violence and Victimhood

For the Clinton administration and NATO, the haunting consequences of declining to use force in both Bosnia and Rwanda, and their continuing impotence in the face of Milošević's manipulations in Kosovo, were becoming untenable. The spectre of another cycle of violence in Kosovo, so soon after the brazen actions of Serb forces in Bosnia, which among other brutalities had seen the ruthless siege of Sarajevo and the mass slaughter under the U.N.'s nose in Srebrenica, was truly alarming. The events also cast the shadow of destabilizing effects across the region, endangering the fragile peace in Bosnia and threatening to spill over to neighbouring countries like Albania and Macedonia.

But Kosovo did not loom large in the Western imagination. Americans knew next to nothing about the small territory, and while some had learned about Bosnia from recent events there, Kosovo was another story. If NATO was going to wage war for humanitarian reasons, they would presumably need to make the case.

The Clinton administration and other proponents of intervention argued that the events in Kosovo would destabilize the region, invoking the metaphor of Kosovo as the "powderkeg" of the Balkans and raising the historical spectre of the domino events that led to World War I. They leaned most heavily, however, on the language of atrocity from World War II, frequently invoking Holocaust imagery. A number of officials, Secretary of State Madelaine Albright chief among them, cited the "lessons of Munich" to convey the necessity of standing up to Milošević, rather than ignoring or appeasing him as world leaders had once done with Hitler. The public was reminded that NATO itself was "forged in the aftermath of the Holocaust" to prevent further war.[14]

The Congressional record from the time contains numerous direct references to World War II and the Holocaust, to the point that some of the members began to openly question the comparison. It seemed, in many ways, that the question of whether the United States should go to war would be determined by how appropriate the analogies to World War II really were.[15] As Roland Paris found in his study on the use of metaphors preceding and accompanying the Kosovo War:

> If the U.S. Administration, other members of Congress, opinion leaders, and the public could be convinced that the complex situation in the Balkans was in at least a few important ways analogous to the Holocaust or to Nazi aggression (if these constituencies could just be persuaded to think about the Kosovo crisis in the light of World War II) then it would be difficult to oppose U.S. Military intervention in the crisis.[16]

The exact inverse of this perception, however, seemed to be operating in the minds of the Serbian regime, which had long invoked the rhetoric of the Holocaust — both in reference to Kosovo and to Croatia — but with *Serbs* placed in the role of the victim. Before and during the conflicts that raged in the former Yugoslavia through the 1990s, nationalist Serb leaders and writers frequently invoked persecution imagery that aligned Serbs with the Jews as a targeted, victimized, and imperilled group throughout history — continuing to the present day.[17] They drew on the very real atrocities that Serbs had suffered during World War II under the Croatian Ustaše government that co-operated with the Nazis. They invoked the spectre of violent persecution by ethnic Albanians in Kosovo.

They pointed to the international community's ongoing condemnations of Serbia's actions in the 1990s as further evidence of persecution. Dobrica Ćosić, the first president of the Federal Republic of Yugoslavia, explained the "Serbophobia" he saw targeting and victimizing the Serbs this way: "We Serbs feel today as the Jews did in Hitler's day…. Today, Serbophobia in Europe is a concept and an attitude with the same ideological motivation and fury as anti-Semitism had during the Nazi era."[18]

In reality, however, the Serb forces still held all the cards in Kosovo: a powerful military, a heavily equipped and well-trained police force that could be deployed like an army, a newly armed civilian population that could be enlisted on the ground, violent and battle-hardened paramilitary groups eager to join the cause, and a centralized command to coordinate their operations from the top.

III

# This Means War

The last hope to stop the escalating violence and a descent into all-out war in Kosovo came with peace talks organized by the international community in Rambouillet, France in February of 1999. The talks were drawn out over three long weeks and followed a "shuttle diplomacy" procedure in which the Serbian and Kosovar delegations met indirectly through third parties.[19] As the negotiations unfolded, the level of violence on the ground in Kosovo was noticeably reduced. At the same time, however, Serbian authorities were rolling out extensive and coordinated plans for a large spring offensive. Beginning in February, international observers and local civilians watched as the military began to heavily fortify and reinforce its units, deploying brigades inside Kosovo and massing along its borders. Late February and early March saw the arrival of convoys of tanks and armoured military vehicles, as well as brigades of special forces police equipped with automatic weapons and combat gear. When new soldiers were rotated into Kosovo for duty, the men they were replacing had their service extended and thus remained in place. The result was the build-up of thousands of additional troops.[20]

The Rambouillet negotiations failed. Both KLA attacks and joint operations by Serbian military and police followed. When peace talks were reconvened in Paris, they broke down almost immediately.[21]

On the ground, international observers described a shift in the behaviour of Serb forces: their strategy changed from responding to KLA expansions and attacks to initiating operations against the Kosovo Albanian population more broadly. In late March, with the conflict escalating and NATO attacks seemingly imminent, international organizations operating in Kosovo began to withdraw. The Kosovo Verification Mission left on March 20 and the UNHCR left on March 21.

On March 22, the renowned diplomat and negotiator Richard Holbrooke was sent to Belgrade to convince Milošević to change his mind, stop the escalating attacks on Kosovo, and thereby avert a NATO bombing. Milošević refused, telling Holbrooke that he was fully aware of the consequences.[22]

On March 24, President Clinton announced that NATO attacks were underway. He identified three goals: "To demonstrate the seriousness of NATO's opposition to aggression," to deter Milošević from "continuing and escalating his attacks on helpless civilians," and, if necessary, "to damage Serbia's capacity to wage war against Kosovo by seriously diminishing its military capabilities." He also made it clear, however, that he did not intend to send in troops on the ground.[23]

# 10

# PODUJEVO

## I

### Podujevo

The acts that took place in Podujevo were among the darkest of the war. They were also among the most notorious — in part, at least, because they were so difficult to justify or deny. The fact that these acts were ever prosecuted, beginning with an entirely unprecedented local trial in Serbia, was owed to the bravery and tenacity of several young children who had survived the killings, and to one of the perpetrators who broke ranks and came forward against his former colleagues. But the road to justice for the events in Podujevo was long, tortured, and controversial. The events, and the attempts at justice that followed, came to seem somehow emblematic of the reactions to the conflict more broadly — emblematic of competing forces within Serbia, emblematic of barriers to acceptance and justice, and then emblematic of a genuine potential for hope.

———

Saranda and Fatos Bogujevci were cousins. In March of 1999, Saranda was fourteen years old and Fatos was twelve. They had gone to school together, a grade apart, and lived in the same house in Podujevo, Kosovo. Their town lay on a crucial supply route between Priština and the Serbian city of Niš, giving it tactical significance for both Serbian forces and the KLA.[1]

Saranda and Fatos lived in a family compound that contained three homes, a common living arrangement amongst Kosovo Albanians. On March 26, with rumours circulating that Serb forces were targeting and killing Albanian men, the women of the Bogujevci family urged the men, and in particular Saranda's father Safet, and Fatos's father Selatin, to hide elsewhere in the town. Of the nineteen people left in the compound — twelve in Saranda and Fatos's house, seven in the other — only one adult male remained, seventy-year-old Hamdi Duriqi. The family stayed indoors with the curtains drawn.

March 28 was Bajram Day, a religious holiday for ethnic Albanians.[2] At about 7:00 a.m., the families noticed an armoured personnel carrier (APC) pulling up to the front of the compound. Terrified, the adults decided to move everyone into Saranda's uncle's house, which was set off from the street and seemed somehow safer. They joined the Duriqi family there, all nineteen of them now in the same house, nervously waiting. They watched from inside as Serb forces began to enter the houses around them and bring people out onto the street.

Soon a group of four or five men wearing green camouflage walked into their compound, and Saranda and Fatos found themselves walking outside with everyone else. They had packed bags of food to bring with them, but were told to raise their hands and leave the bags there.

It was a cold morning and Saranda put her hands in her pockets to keep them warm. Seeing this, one of the men pulled her to the side and searched her pockets. Soon members of the family were being searched all around her. Her younger brother Shpetim had marbles in his pocket; when one of the soldiers found them he began bouncing them out onto the ground, one by one. Her mother, unsure of what to do, bent down and tried to gather them up as they scattered.

The men told the older women to take off their headscarves, then snatched the traditional *plis* hat off of Hamdi Duriqi's head. Fatos looked on as one of the men took money out of his mother Shefkate's pockets, then pulled her away towards a shed.

The men walked the rest of the group from one neighbour's garden to another, then out onto the street by the police station. Serb forces wearing mixed uniforms shouted, swore, and smashed the windows of the local shops and coffee houses. There were some sarcastic chants of "KLA, KLA!"

Saranda watched as a soldier removed Selman Gashi's *plis* and directed him inside a coffee shop. A short man wearing half of a police uniform — a brown shirt atop police trousers — said something to Hamdi Duriqi and then slapped him across the face. He led Hamdi inside the same coffee shop. Then both Saranda and Fatos heard gunshots. They never saw either man again.[3]

Saranda, Fatos, and the rest of the group were led along a small path that took them back through the courtyard. There were a number of men milling about, yelling at them in Serbian. One of the men took out a scalpel — Saranda thought it looked like something you would use in surgery — and brandished it at Fezrije Lugaliju. She thought the man said something about not having a heart. As they passed their house, Saranda could see that the furniture inside had been piled in the centre of the room.

Fatos saw his mother being dragged out of the shed, a soldier gripping her by the neck. She was crying. She said something in Serbian that neither Fatos nor Saranda understood, though they could make out the last part: "They are only children."

Fatos and Saranda watched as the man shoved Shefkate in the back, then raised his AK-47 and shot her. She collapsed to the ground and the man fired again into her upper body. Fatos started screaming, as did his sister beside him. The man tossed his gun to the ground, empty. Then he took another AK-47 from one of the men standing nearby.

There were now about ten men standing in the courtyard. The group of women and children, including Fatos and Saranda, found themselves up against a wall — the side of one of the houses in the compound. Saranda was directly in the middle of the group. Fatos was standing at the edge, though he was pushed towards the centre as well.

The same man pointed his gun at the group. From about four or five metres away, he opened fire. Saranda described what happened next:

When he started shooting, I just leaned on the wall and just slided down and then it hit me on my right leg, the bullets, and then after a while the shooting stopped; and there was a sound from someone, the kind of sound where you're struggling to breathe, and then the shooting started again. And then when the shooting started again, it hit me in my arm and in my back. And then after a while, the shooting stopped, and then it was quiet, so I wasn't sure whether the soldiers were still there or had gone. And then I decided to lift my head up. And then I just — I looked around and I saw my cousin Genc, who had lifted his head up as well, and I saw my brother Shpetim, who was nine years old. He was lying face-down on my feet, and he was shot on his head, half of his head was missing. And I also saw Fatos, my cousin Fatos, he was in front of me and there was something behind his back and it looked kind of — it was something from the inside of the body, something from the body. So I thought the, you know, he was dead, but then he lifted his head up as well and I realised then that he was alive. And I also saw Enver's son, the old one, and he was shot in his face. I couldn't really tell where his eyes was or his mouth. And I also saw my grandmother, she was lying down, and she was facing me, and her eyes were opened.[4]

Fatos, for his part, had pretended to be dead. When the shooting started, everyone had tumbled down in the same direction. He had just stayed down. When the shooting stopped briefly — he thought it was so they could reload — he could hear Fezrije breathing as well. Then the shooting started again. He was hit several times but he stayed conscious, lying still. Then the shooting finally stopped.

Saranda turned to her cousin Genc, Fatos's brother, and told him to stay down. The two of them lay still on the ground. They could hear voices talking. Saranda thought she could make out someone saying, "Children."

With his eyes still clenched, Fatos could hear voices crackling over a radio. He heard some of the men shouting and swearing at each other.

He assumed the radio had told them to stop. The men left the courtyard and it was silent for several minutes.

Both Saranda and Fatos were riddled with bullets. Saranda had been shot twice in the right leg, once in the back, and thirteen times in the left arm, which she had reflexively held up to protect herself. Fatos was shot three times in the left leg and twice in the right.

As she lay there, Saranda could see that there were men — different men, it seemed, wearing different uniforms — who were collecting some of her cousins, still alive. She felt numb. She could see holes in her coat and a hole in her hand.

At some point, she decided she would try to move. As she did she felt and heard something click in her elbow; the bone had broken. She saw two men moving quickly towards her and before she realized what was happening they had pulled her out from amongst the other bodies. They laid her on the ground and looked at her wounds, cutting the trousers from one of her legs and examining her arm.

Five of the children had survived: Saranda and Fatos, Fatos's brother Genc, and his sisters Jehona and Lirije. Fatos watched as five men swarmed around them, cutting open their clothes to get at the bullet wounds and keeping them warm. Someone gave him a glass of water.

The men carried the children to a Pinzgauer,[5] then to what looked like an ambulance. Fatos remembered sitting on the edge of the ambulance and watching soldiers, police, civilians, and men in mixed uniforms talking on the street, breaking shop windows, and looting. He recognized some of the men, including a local police officer, as Serbs from the town. As he sat there he watched one of the stores being emptied out, the food loaded into a lorry parked out front.

Fatos was stacked underneath his injured sister in the ambulance; a soldier sat with him and tried to keep him distracted.[6] Saranda only remembered her vehicle starting to move. She closed her eyes and then woke up in the Pristina Hospital. There were people shouting around her, removing her clothes and asking where she was from — "Kosovo Polje?" "No, Podujevo." For a while she didn't know whether it was day or night.

None of the other women or children survived the shootings in the courtyard. Fourteen people were killed, all of them women and children. Many of the victims were members of Saranda's family: her mother Sala, her grandmother Shehide, her brothers Shpend (twelve years old) and Shpetim (nine years old), her father's aunt Nefise, and her daughter-in-law Fezrije.

Fatos lost his mother and his sister Nora. Seven members of the Duriqi family, who had been hiding with the Bogujevicis, were killed as well. All of them were buried on the outskirts of Podujevo.


The surviving children were treated in the Pristina Hospital, which was under Serb control. The doctors knew who the children were and why they were there. It soon became apparent that as survivors of the massacre they posed a public relations problem to the operations in Kosovo.

Saranda remembered two policemen being stationed in her hospital room. One of them told the nurses not to give her any food. When she did get food it was inedible: "even animals wouldn't eat the kind of food they brought in," as she put it.[7] She was moved from room to room and left to lie in bed alone, day after day.

Serbian journalists came to visit the children in hospital, and before they arrived they were transferred to nicer rooms. Doctors told the children to say they had been the victims of a NATO bombing. They were afraid to say otherwise. They were put on show to illustrate "the consequence of NATO."

Wondering what had happened to her father, Saranda tried to send a message to him from the hospital. With time, the message managed to reach him. When he realized his daughter was in the hospital, he walked through the mountains and then into the heart of Serb-controlled Pristina to see her.

Having been in the hospital for a month, Saranda looked up one day to see her father walking into her room. What was a joyous occasion for her, Safet described as the most difficult moment of his life. He looked at his daughter, lying in the hospital bed, "in total shock." He didn't yet know what had happened to his family.[8]

On June 12, Saranda's birthday, the family learned that the war had ended and that NATO was taking back Pristina. After NATO moved in, a British army doctor who learned about the children made arrangements for them to be airlifted to England for treatment. In September, all five children were flown to Manchester and underwent major surgery. Saranda had multiple operations, and though her left arm was infected and immobile when she arrived, over time she regained the ability to use it. The children were eventually granted asylum in England.

ǁ

## Vacation at the Savage

Although Saranda and Fatos didn't know it at the time, the men who opened fired on them that day were members of the Scorpions, a notorious Serbian paramilitary group that had been involved in ethnic cleansing operations in both Bosnia and Croatia throughout the early to mid-1990s. Four years before their arrival in Podujevo, the Scorpions had been deployed to Srebrenica, where they served as an execution squad.[9]

Also unknown to Saranda and Fatos at the time was how the Scorpions, who were disbanded after the war in Bosnia, found themselves reconstituted and deployed to Podujevo four years later. The answer led back to the Serbian leadership and directly to Vlastimir Đorđević's doorstep at the Serbian Ministry of the Interior. It would form an important part of the trial.

The key prosecution witness for this aspect of the case was a man named Goran Stoparić. On the witness stand he looked like the consummate professional, dressed sharply in suits and crisp-collared shirts. He kept his thinning hair short, military style, and he spoke firmly and decisively, always straight to the point. Stoparić had served and fought as a member the Scorpions. Now he was testifying for the prosecution, informing on his former colleagues.

After the Dayton Accords ended the Bosnian War in 1995, the members of the Scorpions had returned to Serbia to resume ordinary lives. Back in his hometown of Šid,[10] along the Croatian border in northwest Serbia, Stoparić had opened a cafe called "Baby Blue" with his girlfriend Tanja. With a number of former Scorpions living in and around the town the cafe became a popular gathering place, the men often reuniting to share a drink, recount old adventures, and talk about what was going on in Kosovo. Customers would often ask Stoparić if he might enlist to fight again. He always demurred. He was too busy, he liked to say, running the cafe.

But returning to action was on his mind. The men of the Scorpions, himself among them, missed war. As he would later put it: "At the time, the word was that the Scorpions had been resting for four years, and now they craved war. That was literally the feeling. During those four years, we were in a stand-by status and missed war. There would have to be bloodshed."[11]

As Stoparić was testifying, an unusual mistake appeared briefly in the live transcription. It recorded him incongruously speaking the phrase, "Vacation at the Savage," although he had said no such thing. The strange phrase was corrected and soon disappeared from the transcript. But it remained firmly stuck in my head. It seemed to somehow capture the lives these men found themselves living: bored in their conventional lives back in Serbia, then travelling for extended periods of extracurricular recreation in war zones across the Balkans, where they engaged in murder, rape, and plunder.[12]

Several days before the outbreak of the Kosovo war, Stoparić's old boss in the Scorpions, a man known as Boca, paid him an unannounced visit. Stoparić wasn't home and his girlfriend chased Boca and his bodyguards out onto the street. But Stoparić encountered them there a few minutes later. Boca told Stoparić that the "Yankees" were going to strike Serbia and that his country needed him. The Scorpions were going to be re-formed and deployed to Kosovo. This time, Boca explained, the unit was going to be directly incorporated into the SAJ, the elite anti-terrorist wing of the police. Stoparić was surprised, though he didn't say it. Zealous though they could be, the Scorpions were a group of predominantly untrained civilians. The SAJ, on the other hand, were the best-trained operatives in the Ministry of the Interior — they were heavily armed, well equipped, and functioned more like a commando unit.

Stoparić didn't give Boca his decision right away. He wandered back to his cafe, only to find it full of his former Scorpions colleagues. His old friend Milovan Tomić, who was assigned to run the reconnaissance unit, handed him a notebook and relayed Boca's explicit instructions that he was to take down the names of men wanting to join the Scorpions to fight in Kosovo. Before he knew it, Stoparić had over a hundred names, some of them former members and some of them new recruits.

As Stoparić tells the story, he was still reluctant to join up himself, continuing to claim that he was needed at the cafe. But Boca was insistent, saying that if he didn't volunteer he would find himself served personally with a mobilization order. Boca wanted Stoparić to head up the Scorpions' reconnaissance unit along with Tomić. He told Stoparić that the buses would be leaving at 5:00 p.m. the next day and to be there.

The following day, three civilian buses pulled into the local park and a varied group of men piled in, about 120 in total. The majority of the town showed up to see them off. As the bus sat there, Stoparić looked around at the other men. They were all in civilian clothes and many of them had no combat experience or training at all.

The men had been told to leave any weapons and equipment at home, since they would be fully armed and equipped as part of the job, but Stoparić brought his night-vision goggles along anyway. The buses rumbled away to waving and cheering; down the road they picked up Boca and his brother Dragan. A man known as Mrgud, Boca's boss and a long-time backer of the Scorpions, drove his BMW out in front of the convoy of buses.

Just south of Belgrade they pulled off the road and into a dark field, where they found police officers sitting at desks. The officers issued them uniforms, combat vests, and boots. On one arm of the new uniforms was the SAJ patch, on the other the Scorpion insignia. The men were given a cap with the Serbian MUP police emblem and issued black woolen ski masks with eye holes. Weapons were loaded into a light-blue truck that followed in behind them.

The men spent that night and the next in a spa hotel in Prolom Banja, just north of Kosovo, where the SAJ maintained a logistics base. The men traded uniforms amongst each other to get a better fit. Stoparić conducted a brief training session for the new recruits, teaching them the basics of "house and street fighting." One of the men, a former Scorpion and current army officer, issued everyone weapons: M70 automatic rifles, grenades, and hand-held rocket launchers.

Then they were driven towards Kosovo. Partway there, they pulled off the road and Boca outlined the mission to the unit commanders. They were told they were going to Podujevo, where half the town was under Serb control. Their orders were to "clear up the other half."

The Scorpions arrived in Podujevo between 3:00 and 4:00 p.m. Boca told them to find places to sleep in the town's abandoned houses and that their mission would commence the next morning. The regular SAJ officers were already there, the town bustling with soldiers and police. Stoparić estimated there were five hundred men there; many were already milling around on the streets or searching compounds. Shortly after arriving, a number of the Scorpions joined in the anti-Albanian activities taking place all around them.

Stoparić searched for somewhere to spend the night, eventually finding a messy but suitable abandoned house. As he described it, he and Tomić saw through the back window that some of the Scorpions were bringing a group of nineteen terrified Albanians — one of them an elderly man and the rest women and children — out to the yard at gunpoint. This was clearly Saranda and Fatos's group. Stoparić testified that he grew concerned about what the men were planning to do. He decided to send them to Boca, he testified, so he went out to the group, walked the men out to the main street, and pointed them in Boca's direction.

According to Stoparić, he and Tomić "had moved away into an alley leading to an adjacent street and were not far away," when they heard the sound of automatic gunfire. It lasted for a minute or a minute and a half.[13] He and Tomić came running back through the alley. When they got to the courtyard, the shooting had just stopped.

Lying crumpled against the foot of the wall were the bodies of the women and children they had seen earlier. He assumed none of them had survived. Four of the men stood in the courtyard, discarding and replacing their rifle magazines. Stoparić thought they were going to "stamp" the women and children, shooting them individually in the forehead to make sure they were dead. They didn't, however, and Stoparić believed it may have been his arrival with Tomić that stopped this from happening.

The mood shifted rapidly as others arrived on scene and saw what had happened. One of the SAJ officers, Spasoje Vulević (known as Vuk — "Wolf"), ran to the group of bodies and carried a small girl out from amongst them, laying her on the road. The SAJ doctor, Dr. Marković, arrived to treat the handful of survivors.

The Scorpions' platoon commander ordered the men to get into formation. Then Boca arrived, along with his deputy, "Tutinac." Tutinac was enraged. He screamed at the men and told them they were going to be sent back. Thirty minutes later, the Scorpions were put on a bus and returned to Prolom Banja.

Even in the context of what was unfolding in Kosovo, the sudden, public, and indiscriminate slaughter of women and children had shocked some of the other men. The SAJ were an elite and well-trained unit, which must on some level have resented the incorporation of these overeager amateurs into their ranks.

Stoparić identified the four men who had been standing in the courtyard and reloading after the shooting. They were Scorpion members Saša Cvjetan, Dejan Demirović, Dragan Borogjević, and Dragan Medić. The last of these men was Boca's brother. Stoparić identified Saša Cvjetan as the man who had initially brought the women and children into the yard, at gunpoint, before he had sent them back out. He also identified two Scorpions on a balcony overlooking the courtyard: Zdravko Smiljić and Saša Dabić. He described Scorpion Miodrag Šolaja and a uniformed local police officer standing behind the shooters.

There was a dispute on the bus as the Scorpions were returned to Prolom Banja. "What did they expect," Boca asked rhetorically as they drove, "we are at war, people get killed in war."[14] One of the men was enraged, yelling at the group that he had children of his own, demanding to know who had done the killing. Dragan Medić stood up.

"I did it," he said. "Shut up."


Executing ethnic Albanian women and children mere minutes after their arrival in Kosovo didn't end the Scorpions' tour of duty. Although they were disbanded after being sent back to Prolom Banja, almost all of them were re-gathered about a month later and redeployed to Kosovo, once again operating as part of the SAJ.[15] The men were rearmed and provided with special equipment: night-vision goggles, bulletproof vests, and silencers.

They were sent to Kosovo Polje and the municipality of Suva Reka, moving northeast from there. Stoparić accompanied the reconnaissance unit, about twenty to thirty men who did most of the actual fighting. Their operations involved driving the KLA out of the territory and seizing villages. They met with little resistance and the villagers would often withdraw as they approached. The other Scorpions, along with PJP police units, would follow in a rearguard position and then take the villages, setting fire to the Albanian houses as they moved. The men quickly perfected their technique: using gasoline as an accelerant, they would start by igniting the curtains and couches.

Stoparić's Kosovo tour ended when a KLA fighter shot him in the arm, shattering his elbow. He was loaded onto a horse that carried him to the nearby town of Strpce, then put in a Jeep that raced to the hospital. He was taken to the Pristina Hospital — the same hospital where Saranda, Fatos, and the other children were still recovering.

I do not know whether they crossed paths at the hospital — that question seemed of little legal relevance, and court time is scarce, though I would come to wonder about it later. Perhaps they did cross paths, or perhaps Stoparić merely learned about their treatment in that same hospital. Perhaps it was not lost on him that Saranda suffered the same injury as he did, albeit in a much more severe form, her arm shattered by thirteen bullets while his was hit by one.[16]

What Stoparić did say was that he was transferred to a special unit for MUP patients and that they received preferential care. A Serbian nurse reassured him that the Albanian staff had either left or had been expelled, so that he had "nothing to worry about."[17]

Stoparić was transferred to Belgrade to undergo surgery. He received skin grafts, just as Saranda eventually did. Deemed medically unfit to continue fighting, Stoparić never returned to Kosovo. He would later receive a formal commendation from the commanders of the SAJ, Simović and Trajković, for his role in the operations.

Over the next twelve months, Stoparić would drive from Belgrade to nearby Batajnica, where the SAJ maintained their headquarters. There he was paid his Scorpions salary in cash.

III

# The Long Road to Justice

The lives that Saranda and Fatos lived in England must have seemed a world away from Kosovo. But with the killers still free, Saranda began to speak about pursuing justice.

In May of 2000, both Saranda and Fatos met with an investigator from the ICTY and gave interviews explaining what had happened. In March of 2003, Saranda travelled back to Podujevo for a commemoration of the massacre, attended by hundreds of people. She returned more focused than ever on the need to speak out about what had happened. As she told the BBC, which made her the subject of a documentary for the program *Real Story*:

> I want everyone to know. I want them to know because maybe that will help them understand things more, and maybe that will help them change their mind and think really carefully of what they're doing and that this is something really bad, and that it's not something that people should do. No matter where you're from or what colour you have, or what religion, that doesn't matter. It's about the person you are inside, and that you have to try and love and not hate. You know, just to make people understand.[18]

In July of 2003, four years after the shootings, the children who survived the Podujevo massacre agreed to travel to Belgrade, to testify in a domestic Serbian prosecution of one of the perpetrators.

That a local prosecution was proceeding at all was a shocking development. At the time of their testimony, to say that that the court system in Serbia had ignored the ethnic cleansing of Kosovo would be an understatement; the atrocities in Kosovo were being very actively avoided. Although the Serbian military courts were fully operational and responsible for charging and punishing crimes committed during wartime, they focused exclusively on crimes committed against the army: acts like desertion, refusal to obey orders, or petty theft. Serbian prosecutions of police, military, or paramilitary members for acts committed against Kosovo Albanians were virtually unheard of.

The case began, like many of Serbia's investigations during the Kosovo conflict, as a seemingly hollow procedure destined not to lead anywhere. On May 23, 1999, a criminal report had been filed against two of the Scorpions: Saša Cvjetan and Dejan Demirović. The men were detained, but then released ten days later. Demirović left Serbia for Canada. Cvjetan went back to his life.

Though this may have been frustrating, it should not have come as a surprise. After the killings occurred, no one had expressed any interest in the crime scene, the perpetrators were immediately evacuated from the town, and on their return to Prolom Banja none of the men were questioned about what happened.[19]

Yet, beginning in 2002, and then continuing in 2003, proceedings against Saša Cvjetan actually went ahead. One is left to wonder why. My own view is that there were a number of contributing factors. On the one hand, with Saranda, Fatos, and the other children surviving to tell their stories and then being relocated to a Western country, the optics were particularly bad. This was without question a serious crime and it was difficult to see even a purported basis upon which it could be justified. With the surviving children riddled with bullets, the traditional propaganda-machine retort that the incident was caused by NATO bombing made no sense.

At the same time, it seemed that one of the unwritten codes of the Kosovo operation had been violated. The *modus operandi* of the Serb forces had frequently been to separate the civilian men from the women and young children, then to kill the men and expel the women and children from the town, directing them towards the border. There had been a number of notable exceptions to this, of course, in which women and children were killed as well — many of these acts were the subjects of our indictment. But not all of the forces on the ground could be painted with the same brush. For some, certainly, it was one thing to have killed men, quite another to execute young children and their mothers. The angry responses of many of the officers in Podujevo made this clear enough.

There was also a third factor, however, that operated on a more general level. Prosecuting one individual for the killings was consistent with what was in fact a broader exculpatory narrative: that the crimes and killings in

Kosovo were not the clear and entirely foreseeable result of express political, military, and police planning, but were instead the actions of a handful of individual criminals who acted on their own. This was a narrative frequently repeated in public and a defence frequently advanced at the ICTY.

Any or all of these factors may have prevented these proceedings from being quashed at an earlier stage. But one should never discount the fact that once a very human process like this has been initiated — an actual case pushed ahead by deeply motivated witnesses, a determined Belgrade judge, and humanitarian groups who monitored and assisted with the process — it can develop a momentum all its own.[20]

The way the trial unfolded was bizarre and emblematic of the powerful competing forces then operating in Serbia.

In October of 2002, Cvjetan was brought to trial in the southern Serbian town of Prokuplje. Goran Stoparić was called as a witness at the Prokuplje court, and in his testimony at the ICTY he described what transpired there. According to Stoparić, prior to the Prokuplje trial Boca had brought him and two other witnesses to his farm, threatening their lives if they spoke out about what had happened. An attorney provided them with a pre-written statement, setting out an exculpatory version of events. Stoparić was to claim that Cvjetan was running beside him when the shooting took place and that the only shots Cvjetan had fired were warning shots into the air some fifteen minutes earlier. Fearing for his safety, Stoparić did as he was told.[21]

The trial in Prokuplje, however, was never completed. On November 27, 2002, the case was transferred to the District Court in Belgrade. It was recommenced in Belgrade on March 12, 2003.

On what was to be the first day of the new trial, Serbian prime minister Zoran Đinđić, notoriously tough on crime and the man who had extradited Milošević and other members of the Serbian regime to the ICTY, was assassinated by a group of hardliners led by Milorad "Legija" Ulemek, who had a long history of close ties with paramilitary groups.

When the case resumed, the Bogujevci children flew to the Serbian capital and became the first Albanian witnesses to testify in Serbia about war crimes in Kosovo. Although the trial would be attended by media and human rights monitors, the children were concerned for their safety. If the Serbian government couldn't keep the prime minister safe, how could they be protected?

When they landed in Belgrade they found that the entire airport terminal had been sealed off as a security precaution. They were guarded by over thirty Serbian Secret Service agents, with the entire floor of their hotel closed to the public.

The next morning, Genc — only ten years old — became so scared about seeing the killers again that the family felt it best to send him home to England. The remaining children were taken to the Belgrade Prison, where they were asked to try to identify Cvjetan from a lineup.[22] The next day they were driven to the courthouse in a convoy of security vehicles. They testified over two days, with both Saranda and Fatos giving their evidence in English.

Saranda described the shootings to the Belgrade court in moving detail.[23] Fatos's description was more sparing, but clear and direct.[24]

Stoparic was also called as a witness. Before he took the stand he was approached once again. Cvjetan's lawyer told him to claim that he didn't remember much and that the victims were likely killed by NATO. Boca showed up at the courthouse, flanked by his bodyguards, and offered him money not to implicate his brother Dragan. Stoparić refused and instead requested security measures from the court to protect him. When he took the stand two days later he implicated the four Scorpions he had previously identified, including Dragan.

Stoparić told the court that by testifying he would be seen as a traitor to the Serbian people and that he had effectively painted a target on his back. "I will probably be hunted," he said, "but if I have to die I won't be sorry."

Judge Sinanović ordered the Serbian Interior Ministry to use all means at its disposal to ensure Stoparić's safety. But there were reports that the judge herself had found threatening messages attached to her car and that her tires had been slashed.[25]

On March 17, 2004, Cvjetan was convicted for the Podujevo murders and received the maximum sentence, twenty years. That decision, however, was then overturned by the Supreme Court of Serbia, which sent the case back to the Belgrade District Court for a new trial. On June 17, 2005, without presenting new evidence, the District Court pronounced the same verdict again, imposing a twenty-year sentence once more. On December 22, 2005, this judgment was confirmed by the Supreme Court.[26]

By the time Saranda and Fatos were called as witnesses at the ICTY, they had already told their story a number of times. These retellings came in different contexts and through different filters. The media had focused on conveying the human face and the enormous personal tragedy of the events they had suffered. In the Belgrade court, the focus was on the immediate perpetrator — the man (or at least one of them) who had pulled the trigger. At the ICTY, the focus was cast more broadly: on whether and how the Scorpions were re-formed and then deployed by the state as part of a calculated plan.

For these purposes, the plain facts of the killings — the events that Saranda and Fatos testified to in detail, that Goran Stoparić corroborated, and that were buttressed by clear forensic evidence — were difficult to dispute.[27] More controversial, at least from a legal perspective, was the question of how the Scorpions fit in with the alleged joint criminal enterprise of the Serbian leadership to ethnically cleanse the territory. How foreseeable was it that a group of men like the Scorpions, deliberately placed into this cauldron of ethnic tension and violence, would engage in murder?[28]

It was difficult, in the end, to know just what to make of Mr. Stoparić and his tours of duty with the Scorpions. There is no question that his evidence was extremely valuable and that it required no small amount of courage. It also provided a rare and often fascinating insight into the actions and motivations of some of the most notorious perpetrators of ethnic violence in the Balkans.

With respect to his credibility, the Đorđević Trial Chamber wrote the following in its final judgment:

> With respect to Goran Stoparić, the Chamber concluded
> that his testimony was coloured by an effort on his part

to minimize his own role in the events, to limit the responsibility for the shooting to specific individuals and not to implicate others. It notes, however, that despite these issues, other aspects of his evidence are reliable. In particular, it serves to confirm and better develop the account of events involving the killings that occurred in the courtyard on 28 March 1999 as described by the victims, Saranda and Fatos Bogujevci, including the identification of forces involved in these killings.[29]

# 11

# DISTURBED EARTH: ĐAKOVICA

I

## Heard for the First Time

Lizane Malaj came to The Hague to testify about the ethnic cleansing of her home village, Korenica, in which her husband, brother, and eldest son were killed. Her appearance at the Đorđević trial would mark the third and presumably final time she would testify at the Tribunal. The first time she had testified against Slobodan Milošević, and the second time against the Kosovo 6. For the third, she would be testifying against Mr. Đorđević, a man she likely hadn't heard of before he was indicted.

Her testimony at this final trial would be of particular significance, however, for two very different reasons. The first was straightforward: Mr. Đorđević had command responsibility for the Serbian police, including the men who had descended on her house that fateful morning, and was also alleged to have directed the operation that abducted the bodies of her murdered family members. The second was a surprise, which we learned about just moments before she was to testify. Looking down at her young son, who she had brought with her from Kosovo, she told us that he had never heard the story of what happened to his father and brother. She wanted him to hear it now, through her testimony. As she walked to the courtroom, a support worker guided her son to the public gallery.

Lizane married a farmer, Vat Malaj, when she was nineteen years old. The two of them had five children and lived in Korenica, a small village of about seventy houses. Unlike most Kosovo Albanians, who are predominantly Muslim, the Malajs were Catholic.

Ms. Malaj was one of a number of witnesses who testified about events in Đakovica, a municipality in western Kosovo with a population of approximately 131,700 people, 93 percent of whom were ethnic Albanian. Bordering on Albania, the municipality was a particularly active zone for the KLA, with arms and supplies frequently smuggled across the border.

After the NATO bombing commenced, Serb forces had hit Đakovica hard. A coordinated operation swept through the area, destroying homes and shops belonging to Albanians. The forces targeted religious and historic Albanian sites in the town of Đakovica, including shops in the old bazaar, the library, an Islamic school, and the Hadum mosque. The presence of the KLA during these events was minimal.[1]

The Malaj family had lived through Serbian offensives before. In May of 1998, in what was termed the "spring offensive," Serbian forces had deployed tanks, APCs, and Pinzgauers along the main road to the village and were firing as they advanced. Lizane and her children had fled to the neighbouring village of Guska for safety, while her husband and other men from the village had fled into the mountains.

On April 4, 1999, Easter Monday, a uniformed officer named Milutin Prascević knocked on the Malaj's door and again ordered their family to leave. They got as far as the nearby village of Suhadoll, but there the police abruptly turned them around and sent them home. Confused, the villagers returned to Korenica.

Three weeks later they would not be so fortunate. Malaj described April 27, 1999 as a "horrible, horrible day." She awoke that morning at 5:00 a.m. to find that police, soldiers, and paramilitary men with ribbons tied to their arms had descended on her village. Some of the men wore masks, others had their faces painted, and all of them were heavily armed. She counted roughly thirty-five men surrounding her house, flanked by tanks and Pinzgauers.

They had appeared so quickly that her eldest son, fifteen-year-old Blerim, found himself trapped outside the house in the bathroom. The men spotted him as they encroached and forced him to lie on the ground outside, shouting and yelling. Her husband Vat went out to the courtyard to stand by his son, the two of them surrounded. The men told Vat to tell the rest of his family to leave the house. He turned and called out to them, then Lizane came out with the children. The men ordered Vat to lie on the ground next to his son.

The police went next door, to the house of Lizane's brother Nikoll Kabashi, breaking the door down and forcing his family into the courtyard. They demanded that the men produce their identification, then they forced Nikoll and his son Andrush to the ground as well.

Lizane counted seventeen people in the courtyard — twelve women and children still standing and five men and boys lying on the ground. The armed men pointed the women and children down the road, ordering them to begin the journey to Albania. Lizane started walking along with the other villagers, leaving behind her husband, her son Blerim, her brother Nikoll, and her nephews Andrush and Arben.

She had walked about fifty metres down the road, out of sight of the house, when she heard gunshots and screams. She thought she recognized Blerim's voice. She turned to run back but a policeman perched on a nearby tank pointed his gun at her chest.

"Better to continue on with your children than turn back and be killed," he told her.

She took a last look at the distant village, many of the houses now in flames, her fellow villagers flooding out along the road. Then she turned and continued towards Albania. As they walked they were joined by people from other villages, the police and military shepherding them forward. They were directed towards Prizren, then to the Albanian border. Before they crossed they had their identification documents taken away; those with vehicles also had their licence plates removed. Lizane crossed the border into Albania on April 28. She would never see her husband, her son, her brother, or her nephews again.

The trial would hear from other sources that the events in Ðakovica were part of a broad deployment known as Operation Reka, a joint operation that involved multiple battalions of the military, over four hundred police personnel, and various paramilitaries. Its motives were both broad and personal. Milutin Prascević, who had come to the Malajs' door back on April 4, had been ambushed and killed by KLA fighters just over two weeks later, along with three of his colleagues. According to military captain Nike Peraj, police and military officials held an informal meeting in the days after Prascević's killing, presided over by Momir Stojanović, who was one of Prascević's relatives. In an "emotional outburst," Stojanović declared that they needed to take revenge: at least one hundred heads had to be eliminated, with the Albanian houses burned to the ground. An order was issued on April 26, 1999 to "clean the area from Albanians."[2]

On July 3, with the war over, Lizane returned to Korenica. She found her family's house, burnt to the ground. There was no sign of her husband, her son Blerim, or any of the other men who had been held on the ground. She feared that they had been killed. But there was no sign of the bodies.


After Lizane finished her testimony, we met her in a small debriefing room around the corner from the courtroom. She was sitting on the sofa with her son, while the two of us, still in robes, sat in chairs. We thanked her for coming to testify and told her how appreciative we were once again. Her son was looking at her with unmistakeable pride, eyes wide open, smiling, seemingly excited. We made small talk for a short time, about when they were returning home and whether she would have time to take her son to Madurodam, an interactive miniature park near the Tribunal that has seen its share of ICTY witnesses and their children. When the court staff arrived to take them back to their hotel we thanked each other again, profusely. Then she left, her son holding her hand as they walked down the hall.

I would like to believe that her testimony was an unequivocally positive experience, but I know it isn't that simple. Just because the moments after testifying are usually positive — suffused with relief, if nothing else — this doesn't mean that it remains this way. I certainly hoped it had been worth it. Perhaps it felt like a duty, a responsibility to be borne with pride. Perhaps, looking back, it might even seem like a sort of vindication. Or perhaps not. You never quite knew.

## II

# Millosh Giliq Street

One of the most important witnesses to the crimes in Đakovica was just ten years old when the events took place.

Dren Caka and his family lived on Millosh Giliq Street. When the NATO bombing commenced, he and his family went to stay in the basement of Luli Vejsa's pool hall, which they hoped would be safe. Dren was young enough that he hadn't noticed much that was unusual until then. He could recall that on one occasion he and his sister had been playing marbles when a police officer came by the house and told them to go inside. Until they moved to the pool hall, this was the only thing that stood out in his mind.

The pool hall's basement was a single small room. As Dren pointed out, it was about half the size of our moderately sized courtroom. The two side-facing windows had been boarded shut so the only way in or out was through the door leading upstairs. There were twenty-one ethnic Albanians sleeping there, the members of five families: the Cakas, Hoxhas, Vejsas, Haxhiavdijas, and Nucis. All but one of them, an older man, were women and children. Dren, his mother, Valbona, and his sisters, Dalina, Delvina, and Diona, had been staying there for four or five nights.

The word on the street was that the police were only looking for men and that they would spare women and children. The men of the group, including Dren's father, Ali, thus stayed above ground in the same building, watching for the police and ready to flee at a moment's notice. They would stay up all night, some taking shifts to rest while the others stood guard.

In the early evening of April 1, Dren went down to the basement with the women and children, and they shut the door behind them. He remembered that it was hard to sleep and that he was given sleeping pills. He fell asleep just before midnight.

Unbeknownst to Dren, just after midnight the police had begun knocking on the doors of Albanian houses along Millosh Giliq Street and then setting them on fire, the flames illuminating the night sky.

At about 2:00 a.m., Dren was abruptly awoken by his mother. "Wake up," she said, her voice urgent but hushed, "police officers are here." He could hear the men moving above, their boots heavy on the floor. He held his breath to keep quiet. Then the door opened — Serbian police, clad in blue camouflage and armed with AK-47s. Dren thought he recognized one of the men from his street. The officers ordered them out of the basement.

They were walked single-file out of the basement and towards the house. As they moved briefly outside to use the house's exterior door, Dren saw a car on fire. It was the only source of light on the street and he watched it burn, the flames tinting everything orange. When they reached the door of the house, one of the policemen pulled out his gun and shot the door down.

The police ordered them inside. Most of the group sat on divans in the living room, with three or four of them outside in the hallway. They lit candles so they could see. There were two policemen in the living room and another stationed outside.

As one of the young women stood up to make tea, the killing commenced:

> A. … and Flaka decides to go and make tea. And as she's walking, a police officer kind of like pushes her and fires and she's gone. And her mom, around the corner of the door, ran out and she — she was gone too. And also then —
>
> Q. When you say "she was gone," what do you mean?
>
> A. Like, she got shot, too, right after her daughter.[3]

Dren described the events in flashes, short moments lit only by flickering candles. A police officer opening fire on everyone in the room. Other shots coming in through the window. Dren shot in the right arm, the other bullets fired in his direction hitting a woman named Dushi, who happened to be standing in front of him. Luli's wife shot holding her baby daughter. Dren's mother, in the middle of changing his two-year-old sister, shot in the back, collapsing. Police firing into the closet. The house going up in flames. Smoke filling the room.

The smoke spread quickly as the shooting continued. In the chaos, Dren's older sister appeared and handed him her glove so he could hold it over his mouth and breathe. Then she seemed to disappear. He would not see her again.

He realized he needed to get up. He remembered trying to help five-year-old Arlind Vejsa, who was lying on the ground, and then watching as Arlind stopped breathing. He could hear his baby sister Diona crying, trapped underneath his mother's body, which had toppled forward. He moved over and tried to pull Diona out, but he was small, his mother was large, and his arm was broken. As the smoke thickened and he could no longer breathe, he realized it was pointless to continue.

He went out into the hallway and saw Behar Haxhiavdija's wife frozen in an embrace with her daughter, both of them dead. Dren took off his jacket and lay down on the floor, pretending to be dead himself, but smoke continued to fill the hallway and after two or three minutes he moved into the bedroom next door, where the windows were open and he could breathe. He lay down on the floor again, catching his breath and trying to be still. He knew he needed to escape the house. After what he estimated was ten or fifteen minutes, he stood and jumped out the window.

Twenty people were killed in Luli Vejsa's house that night. Twelve were children, seven were women, and one was a fifty-year-old man named Hysen Gashi who was mentally impaired.[4] Dren was the only survivor.

Once out the window, Dren looked around for the police. Peering around the side of the house, he saw the three officers who had been inside, now standing and smoking. It was dark, but he worried they would see him. He saw there were cases of beer on the ground and he stacked them one atop the other, then used them to jump the wall into the adjoining compound. He knew the terrain well, clambering and weaving through the cluttered yard, ducking into little alleyways, and heading back towards his own house, where he hoped to find some of his relatives.

Two houses down, Dren abruptly came upon his aunt Nimete. He called out to her for help but she turned and ran away, not recognizing him. When he called out again she recognized his voice. "Dren?" she asked, startled to see him outside all alone. "What happened?"

In his testimony, Dren recounted his attempt to answer her, a story within a story: "And I said: 'Oh, everyone is gone. Everyone's dead.' And she said: 'No, I think you've had a bad dream.' I said: 'No, I don't think I've had a bad dream because it just happened right before my eyes.'"[5]

From the mouth of a ten-year-old it seemed unreal. He had only been two houses down, she knew, but what was he doing outside by himself? As she hurried him back inside, Dren momentarily fainted. He woke up again when she returned to see why he was lagging behind. He told her he was okay but that he'd been shot and had lost a lot of blood. She looked at him strangely, not knowing what to make of his account. "It's probably just the sleeping pills," she told him.

She brought Dren into the house and he sat with his grandfather, grandmother, and uncle in the kitchen. He tried again. "Everyone's gone," he said, as simply as he could. "Everyone's been shot dead."

His grandfather looked at him again, refusing to believe what he was saying. Dren held out his arm. It was dark in the room and his grandfather held out a candle, straining to see.

"Oh my God."

His grandfather scrambled for a knife from the drawer and cut through Dren's shirt, which was soaked through with blood. They finally understood.[6]

They also understood, immediately, that they were in danger. They moved into Dren's uncle's room, lighting a single candle. When they heard any noises nearby they would blow it out and sit uneasily in the dark. They spent the entire night that way.

In the morning, Dren's father Ali came home. It was clear they had to get Dren to a hospital. It was too dangerous to drive, and an able-bodied man like Ali couldn't risk being seen in the streets, so Dren's grandfather and aunt wrapped a blanket around him and then put him on a bicycle, which they pushed to the hospital. They passed two police officers en route. When asked where they were going, Dren's grandfather said Dren had hurt himself playing and had to go to the hospital. They were allowed to proceed.[7]

When they arrived at the hospital they encountered a Serbian soldier. With the blanket no longer covering Dren's arm, the wound was visible; when the soldier asked what had happened, Dren's grandfather told him he had been shot. The soldier was shocked. "We shouldn't be hurting women and children." He arranged for Dren to get help right away.

Dren's arm was X-rayed and the doctor told them what they already knew: it was broken. They never set the bone, however; they wrapped it in cloth and Dren was released. In court, Dren stood and showed the judges where he had been shot, holding out his right bicep.

On his return, Dren and his remaining family members decided to sleep at a different house. The nights were uneasy, spent listening for noises. On the second or third night, they thought they heard people approaching and they ran wildly out the back of the house, scrambling up a steep hill. His aunt broke her leg in the panic. When they realized it was quiet again they returned to the house. The next morning they packed and left for Albania, crossing the border with other refugees at Kukes. Their passports, registration papers, and licence plates were taken from them as they left the country.

As soon as Dren came across the border, a medic rushed him to a medical tent for treatment. He was recorded on video explaining what had happened to him. In between recounting the events, he could be heard worrying about the scissors being used to cut his bandages, afraid to have surgery. He fell asleep shortly thereafter and was rushed to Tirana by helicopter. He spent two months in the hospital.

Although he was the sole survivor from the pool hall, Dren's testimony about the events that night was supplemented by other witnesses. Two of the men who had been staying above the pool hall that night, Luli Vejsa and Hani Hoxha, also gave evidence. Vejsa had fled through a small back window as the police neared, while Hoxha watched eight to ten uniformed men break into the compound before he climbed two walls into another yard. Hoxha spent seven or eight hours hiding there under wooden boards, where he heard gunshots, yelling, and someone shouting, "Spare me, don't kill me," in Albanian.

The next morning, Hoxha and Behar Haxhiavdija returned to the house to find it completely burnt down, the basement still smouldering. They knew that people had been killed there, but the bodies were gone.

Fred Abrahams, a researcher with Human Rights Watch, would later discover that workers with the Đakovica Public Works Department had taken the burnt remains of the bodies from Vejsa's house, along with a number of other bodies, and moved them to the Đakovica Public Cemetery.[8]

III

# Disturbed Earth

Conducting a cover-up operation of this size and scope required manpower. Police officers, soldiers, and militia men, it turned out, were not always enough. There were also civilians who played key roles: labourers, skilled workers, drivers, heavy machine operators. Some had worked willingly and some had little choice but to co-operate. Finding witnesses from these ranks was crucial, but no easy task.

K72, a Serb civilian and an excavator driver, provided a view into the nature and scope of the cover-up operation on the ground in Đakovica. He testified using a codename but gave his evidence in open session, where it could be seen and heard by the public.[9]

His wartime work for the police had started unremarkably enough, digging tactical trenches and sometimes working with the local civil protection unit to remove the carcasses of animals killed in the conflict. The police paid him in cash, with a man he called "the treasurer" sometimes dispensing the money out of a suitcase. It wasn't much. But payment or not, these were not jobs you could turn down. "The moment they came to pick me up," he explained, "I knew I could not refuse."[10]

On a night in April, things would change. He heard a knock on his door at around 8:00 or 9:00 p.m., opening it to find a uniformed policeman who told him he was needed for a "delicate job." He grabbed his coat and the man drove him to the police station, where his excavator machine was parked and waiting. He wasn't told where they were going and he didn't ask. The officer pulled out to lead the way, then he got into the cab of the excavator and drove it behind.

When they reached the area of the Bistražin Bridge, just outside of Đakovica, he began to notice police officers all around, securing a perimeter. The car turned off the main road, then came to a stop. As K72 pulled his excavator in, one of the officers pointed to a spot up ahead — a patch of earth that was already disturbed. The officer told him to start digging. The other policemen hung back as he rolled forward, and as he drew near he was overwhelmed by a terrible stench in the air.

He worked in the darkness, the scene lit only by the headlights of his excavator, which he kept on short beam so they would be minimally visible to any NATO planes that might be circling overhead. As he plunged the fork into the earth he could see human bodies in the ground, intermingled with the soil. There were four or five Roma workers — "gypsies" as he called them — who were assisting with the operation on foot. They would pull the bodies apart so the excavator shovel could gather them in its scoop. If the workers found valuables — "a little ring, a chain with a locket" — then they collected them. Once the bodies had been pulled from the ground he would unload them to the side. From there the men would pile them into two white-boxed trucks. Police supervised from the sidelines, standing back from the scene because of the overpowering stench.

The excavator's lights were bright enough that he could see the human cargo as it was lifted. These were men, dressed in civilian clothing. They were caked in dirt but he could still make out parts of some of the faces. The bodies were not yet badly decomposed, but the excavator's teeth were severing arms and legs as they dredged the earth.

He vomited more than once as he worked. Hoping to finish quickly, he asked one of the policemen how many bodies there were. "Not many," he was told, "100 or 120." The work lasted for two or three hours. When they finished he drove the excavator back to the police station and was given a ride home.

For the next couple of weeks, he went back to an ordinary routine of life and work as best he could. Then, late one afternoon, the knock came again; it was a different police officer this time. He took K72 to an elementary school, where his excavator was waiting, and they stayed there until nightfall.

When it was dark, the officer pulled out in front and K72 followed, driving to the public cemetery in Brekovac. When they arrived there were ten to twenty policemen securing the perimeter of the scene. He was directed to dig up graves, one at a time. It was clear that these bodies had been recently buried; the earth was fresh and makeshift gravestones had been improvised with planks. The names they bore were all Muslim and male.

K72 pushed his excavator shovel into the ground, unearthing the bodies one by one. They had been dumped directly into the earth, without caskets. The workers on foot formed a crude assembly line, with two men unloading the bodies out of the excavator's shovel, and then piling them into a tractor-trailer. The tractor-trailer took the bodies to a larger truck, covered with a tarpaulin, that was parked outside the cemetery. Another two workers transferred the bodies into the final truck.

The work was exhausting. The graves had to be dug up individually, then filled back in with earth once the bodies had been removed. The operation took twelve to thirteen hours to complete.

Only two days later the police collected K72 again, for what would be his final exhumation. This time they led him to the village of Guska, where he dug up a series of unmarked graves. There were "around ten bodies lined in three rows, three or four per row."[11] Once again, workers loaded the bodies into a truck. When that was finished he was led to another site, this one further into the woods, where the graves were scattered. One of the officers used a flashlight to show him where to dig.

When the job was done, and he was resting alone in the excavator, one of the officers approached him. The man told him bluntly that he would "lose his head" if he talked to anyone about what they had been doing.

K72 was well aware of how precarious his position was. He wasn't a police officer or a soldier, just a civilian. He had been conscripted into what was obviously a clandestine operation. Even if he didn't know the circumstances in which these people had been killed, he still presumably knew too much. He told the officer that he had spoken to a lawyer about the work he had done — although he hadn't actually spoken to anyone. He told the officer as confidently as he could that if he were to disappear, people would know what had happened. The officer didn't respond. Soon after the end of the war, K72 left Kosovo with his family.[12]

When he testified in The Hague, he gave his evidence plainly and without much emotion. The work was surely sickening. The overpowering stench, too strong for the police at the scene. The sight of bodies being pulled apart. The ever-present awareness that he was taking bodies from the grave. He didn't dwell much on the descriptions. If he was resentful or angry that the police had enlisted him to conduct this unspeakable work, or that we were now compelling him to revisit it, he didn't show it. He seemed resigned to explaining what he had seen.

He did notice that the cover-up was sloppy — maybe because of the unpleasantness of the work, maybe because they'd been forced to work at night, or maybe because no one wanted to be there. Whatever the reason, when they finished they left clear signs that the graves had been disturbed.

K72's evidence provided a detailed and up-close account of one of the unearthing operations, but other evidence at trial provided glimpses into something more widespread. Across the municipality of Đakovica, various witnesses saw workers collecting bodies, soldiers loading bodies into trucks, and tarpaulin-covered trucks transporting bodies. In July of 1999, Fred Abrahams of Human Rights Watch visited another cemetery in the town and found dug-up earth and track marks from what looked like heavy machinery. Đakovica Public Works employees told him that Serb forces had removed seventy bodies from that site in May.[13]

# 12

# THE OTHER FACE OF JUSTICE: REDUX

|

## Revenge Is Sour

In his 1945 essay "Revenge Is Sour," George Orwell explored the relationship between violence, victimhood, and revenge. He wrote of his time in Germany in the immediate aftermath of the liberation of the concentration camps, where some of the Jews who had been prisoners now found themselves acting as prison guards for captured Nazis. Orwell was given a tour by a Viennese Jew, who identified one of the captives as an SS general who had almost certainly been in charge of concentration camps. By now the "Nazi torturer" was little more than a "pitiful wretch" with deformed feet. Even as the Jew kicked the man and demeaned some of his colleagues, Orwell sensed that he wasn't really able to enjoy his newfound power. Instead, he was trying to behave "as he had planned to behave in the days he was helpless."[1]

There was, Orwell concluded, "no such thing as revenge." By this he meant that as soon as punishment actually becomes possible, it ceases to seem attractive: "Revenge is an act which you want to commit when you are powerless and because you are powerless: as soon as the sense of impotence is removed, the desire evaporates also."[2]

As soon as one is in an actual position of power, in other words, taking revenge tends to lose its appeal. It becomes an obvious act of cruelty; bullying. It feels wrong.

What is most interesting about Orwell's observation, however, is that despite the inversion of the power dynamic, and despite the fact that revenge may become sour, there are certain situations in which the desire to do violence does not evaporate with the assumption of power. In these situations, despite having power and control, the other does not cease to seem threatening, the impulse to violence continues to thrive, and the sense of justification for one's actions persists. These are the most dangerous of situations, where the men with the ability to kill, rape, and torture ruthlessly and uninterruptedly — the ones with the weapons and the tanks and the access to the resources of the state — continue to act as if they are the victim, as if they are threatened, as if they are suffering the injustice. These are the situations, relatively rare though they may be, where we tend to find genocide, crimes against humanity, and violence on a staggering scale.

This is not the same as revenge. To take revenge is a temptation, but one we know we should not succumb to; we know, at least in our modern societies, that one is not justified in doing violence simply to avenge another act. If one can cast himself differently, however — as a victim still suffering in the throes of a broader narrative of injustice, as under attack, as acting defensively — then acts of violence and oppression seem easier to defend.

This is not to say that other factors are not at play, or that the marshalling of notions of injustice and victimhood is the exclusive cause of mass violence or genocide. There are a great number of contributing factors, and certainly a range of different scenarios, that have led to the many mass atrocities with which we are now all too familiar. But what one also invariably finds, amongst all of these remote and proximate causes, is something so powerful and deeply rooted that it will not only impel people to violence but enable them to justify it to themselves.

This may involve revenge, but it is not *just* revenge. As Orwell described, the desire for revenge tends to evaporate when one is in the position of power, and having that power is a necessary precondition to committing systematic and large-scale atrocities. It may involve dogma, but it is not just any dogma that can motivate and perpetuate otherwise unthinkable acts of violence. It may involve hatred, but it must be the type of hatred that enables people to hate along broad lines of division — not personally but generally, even conceptually — and to justify seemingly civilized people to take the lives of others. Finally, it may involve acting pursuant to the belief that "the end justifies the means." But under what rare circumstances would such inhumane means be justified by *any* end? At the heart of that dangerous phrase we encounter this same word: *justifies*. To sanction such acts, and to continue perpetuating them when holding the reins of power, seems to involve stimulating our sense of injustice and victimhood and thereby activating an impulse to anger and violence that somehow seems inherently justified.

It is also true, surely, that once one begins to treat other human beings as less than human, and thus make them *seem* less than human, it becomes all too easy to continue on this course. Over time, and certainly after the repetition of such acts, our conscience tends to tug less and less on our heartstrings. But something has to propel us along this path.

Committing atrocities on this scale requires people — large numbers of them — to do the actual work. It requires motivating soldiers and civilians to make incredible sacrifices, often to risk their lives in furtherance of a cause. Direct orders can go a long way, but they're seldom the whole story. Focusing only on how the leadership is able to orchestrate violence on this scale also leaves an important question off of the table: how and why these leaders came to convince *themselves* that such violence was necessary and justifiable. What must seemingly persist, to pave the way for violence on this scale, is some belief in the rightness, necessity, or even nobility of one's mission — no matter how objectively wrong the actions it may entail.

## II

## The Ethnic Cleansing: A Bird's Eye View

March 24, 1999 was the day the operation in Kosovo began in earnest. When the NATO bombing commenced the Serbian forces rolled out their operation: a preplanned and well-orchestrated joint campaign involving the police, army, paramilitaries, and armed civilians. The enterprise was prepackaged within the same story that Milošević had ridden to power and that had already been used to justify violence across the former Yugoslavia: that ethnic Serbs were the imperilled victims of injustice and that in deploying its formidable forces to Kosovo, Serbia was acting defensively. Now there was an additional dimension: that Serbia was the victim of NATO aggression.

Serbian forces moved across Kosovo in a coordinated operation to expel the ethnic Albanians. To do so, they murdered, abused, and persecuted thousands of civilians, destroyed religious and cultural property, and burned houses and entire villages to the ground. The leadership took pains to make it look like a legitimate operation against the KLA and to describe it as such.

In the two and a half months that the operation lasted, Serbian forces drove the vast majority of ethnic Albanians out of their homes and managed to forcibly deport more than 800,000 civilians from Kosovo, almost half of the total population. According to the UNHCR, 860,000 people flooded across Kosovo's borders, with 444,600 streaming into Albania, 345,500 into Macedonia, and 69,000 into Montenegro.[3] The images were staggering: long, winding lines of ethnic Albanians from all across Kosovo — children, adults, the elderly, the disabled — walking with their suitcases and belongings, flanked by thousands of tractors, moving in mile-long columns that snaked slowly to the borders. The operation was described by journalist and human rights scholar Samantha Power as "the largest, boldest single act of ethnic cleansing of the decade."[4]

The central claim from the Serbian regime — repeated by the defence in the Kosovo trials — was that the Albanians had left Kosovo because they were fleeing from NATO bombs. When this didn't seem enough there were additional or alternative claims: that the Albanians fled out of fear of the KLA, that they had only *pretended* to leave, and even that they had left from fear of the depleted uranium in NATO bombs.[5]

The events on the ground, however, revealed a clear pattern unfolding across Kosovo: expulsions that were forced, well coordinated, and part of a systematic campaign. Heavily armed Serb forces moved from village to village and from house to house. In the typical pattern the military would target a village for shelling and then the police, often accompanied by paramilitary and/or military forces, would advance through the village on the ground.

Murder was rampant. In many villages the men were separated and executed while the women and children were expelled from the town. Serbian forces looted houses and raped women. They burned villagers' houses as they advanced, torching Albanian homes to drive them away and to dissuade them from returning. The houses of Serb civilians were generally left untouched.

By June of 1999, almost half of the 568 functioning mosques in Kosovo had been destroyed, with virtually all of those still standing having suffered some form of damage. Though Serbian authorities claimed this was the result of NATO bombing, the evidence showed otherwise. Andras Riedlmayer, a specialist who surveyed cultural and religious buildings across Kosovo, found extensive evidence of targeted Serbian ground attacks on religious institutions and on mosques in particular — destruction by artillery, fires started from the inside, and explosives planted inside minarets.[6]

When the Albanians reached the borders, the police, military, and paramilitary forces manning the crossing points systematically took away their passports, driver's licences, and identification cards so they could never return. When international observers returned to Kosovo at the end of the war, they found piles of these documents burning in large bonfires outside of police headquarters.

III

# Operation Allied Force

Operation Allied Force, NATO's seventy-eight-day war against Serbian forces, ran from March 24, 1999 to June 10, 1999.

The operation was NATO's first extended use of military force and the first war conducted for humanitarian reasons against a country committing acts within its own borders.[7] It marked a notable shift in approach, following the abject failure of the international community to stop ethnic cleansing and genocide throughout the 1990s, most spectacularly in Rwanda and Bosnia. The willingness of the international community to take meaningful steps to stop mass violence was an open question, and the Serbian regime's continuing defiance was beginning to raise serious questions about NATO's credibility.

The scope of Operation Allied Force was extensive — since World War II, only Operation Desert Storm and the Vietnam War had seen a greater mobilization of air power. The deployment of ground troops seemed politically untenable, however, and so the war was fought entirely from the air. The U.S.-led decision to launch strikes at all was surprising given the clearly hesitant political administration, the divided Congress, and the generally uninterested domestic population. A campaign fought remotely from the air, and with limited casualties, had surely seemed the best compromise available.

A remote "virtual war,"[8] however, proved unable to stop the coordinated ethnic cleansing operations being conducted on the ground. Kosovo's terrain of mountains and valleys, along with low cloud cover, fog, and bad weather throughout the campaign, made it difficult for NATO to identify and destroy tactical targets. Serbia's surface-to-air missile batteries, portable air defence systems, and anti-aircraft artillery forced air crews to conduct most of their bombing from above fifteen thousand feet, making the clear identification of enemy targets especially challenging.[9]

Serbian forces were able to disperse and hide their tanks and APCs, making them difficult for NATO to identify and target en masse. They often sent smaller numbers of troops, paramilitaries, or police into villages instead; given their overwhelming superiority on the ground, this was more than sufficient. Had NATO showed the intention to pursue a ground attack, Serbian forces would likely have had to position tanks and heavy armaments to secure key roads, making them easier targets.[10] But the Serbian forces proved adept at hiding and NATO proved largely unable to stop their operations. The air campaign, which NATO leaders had hoped would only last a matter of days before shocking Milošević into compliance, endured for over two months.

As the war developed and NATO saw little progress in its attempts to prevent or even discourage Serbian forces from expelling the ethnic Albanian population, it began to broaden its targets to Milošević's power base and Serbia more broadly. Cruise missiles hit targets that included Belgrade radio and television sites run by Milošević's wife, key political offices, and Belgrade's national command centre. NATO began targeting oil refineries and depots as well as key factories and bridges. They attacked telephone and computer networks, transformer yards, and a number of other infrastructure sites, cutting power to broad swathes of the country. By May 24, power was cut off for 80 percent of Serbia, leaving many without electricity or water.[11]

The bombings in and around Belgrade were a particularly stunning development: a Western attack on a major European capital at the end of the twentieth century. The shift in strategy had immediate and profound impacts on the general population and the already-struggling Serbian economy. The disruptions also had a strong effect on morale.[12] The shift in strategy marked the beginning of the end of the war.

On June 2, Russia's envoy to the Balkans travelled to Belgrade with the president of Finland and an EU representative, to encourage Milošević to surrender and to provide him with a proposal to end the conflict. It is difficult to know what, exactly, led Serbian authorities to capitulate. The loss of backing from Russia represented a significant political shift, surely. The bombing campaign was taking its toll and showed no sign of stopping, and the expansion of bombing targets had a clear impact on Serbian citizens. There was talk that Milošević had come under increasing pressure from various Serbian elites to stop the operation. Serbian authorities may also have feared a potential ground operation on top of the ongoing air attacks.

In the end, Milošević accepted the terms to end the conflict: he would withdraw all of his forces from Kosovo, permit a NATO-led security force to operate on the ground, allow the ethnic Albanians to return to their homes, and enable a regime of self-rule for the Kosovo Albanians. The Serbian Parliament ratified the agreement the following day. Although it took almost another week for military officials to agree on the precise terms of the withdrawal, the official agreement ending the war was signed on June 9, 1999 at a NATO airfield in Kumanovo, Macedonia. The U.N. Security Council approved the implementation of a new peacekeeping force on the ground and NATO declared victory.[13]

Although the war between NATO and Serbia had been remarkably one-sided — NATO lost only two aircraft to enemy fire over the course of the operation[14] — it wasn't until Serbia actually capitulated that NATO's humanitarian goals were achieved and the violence was stopped.

The ethnic cleansing campaign had been deliberately timed to coincide with the NATO bombing. This was neither ironic nor coincidental — it was intentional. The international intervention provided further seeming justification for a broad military initiative and a smokescreen for a very deliberate push to rid the territory of ethnic Albanians.

Following the end of the war, displaced and expelled Albanians returned to their devastated communities and what was left of their homes. As they returned, a great many of them — across Kosovo, in different cities, towns, and villages, and in markedly different circumstances — found that their family members and friends had disappeared.

IV

# Indictments and Arrests

On May 27, 1999, some two weeks before the end of the war, the ICTY's prosecutor, Louise Arbour, had announced that the Tribunal was indicting Slobodan Milošević, along with Milan Milutinović, Nikola Šainović, Dragoljub Ojdanić, and Vlajko Stojiljković. The initial indictment was solely for actions in Kosovo in 1999. More than two years later, the Tribunal issued a new indictment charging Milošević with the ethnic cleansing of Croatia, and a month after that the allegations were expanded again to include the brutal crimes committed in Bosnia and Herzegovina. Milošević's case was severed from his co-accuseds and he stood trial alone.[15]

Those proceedings began on February 12, 2002, requiring a formidable push by the prosecution to prepare such a massive case in a short window of time. On March 11, 2006, after the prosecution's case had concluded and in the midst of the defence case, Mr. Milošević passed away. Three days later, the Trial Chamber abruptly terminated the proceedings. It was, to be sure, a striking and disappointing anti-climax. No factual findings were made and no verdict was ever delivered.

On October 2, 2003, the ICTY had issued another indictment relating to the ethnic cleansing of Kosovo, this time charging Generals Pavković, Lazarević, Lukić, and Mr. Đorđević. On July 8, 2005, this case was joined with the other Kosovo case that had been severed from Milošević — Milutinović et al.

As this Kosovo case moved to trial, however, there were two glaring omissions. Both struck at the core of the prosecution's ability to uncover and prove the secret operation to conceal the bodies of thousands of murder victims.

The first was that former Minister of the Interior Vlajko Stojiljković, Đorđević's boss and the man who had reported most directly to Milošević about the concealment operations, had killed himself before he could be brought to The Hague and prosecuted. On April 11, 2002, the federal Parliament in Belgrade had adopted a motion to arrest indicted war crimes suspects still in Yugoslavia, including Stojiljković, and extradite them to The Hague. Mere hours later, at around 7:00 p.m., Stojiljković walked out to the steps of the Parliament building, hesitated, then drew a pistol and shot himself in the head. He died in hospital two days later. Stojiljković left a scathing fifteen-page suicide note, written by hand. In it, he included a list of the people he held responsible for his death, including Serbian prime minister Zoran Đinđić and Yugoslav president Vojislav Kostunica. He ended ominously: "Patriotic citizens of this country will know how to avenge me."[16]

The second problem was that the Tribunal still didn't have Mr. Đorđević, who had gone into hiding. With Đorđević missing in action, he was severed from the proceedings, to be tried at a future time if he could be captured. The Milutinović et al. trial started on July 10, 2006. It would be known as the Kosovo 6.

On June 17, 2007, Đorđević was arrested in the coastal town of Budva, Montenegro by Montenegrin police working with Serbia and the ICTY. Local reports were limited but he was said to have been working in construction. The arrest had unfolded quickly. Two days earlier a "female companion" was said to have been arrested by Serbian border police trying to smuggle alcohol and cigarettes from Montenegro to Serbia. She allegedly told police that Đorđević had entered Montenegro several months earlier, having assumed the identity of a deceased Kosovo Serb refugee. He was found boarding at the house of an elderly couple, who were apparently unaware of who he was. He was arrested while sleeping that night, then moved under heavy guard to Podgorica and flown directly to the Netherlands to stand trial in The Hague.[17]

# V

# The Other Face of Justice: Redux

The events that unfolded in Kosovo, and across the Balkans more broadly, were clearly a product of very specific forces of history, culture, and ethnicity that could be marshalled by the leadership towards a particular end. But the more familiar I became with the underpinnings of this violence, and the mechanisms of justification that were used to fuel and perpetuate it, the more I began to see clear and disturbing parallels to other global acts of genocide and crimes against humanity. Indeed, despite the radically different sets of cultures, causes, and events that make each historical act of mass violence unique, many of the darkest events of our recent history seem to share a very particular sort of psychology. In each of these situations, the perpetrators and their collaborators have amplified and then mobilized a reaction to injustice in order to motivate and seemingly justify stunning levels of violence. The events in the Balkans were consistent with a much larger pattern.

The powerful use of narratives of injustice was a core aspect of the madness that unfolded in Cambodia after Pol Pot and the ultra-Maoist Khmer Rouge came to power in 1975, imposing their radical vision for a communist agrarian utopia and unleashing murder, torture, and starvation on a staggering scale. In four years of rule before being toppled by a Vietnamese-backed invasion, the Khmer Rouge regime purged and slaughtered, forced their citizens onto collective farms, eliminated money, schools, and religion, and oversaw the resulting deaths of an estimated two million people. Though the cruelty and collective madness that seemed to grip the country during this period eludes any simple explanation, the violence and torture that the regime directed was motivated and justified quite overtly as a response to injustice.

As Alexander Hinton explored in lucid detail in *Why Did They Kill? Cambodia in the Shadow of Genocide*, the senior Khmer leadership both demanded and incited violence as a response to class oppression (“*chih choan*” or “*sangkat*” in Khmer) and foreign imperialism.[18] The regime stoked anger along the lines of socio-economic class, casting their “revolution” within a created historical narrative in which peasants had taken up "their scythes and axes" to drive out the landlords who had taken their land.[19] They invoked the very real devastation of American bombing in the Vietnam War to incite anger against foreign imperialism, which they blamed for the decline of the dominant Khmer culture of the past.

The story told by the perpetrators of the Cambodian genocide was one in which they were revolutionaries fighting for justice, seeking to liberate the peasantry from exploitation. They saw themselves not as the majority group who controlled the machinery of the state but as the impoverished victims of class oppression, fighting an armed struggle against the unjust elite. They made little attempt to hide their use of this self-told narrative to perpetuate violence that they felt was necessary.[20] As the violence continued to escalate, the regime perpetually stoked the anger necessary to sustain it by drawing on these accounts of victimhood and injustice. One of the core tenets of the revolution was known as "constantly burning rage" ("*kamhoeng chap cheh*"), which the leadership nurtured through continuous emphasis of how the elite and imperialist enemy had been oppressing and exploiting them.[21]

One notorious practice of the regime was for interrogators at S-21, the Tuol Sleng torture centre, to beat, burn, electrocute, hang, choke, and humiliate their captives for days on end in order to manufacture "confessions." The extent to which they genuinely believed these forced statements to be true, and the extent to which they were more transparently self-serving, is difficult to know. What is clearer is the use to which the confessions were put: the victims were made to write personal narratives in which they described their lives and identified their supposedly traitorous actions.[22] The torturers thus manufactured their own self-serving justifications to execute their victims, casting these men and women as perpetrators of injustice and themselves — in broad terms at least — as the real victims. When they ultimately and inevitably executed these men and women, they could frame these actions as seemingly deserved punishments.

The nefarious use of our instinctively powerful reactions to injustice, and the reinforcement of a very particular type of narrative, was also a core aspect of the 1994 Rwandan genocide, in which tens of thousands of Hutu murdered an estimated 800,000 Tutsi and politically moderate Hutu over just one hundred days. What began as widespread killings committed mostly by well-equipped soldiers and militiamen quickly evolved into a pervasive mass slaughter perpetrated by regular Hutu civilians — men armed with machetes, clubs, knives, or whatever else they could fashion into a weapon.[23] The speed, scale, and brutality of the killings were difficult to comprehend: as the violence unfolded, Rwanda's rivers, roads, and churches were literally overflowing with the bodies of the dead.

Rwanda's brutal history as a Belgian colony, in which the slightly more European-looking minority Tutsis had been cast as ethnic elites, provided fertile ground for modern politicians, leaders, and members of the local media to provoke feelings of injustice, victimhood, and rage amongst the majority Hutu population. That Rwanda had attained independence from Belgium in 1962 and was governed by a Hutu-dominated leadership seemed to make little difference.[24]

The path to genocide was sown with the rhetoric of Tutsi injustices, Hutu victimhood, and the accompanying demonization of all Tutsis. Propaganda was asserted from the top, distributed broadly to the masses over the radio, and pipelined to Rwandan troops by the Rwandan general staff. Modern Tutsis were repeatedly cast as outsiders and as the unjust elite — wealthy, monopolizing credit, taking prestigious jobs and educational opportunities from Hutus, and dominating everything from the government to the church. They were described as *Inyenzi* — cockroaches — and associated with the crimes "of their elders" — murder, rape, and plunder chief among them.[25]

In addition to the emphasis on these historical and contemporary injustices, the extremists' propaganda also continually emphasized the *threat* posed by the Tutsis, constantly reasserting Tutsi intentions to exterminate the Hutu. The Hutu extremists, in other words, accused the Tutsi of precisely what they intended to do themselves.[26] This fear would prove an important tool — with the predominantly-Tutsi Rwandan Patriotic Front (RPF) already fighting against government forces, it was easy to stoke fear about the threat of impending violence. Much of the propaganda addressed the RPF and the Tutsi as if they were interchangeable, and the RPF's intentions were frequently described as genocidal.[27]

With the foundations for a genocide so thoroughly laid, all that was needed was the right spark. The one hundred frenzied days of killing in Rwanda commenced on April 6, 1994, when a plane carrying Rwandan President Habyarimana (a Hutu), was shot down over Kigali. It was never established who shot the plane down, but Hutu extremists immediately placed the blame on the Tutsis and began their campaign of killing right away. It soon became apparent that a detailed roadmap for the genocide — including the arming of the population, the creation of preliminary lists identifying who would be killed, and a logistical plan for the slaughter — had been laid out by Hutu extremists well before Habyarimana was killed. The death of the president proved a powerful rallying point to inflame the emotions and sense of injustice of the local Hutu citizenry, and to drive home a sense that they were threatened themselves and would therefore be acting defensively — despite the fact that the Hutu were the overwhelming majority in Rwanda and firmly in control of the power and machinery of the state.

Although the mass violence that unfolded in Cambodia, Rwanda, and the Balkans now lies in the past, there are ongoing events that exhibit many of the same troubling phenomena. One of the most obvious problems one faces in trying to make any sort of headway into the seemingly intractable Israeli-Palestinian conflict, for example, is that new injustices on either side of the conflict are immediately and almost gleefully integrated into broader narratives of anger and blame, then turned outward as ammunition against the other. The dialogues around the dispute often reek of a sort of demonization — new victims and injustices on one side are deployed to justify actions and initiatives that might otherwise seem unconscionable. For portions of the Muslim world, Israeli injustices against the Palestinians seemingly provide justification for violence, hatred, and terrorism aimed broadly at Jews. For the Israelis, Palestinian or Arab threats and attacks can be mobilized to justify expanded settlements, military incursions, and the perpetuation or worsening of already unacceptable conditions.

Both Jews and Palestinians can cast themselves — and genuinely see themselves — as the imperilled victims of violence and injustice. They do so from different perspectives, each of which is very real — the Palestinians in relation to Israel, the Israelis in relation to the broader Arab/Islamic world surrounding them. Both, in this sense, are correct — to diminish the ongoing injustices suffered by the Palestinians is as misguided as diminishing the victimhood that birthed Israel as a nation and the ongoing threats that it, and Jews, face from hatred, extremism, and terrorism.

But this approach — the misdirection of injustice and victimhood for the purpose of justifying and perpetuating new violence — both entrenches and worsens a situation that each side knows is shameful and unsustainable. These things should anger all of us — the actual victims most of all — because they sacrifice real people and real lives on the altar of perpetuating hatred. What is needed, badly, is a change in both perspective and intent.

Our ability to distinguish amongst the various uses to which "injustice" can be put has been dismal, and it may be getting worse. In this respect, we should be asking not just *whether* genuine injustices took place, but what is being *made* of these injustices and for what purpose they are being marshalled.

The sincere hope for international criminal prosecutions has always been that we could appeal to some higher power — not divine but societal — to see that injustices are exposed, recognized, and condemned in an official, impartial, and neutral setting that represents everyone. The hope is that we can give voice to these accounts of injustice, convey that they should not have happened, and then restore some sense of a whole. The intention is to do so by focusing on the individuals who oversee and perpetrate these unjust acts, not on broad classes of people.

The human response to injustice has a seemingly dual potential: it can be restorative or it can be destructive. Genuine acts of injustice — large-scale atrocities that are experienced collectively — can also be absorbed into a larger framework of anger, hatred, and justification. Justice systems have the potential to act as an important stop to these mechanisms, by acting as a broader arbiter of justice and by serving, ideally, as the leviathan that we all entrust to do justice. But this only works where they are seen to have that legitimacy and where they are viewed not as pawns in a game of inter-ethnic finger-pointing but as institutions that speak for us all.

# 13

# WHERE THEY WERE HIDDEN

That corpse you planted last year in your garden,
Has it begun to sprout? Will it bloom this year?
Or has the sudden frost disturbed its bed?
Oh keep the Dog far hence, that's friend to men,
Or with his nails he'll dig it up again!

— T.S. Eliot, *The Waste Land*, 1922

I

## Where They Were Hidden

There wasn't much to distinguish the training centre from the fields that surrounded it. More green grass, perhaps a sign that I hadn't seen from the car. We turned off the road and drove down a seemingly endless driveway. We were still essentially in Belgrade. One might call this a suburb, though the terrain felt sparse and rural.

We were in the middle of the trial but I had never been to this place. Although eleven years had passed since the events, this was still the active training ground for the SAJ. They remained the elite anti-terrorist unit of the Serbian police — the "best of the best," as Hollywood always seems to describe such teams of crack commandoes. The men looked about as I had expected: huge and hard-jawed, clad in camouflage, and readying for training or walking briskly between buildings.

In the distance I heard machine gun fire. Our escort noticed me listening.

"Training," he said.

We stopped at the administrative building first, where we met some people and shook some hands. I introduced myself as a prosecutor and my colleague introduced himself as an investigator — both from the ICTY, of course, but they already knew that. They'd known we were coming for weeks. Two impossibly large men came out to escort us around the base. They shook hands with the man from Belgrade who had brought us out here, watchers watching the watcher. They were smiling, very pleasant, though they knew we were there for the prosecution of the man who had once been responsible for their unit and the base itself. I wondered how many of the men here had served in Kosovo and which of them had been on the ground through the events we were prosecuting. Some of them had been, surely, though a lot of time had passed. We shook hands, the watchers spoke to each other, and then we went to see where it had happened.

We walked quietly across the dry grass until we came to a shooting range. We stopped at the threshold and looked around. There was a wooden framework to fire from, then a long straight run of empty space before a set of targets way at the back. The range was set between two rounded hills, good for ensuring that the bullets stayed inside the area.

Our escorts pointed down the length of the range and we started on the long walk to the end. Walking the length of a firing range, through terrain where bullets are meant to fly, is unsettling. It wasn't hard to see why they had put it here.

When we were halfway down the range, automatic gunshots rang out. I turned and looked back at where we'd been but there was still no one there. The shots were close, and loud. There were men firing on the other side of the hill, out of sight.

"Training," our escort said again.

The gunshots on the other side of the hill seemed to grow louder and more frequent, then a helicopter flew low overhead. Some distance away, but still in view, it dipped and hovered, a ladder spilled off the side, and a tactical team descended to the ground, machine guns drawn. It was an impressive showing.

*Training*, I thought, but kept it to myself.

We stopped at the end of the range, then turned and walked to the right, and there it was — or what was left of it. A broad area, now just grass and mounds of dug-up earth, grown over in the intervening years. This area had once been crammed full with bodies, hundreds upon hundreds. Large pits that had been crudely dug, filled with human remains, then clumsily covered over again. Who would think to look here, so far from Kosovo? Who would ever be allowed in?

They were gone now. The operation was exposed, the path leading ultimately to The Hague.

II

## Batajnica

At the outset of the war, almost the entirety of the SAJ forces from the 13 Maj base in Batajnica were deployed to Kosovo. Three or four days later, the base was targeted and bombed by NATO planes. As a result, the handful of members of the unit who had stayed behind relocated to a new site down the road. They left the old site sitting empty.[1]

At the beginning of April, K88 dropped into the Batajnica base to check on things.[2] As he walked the grounds he found it abandoned and strangely quiet. He had come to check on a Praga, an armoured ground weapon that he knew should be sitting behind the kitchen hall. But as he neared the Praga he saw there was a civilian truck — a yellow Daimler Benz — parked by the shooting range. It looked strangely out of place. As he approached he saw a second vehicle, this one an all-blue Tatra construction truck — old and rusted, double-wheeled, and with an open top. He noticed a third truck by the dog training area. He was curious but there was no one there to ask; he left without learning what they were doing there.

When he returned several days later only one of the trucks remained. There was a guard stationed at the base and he asked him about it. The man told him the truck had a terrible smell and advised him to keep his distance.[3]

K87, meanwhile, was working at the relocated SAJ base down the road. He had the unfortunate luck to answer the telephone one morning when it rang. The man on the line, to his surprise, was General Vlastimir Đorđević. Đorđević asked him if there were any officers at the base; there weren't and he said so. Đorđević told him tersely to report in person to his office — a temporary headquarters in Belgrade — at 9:00 a.m. the next morning. He didn't say why.[4]

As directed, K87 drove to Belgrade early the next morning. He soon found himself waiting at the Belgrade Bank, Đorđević's temporary headquarters during the war. He was invited in, sat down, and then Đorđević told him he had a job that needed doing. There were two trucks sitting at the SAJ's Batajnica centre, he said, containing human bodies. According to K87, Đorđević told him these were victims of the NATO bombing. Regardless, K87's assigned task was clear: the bodies would need to be buried. There was a skeleton crew of three or four workers at the base that would help him and they would be provided with an excavator. Đorđević explained where to dig: there was an area where the earth was already disturbed, in a remote field off of the firing range. The ground there would be soft.[5] It was to be a secret operation.

When the discussion was finished, Đorđević brought K87 to meet Minister Stojiljković . He introduced K87 curtly: "This is the man who will do the job."[6]

With that, K87 drove out to Batajnica. He found the base abandoned but he saw the trucks. Then he went home.

K87 called K88 on April 8 and told him what they needed to do. The next morning, K88 picked up an excavator that was waiting for them at a nearby construction company. Then the men headed to Batajnica. When they arrived at the centre, two of the truck drivers were there waiting. One of them, Bogdan Lipovac, was Đorđević's personal driver. The other, Dragan Brasanović, drove for an assistant minister.[7]

III

# Reburials

The men were left on their own to figure out the crude mechanics of unloading and burying the bodies. What became clear right away was that the excavator they had wasn't large enough to dig a sufficiently deep hole. K88 improvised, digging a declining ramp about forty metres long so he could dig increasingly deeper as he rolled forward.[8] The earth, at least, was soft and easy to displace. He piled it on either side as he dug.

This first part was like any construction job. But when the hole was deep enough they had to deal with getting the bodies out of the first truck. The smell was so overpowering that the men worked wearing gas masks. To stay as far from the decomposing bodies as they could, they attempted a curious solution: they opened the back of the truck and then one of the men got behind the wheel, reversed down the ramp, and at the edge stepped firmly on the brakes. The jerk of the truck, combined with the slant of the ramp, sent the bodies sliding and tumbling into the pit.

With the bodies now in the hole, the men began to cover them over with earth. This was the easy part, or should have been, but they were interrupted by air raid sirens. The excavator, they knew, ran at high temperatures, so operating it on the base could make it an obvious target for NATO. The men scrambled out of the base and stayed away until the threat had seemingly passed. They returned later that day to finish the job. Once the hole was covered the drivers returned and drove the empty trucks away. Then the workers finally went home, leaving the base deserted.[9]

This, they would soon discover, was just the beginning. The next shipment arrived several days later, delivered in an old and weathered yellow truck with no license plates, driven by two men in blue police uniforms. There was blood leaking through the floor of its trailer. The men left the truck parked as they figured out what to do. By the time they got around to moving it, a large pool had formed under the carriage. K88 and the other men tried burning it away with chemicals, to no avail. Then they poured gasoline over top and lit it on fire. This seemed to work, at least well enough.[10]

The men dug a new pit for the second load, using the same ramp technique. This was a bigger truck, so they needed a new way to get the bodies out without having to deal with them directly. The men drove the vehicle along the side of the new pit, lowered the panels along the side of the truck, and then tried to tilt the truck sideways over the hole. They hoped the bodies would slide off of the trailer's rubberized canvas lining and into the pit, but when they tilted it the entire trailer went crashing into the hole. The trailer was wedged into the grave but still linked to the truck's cab, which was sitting on the level ground.

It took some time but the men were eventually able to pull the trailer back out of the pit, getting the bodies out in the process by pulling and jerking it back and forth. In the struggle they broke the hitch joining the cab and the trailer. With no way to reconnect them, the drivers had no choice but to drive the cab away and leave the trailer stranded at the scene when they returned to the base.[11]

Throughout April and into May, a mismatched array of trucks continued to arrive at the base. They came from across Kosovo, a new truck appearing every two or three days. Each arrival was preceded by a phone call, Mr. Đorđević letting them know there was another truck on its way.[12] The drivers ferrying the bodies to the centre were a mixed bag. Some wore police uniforms and others wore civilian clothes. Some were old men and some seemed relatively young.[13] Once the trucks arrived they would often sit there for days on end, bodies still inside.

After a while the shipments began to blend into one another, though with the passage of time the men grew no better at the crude mechanics of unloading and burying the bodies. The operation only grew more shambolic.

One shipment came in a new Mercedes moving truck with a mechanical ramp door. When the door broke as they were unloading, the men simply left it in the pit and buried it with the bodies. Another delivery arrived in a thirty-ton refrigerator truck with a cooling system. When the men couldn't get the truck open they just broke through its side and scooped out the contents. They noticed a coffin amidst the foul-smelling soil and tossed it into the pit with everything else.[14]

The sloppiness of the operation wasn't limited to the skeleton crew at Batajnica. Two of the arriving drivers, thankful to have made it to the centre at all, told the men that as they were en route their truck's cargo door had fallen open on the highway, spilling around fifty bodies into the open road. They had scrambled to get the bodies back in the truck, even enlisting some passing motorists to help. The reloaded old truck barely made it to Batajnica. Upon its arrival it broke down completely.[15]

The trucks came and went and the crew at Batajnica dug holes and buried bodies. They didn't need to be told about the bigger picture. But K88 noticed that not all of the trucks were unloaded at the site. Some were driven off elsewhere, presumably still containing bodies, with Batajnica seemingly just a stopping point.[16]

There were officials who would drop in from time to time to check on the operation. One of them, from state security, arrived in a Mercedes and told K88 bluntly that if he said anything about what they were doing there he would be killed.[17]

At some point, it seems that K87 had had enough. He went to see Đorđević in his office and worked up the courage to ask if they could stop the operation:

> I asked him if there was a possibility to stop bringing the bodies … because the feeling was unpleasant, and uncomfortable seeing all these bodies being thrown in the hole. I do not remember his reaction or what he said, but after my request I do not think there was any more bodies coming…. I felt better that I had asked him to stop and that there would be no more bodies coming.[18]

Whether this is what actually led to the end of the shipments to Batajnica is not clear. What is clear is that at some point shortly thereafter the trucks stopped arriving and the work crew wound down the operation.

When the work was completed the men returned the excavator to the construction company. The trailer with the broken hitch, which had been left at the site, remained stranded there.[19]

It wasn't long afterward that the war ended. Although NATO forces and international observers entered Kosovo, they didn't enter Serbia proper. The SAJ returned to the Batajnica base when the war concluded and retained tight control over who was admitted to the grounds. There were probably few more secure locations in Serbia.

Shortly after his return to the base, Živko Trajković, still the SAJ's commander, asked Đorđević why there were bodies buried in the corner of his training centre.

"What can I tell you?" Đorđević said, "All of my brave generals buried their heads into the sand and they left it to me to finish this part of the work."[20]

In the ensuing years it was business as usual at the Batajnica base — living, sleeping, eating, and training — only now with mass graves in the corner of the compound.

# IV

# One Local Journalist

In retrospect, it seems hard to believe that an operation of this size and scope, characterized by this level of carelessness, could have stayed hidden. How do you keep so many people from talking? Civilian workers, police officers, drivers, strangers on the highway. Not to mention the thousands who had been deployed to Kosovo.

People were surely talking, or at least whispering amongst themselves. Too many people knew. Publicly, however, nothing was happening.

In the absence of proof and some sort of broader context to situate the rumblings, it was hard to know what to make of the rumours. During the war, the writer Christopher Hitchens had received a letter from a Serbian student, telling him about a family friend who was a long-haul truck driver. The man had described making multiple trips to Kosovo, picking up truckloads of Albanian bodies and hauling them all the way to Vojvodina in northern Serbia. Hitchens, though he was a strong and thoughtful proponent of the NATO intervention, didn't go public with the allegations. Nor did he really know what to make of them. As he would later describe, he opted not to write about the letter because, "although it appeared to be offered in good faith it also seemed somewhat weird and fanciful, and because rumours of exactly this sort do tend to circulate in times of war and censorship."[21]

To uncover more would require someone who not only knew what to investigate but was inside Serbia, well connected, and brave enough to report what had happened. Under the Milošević regime, poking your nose where it didn't belong was a dangerous endeavour.

The unravelling of the cover-up was ultimately sparked by the work of a relatively unknown local Serbian journalist named Dragan Vitomirović. The loose thread that unravelled the entire operation was the refrigerator truck that had surfaced in the Danube.

In September of 1999, Vitomirović published an article in the *Timok Crime Review* (*Timočka Krimi Revija*), a small local paper in eastern Serbia specializing in crime news. Reporting on the rumours that were still being whispered behind closed doors in Kladovo and Tekija, a clearly curious Vitomirović spoke to a number of people in the area who gave bare-boned and sometimes divergent accounts. All of them, however, had a common core, though: a refrigerator truck had been found in the Danube, and when it was retrieved and opened, "dead bodies fell out."[22] Some of the accounts included curious details, like the fact that one of the officials had obtained tablecloths from a "well-known restaurant" in the area to wrap the bodies.

While Vitomirović clearly thought something strange had unfolded, he seemed not to know — or was unwilling to talk about — where the bodies had come from. The article made no mention of ethnic Albanians, instead repeating elements of the misdirection police had promulgated back in April: that these were "probably the bodies of the Kurds or Talibans who had mysteriously arrived on our territory."[23] The article called on the authorities to explain whether the event had actually occurred or not.[24] But the small publication caused no public reaction, only more local whisperings and some nervous phone calls within the Ministry of the Interior back in Belgrade. Life in Serbia went on. Back in Kosovo, thousands of people were still hoping desperately for news, perhaps even some sort of closure.

It wasn't until nearly two years later, when Vitomirović revisited the same story with a follow-up article for the *Timok Crime Review*, that everything changed.[25] The follow-up piece was bold, well-sourced, and surprisingly brave. It began by pointing a finger directly at the police, the investigative judge at the scene, and the top officials in the Ministry of the Interior for covering up the crime.

A man named Đorđević — a different Đorđević — had finally spoken up about the operation. Vitomirović had convinced the diver, Živojin Đorđević (aka Zika), to explain what had happened. In a lengthy interview, Zika recounted the discovery of the truck and the moment it was opened to reveal the human cargo inside.[26] The article named names, all the way up to Golubović and Đorđević.[27]

Two years after the war in Kosovo, the political landscape in Serbia had changed. Milošević was no longer in power, and the new government that had taken power was an anti-Milošević coalition. Just a month earlier, Milošević had been arrested by Yugoslav authorities — not for committing war crimes but on charges of abuse of power and financial corruption.[28] The winds had shifted dramatically, and the national media was newly emboldened. What began as a small local article was picked up by the Belgrade press and widely reported around the country. The allegations in the article, and the detailed description of what had happened, were too much to ignore.

## V

# The Working Group

In response to public clamouring about the truck full of bodies and the obvious cover-up attempt, Serbian authorities formed a "Working Group" to investigate. It was, as often seemed the case in Serbia at the time, a strangely contradictory exercise. The Working Group was formed by Sreten Lukić, who had himself been the senior ranking police official on the ground in Kosovo throughout the war. Lukić had reported to Đorđević, had overseen many of the ethnic cleansing operations, and would ultimately end up being charged by the ICTY for his actions. He surely already knew about the cover-up operation, and would have known that he and his colleagues had much to lose from anything approximating an accurate report. But much had changed in Serbia. The landscape, again, was shifting underfoot.

The Working Group's focus, at least at first, was on trying to identify the victims who were found in the truck, as opposed to the men who orchestrated the operation. But regardless of the intentions when it was set up, the group ended up identifying and interviewing a range of people involved in the operation. It also sought to speak to both Vlastimir Đorđević and Minister Stojiljković. On May 12, 2001, less than two weeks after the article in the *Timok Crime Review* was published, Đorđević fled the country and went into hiding.[29]

On May 25, 2001 the Working Group released a report with findings. It pointed the finger at Minister Stojiljković and General Đorđević for covering up the bodies in the refrigerator truck, which it identified as Operation Dubina II. The report also suggested a much broader operation than this lone truck. It described a meeting held in March of 1999, in Milošević's office, between Minister Stojiljković, General Đorđević, chief of the RDB Radomir Marković, and Milošević himself. Đorđević had raised the issue of "clearing up the terrain" in Kosovo, Milošević had tasked Stojiljković with this role, and Stojiljković subsequently delegated the responsibility back to Đorđević and General Dragan Ilić. The purpose, according to the report, was "removing civilian victims who could potentially become the subject of investigations by The Hague Tribunal."[30]

The Working Group released a second report on June 26, 2001, in which it addressed bodies from the Danube that had been buried at the Batajnica SAJ Centre. It identified this as a subject for further investigation.[31]

The events pushed into the light by Vitomirović's article and the subsequent Working Group reports provided glimpses into what was clearly a disturbing cover-up operation. But the true scope of the operation, and its connection to what had unfolded in village after village in Kosovo, was only slowly becoming apparent. The truth only came into focus once the bodies were unearthed.

# 14

# THE MAN IN THE BACK ROW

|

## The Man in the Back Row

It can be all too easy sometimes, in the ongoing routine of prosecuting a trial on this scale, to forget that the accused is actually in the room. He is, of course, the entire focus of the exercise — at least ostensibly. But in a case of this scope, so far flung from the immediacy and experience of any single person, the proceedings can tend to take on a life and rhythm of their own. The accused is represented by counsel, and it is those counsel with whom you interact from moment to moment, day after day. The accused sits stoically at the back of the room, watching, occasionally passing a note or whispering instructions.

Judged from afar, perhaps read about in the newspaper, accused war criminals can seem like caricatures. They seem an embodiment of the role they performed and the crimes they allegedly committed, little more. But they are, of course, as fully formed and as human as anyone else. In the courtroom there is nothing mysterious or larger than life about such men. To watch the Đorđević trial was to spend day after day in the same room with a man seemingly polite and courteous, patient, well mannered, dignified, and composed.

The trial must have seemed surreal for Mr. Đorđević. Multiple prosecutors, judges, case managers, investigators, analysts, interpreters, registry staff, interns, and of course his entire defence team, dedicating their workday lives to the attempted re-creation of two specific years of his professional life, ten years earlier. A man watching a group of lawyers trying to piece together his actions and their repercussions, the events now recast through a lens of law and procedure. He would watch as a parade of people came to testify at the trial bearing his name: civilians forever scarred by the operations he ordered, former colleagues and friends, members of the Serbian police and military, men and women he had never met. All of this unfolding in a foreign country, under the sometime watching eyes of the world.

As the Đorđević trial unfolded I often found myself thinking about Adolf Eichmann. I would certainly not compare the two men with respect to the nature or scale of their crimes. But to oversee operations with such powerful human consequences as a relatively detached bureaucrat — a man at a desk, away from the action, performing a job — this is a very particular type of crime. Đorđević, not unlike like Eichmann, was a successful professional who had climbed the ranks and sat largely removed from the consequences of his work, issuing orders from afar and attending meetings. He was surely not a weak bureaucrat who "never realized what he was doing"[1] — he had direct knowledge of what was happening, even personal involvement on occasion, and wielded significant power. But Đorđević, like Eichmann, was a middle-manager of atrocity. In the twisted wartime atmosphere in which he found himself, it is difficult to know the extent to which he reflected on the rightness of his actions.

To recognize the ordinary humanity of such men is not, of course, to diminish the acts that were committed. It is, instead, to confront a more troubling reality — that acts with such inhuman consequences can be all too easy to commit. In every instance of genocide, crimes against humanity, or mass violence, there are of course some shockingly brutal and depraved thugs to be found amongst the perpetrators. You hear about many such men at the Tribunal. But men seemingly predestined for such cruelty tend to be the exception, not the rule. To see the politicians, military leaders, chiefs of police, and legions of co-operating civilians up close is to recognize that they do not fit easily with such demonization. While we can, and do, rightly condemn and punish the actions of those responsible, we lose something crucial if we dismiss these perpetrators as monsters and ignore how they came to commit such acts in the first place.

Evil, if we are to revisit such a loaded word, seems not so much an inherent quality of monsters as a consequence — often the result of acts done by ordinary people who have come to feel that their actions are justified and necessary. They can be angry, aggressive, and scheming. They can also be family men, loyal friends, or prudent careerists.

There are these lessons in criminal trials, if we care to listen — in the human stories of individual perpetrators. I began to think that when an accused comes before one of these courts or tribunals, and particularly when he is convicted and sentenced, his story takes the form of a publicly enacted tragedy. It was the ancient Greeks who gave us tragedy as a performance art, once a year gathering their citizens to the Theatre of Dionysus at the Acropolis to listen to stories of events gone terribly wrong. These were stories about individuals who began as heroes, often leaders, whose lives took decisive and fateful turns into epic disaster and death.

As Aristotle would explain, these stories had lessons to teach. They became valuable tools for the moral and behavioral education of a society. As Alain De Botton has described it:

> A work of tragedy would rise to its true moral and edifying possibilities when the audience looked upon the hero's ghastly errors and crimes and was left with no option but to reach the terrifying conclusion: "How easily I, too, might have done the same." Tragedy's task was to demonstrate the ease with which an essentially decent and likable person could end up generating hell."[2]

Like the tragedies of the ancient Greeks, the criminal trial is a publicly accessible recounting of events that have gone terribly wrong. Like tragedy, in the criminal trial there must be consequences for acting wrongly. As Adam Philips describes tragedy: "No one in Hamlet gets away with anything; indeed, that's what tragedies are, dramas in which people, in the most extreme ways possible, don't get away with things."[3]

In the case of our criminal justice system, however, we must impose these consequences ourselves.

While we may have a tendency to cast the perpetrators of such crimes as monsters, we should never lose sight of the lesson that virtually every genocide, crime against humanity, or large-scale act of violence teaches when one looks closely enough: that it is surprisingly easy to succumb to the mindsets, justifications, and acts that lead to such violence and cruelty. The form that such justifications take have a way, it seems, of always feeling new.

## II
# Perpetrators, Denial, and Cognitive Dissonance

I was most of the way through a presentation on the Đorđević trial and the ethnic cleansing of Kosovo when a hand went up in the back of the class. The trial was over and I was presenting to a group of international high school students who were in Toronto for a special school program. I had described the international court process and the experiences of some of our witnesses, and then explained the killings in Ćuška, Podujevo, and Izbica. Some of the students had already contributed questions and comments: one girl had spoken emotionally about her grandmother's experiences of persecution in Russia, another had asked about forensic evidence, and a boy had asked about sentencing. But this girl at the back looked angry, and I had an inkling of what was coming when I called on her.

"I think this was biased," she said rather boldly. I was struck by her confidence. "We are from Serbia, my family, and bad things were done to the Serbian people too. This is biased against the Serbs."

It was clear she had taken the allegations personally, as an attack on her ethnicity and heritage and perhaps an indictment of her family and culture. I imagined discussions her family had already had around the dinner table, shaping this view on the events in Kosovo, contextualizing the allegations against the Serbian perpetrators into a broader narrative

— if not an alternative version — that diminished the events. I thought about my own family, and some of the mixed reactions that a presentation detailing Israeli actions against Palestinians might well provoke.

It was a challenging question to respond to, and one that I often heard, expressed in only slightly differing versions. When I met someone Serbian and they learned I worked at the Tribunal, I often encountered some pronouncement along these lines, seemingly born of a sort of reflexive defensiveness, a reluctance to fully acknowledge what had happened because of the implications for their own culture and collective history.

Sometimes, in its milder version, it went unexplained: "Well, I'm Serbian, so you know … " Sometimes the first thing expressed was outright denial. More often it was some version of, "We were equally victims" — the 'we' referring to Serbs collectively. This last version seemed a more reasonable response, certainly, and yet it directly echoed the very mentality of victimhood-as-justification that led to the conflict and the crimes in the first place.

I knew all of this when the girl asked her question, just as I knew that anything I said wasn't likely to change her mind. But it was also true, surely, that there would be no one more valuable to connect with than someone denying or minimizing these events.

My answer was a little oblique — at least it started that way. I began by acknowledging that crimes had taken place on all sides of the conflict and that many Serbs had also been victims themselves — victims of violence by Croats, by Bosniaks, and by Kosovo Albanians. I described how after we finished the Đorđević trial, several of my trial team members went on to prosecute the ethnic Albanian and KLA commander Ramush Haradinaj, who after the war had become the prime minister of Kosovo. All of these things were true. But it was also true that the mass murders and deportations I had described had happened, and that they had been directed and overseen by Serbian authorities. The evidence was clear. In fact much of the evidence we relied on had been provided by the Serbian government itself.

The distinction that I hoped to draw was between the *individuals* who committed the crimes and a broader, collective notion of blame and accountability that she seemed to be inferring based on ethnicity. That it was not that "the Serbs" had done this to "the Albanians" — as she seemed to be unconsciously framing it — but that these individuals, and in this case these *leaders*, had committed these particular acts against these particular victims.

It was an important notion, and one that the international criminal courts and tribunals have long embraced. As Richard Goldstone, the first ICTY Prosecutor, put it:

> Specific individuals bear the major share of the responsibility, and it is they, not the group as a whole, who need to be held to account, through a fair and meticulously detailed presentation and evaluation of evidence, precisely so that the next time around no one will be able to claim that all Serbs did this, or all Croats or all Hutus — so that people are able to see how it is specific individuals in their communities who are continually endeavouring to manipulate them in that fashion. I really believe that this is the only way the cycle can be broken.[4]

This is true; these actions were committed by individuals, not by entire ethnic groups, religions, or cultures. But regardless of our intentions, members of these groups often react to these prosecutions, and to the identification of blame, as if the entire group is being judged. This is not the case, and it is certainly not the intention at the ICTY. And yet the defensiveness is not hard to understand. Although these crimes were committed by individuals, there were a great many people who were both involved in and responsible for what happened. There were the soldiers, policemen, militiamen, and armed civilians who participated directly. And there were the and other facilitators, supporters, and deniers who participated more broadly. The leaders who orchestrated these acts often enjoyed broad popular followings, as did some of the offensives themselves. These crimes, as is often the case, were in many ways borne on the backs of a popular resurgence in ethnic identity and pride. They were being justified, before they even began, in the language of collective injustice and victimhood.

The girl wasn't buying my answer and she said so, repeating in not so many words that she still thought the presentation was biased against the Serbs. I tried to respond gently, rephrasing some of what I had already said. Then I thought it best to move on. She had been brave to raise her hand and I didn't want my answer to seem in any way like the affront to her ethnic identity that she seemed to have received it as. I wondered afterwards if I should have said more.

The truth is that her answer was a form of denial, not so thinly cloaked in the language of "look what they did to us." It is true that Serb civilians were also victims in the war, and it is a fair criticism of the Tribunal that not enough successful prosecutions have been brought against other perpetrators, Croatians and Kosovo Albanians in particular.[5] But this surely cannot be used to silence the identification and description of the very real atrocities that Serb forces committed — one does not excuse the other. Nor should we need to endlessly point to equivalencies in blameworthiness between perpetrators from different ethnic groups. The point is to move away from identifying and distinguishing based on ethnicity, towards some shared recognition of what is right and wrong.

There is, I think, a very fundamental issue of identity at play in these situations, which runs a strong interference on our ability and willingness to recognize injustice. It is a problem of what psychologists call cognitive dissonance.

When a national, ethnic, or religious/cultural group that one belongs to is alleged to have committed terrible acts, the result can put two seemingly contradictory notions into conflict. The first is the belief that these terrible events happened — that the Serbian government, for example, with the assistance of a number of Serb individuals, committed terrible crimes against the Albanian people in 1999. The second is the belief we have in the goodness and virtue of our ethnic group itself — in this case that the Serbs are a great people, with a remarkable history, strong values, and rich culture and traditions. These two beliefs, at least on the surface, do not seem to sit well together.

To flip that around, these two beliefs can be experienced as dissonant:

1. Serbs are a great people. I am proud to be a Serb.
2. Serbs committed terrible crimes against the Albanians.

Cognitive dissonance theory tells us that holding two beliefs that we feel are contradictory causes us great mental stress and discomfort.

If two such notions are at odds with one another — seemingly anti-thetical — surely they cannot both be true. Our natural and largely unconscious tendency is to do two things when we encounter such contradictions: to seek to reduce this stress by making the beliefs consistent, and to avoid information that would seemingly increase the dissonance between the two beliefs.[6]

The two beliefs I've described are not, in fact, inconsistent. But what needs our attention, if we want to understand the denial and justification of collective crimes on this scale, are the ways in which we try to resolve the tension between such seemingly oppositional beliefs. To take pride in one's culture, heritage, history, traditions, and family is fundamental. To take a positive view of such basic questions of our own identity — to see oneself and one's family and friends as good people — is not, understandably, something that people are willing to give up. It is not moveable, nor does it need to be.

If these two beliefs are seen to be inconsistent — and therefore dissonant — it is the other belief that must change. If the recognition or acknowledgement that such atrocities happened seems to threaten our own self regard and our very conception of our faith, culture, or identity, then the easiest way to resolve this tension is to deny that the acts were committed.

We are all prone to the disruptive impact of these mental pressures. But if we give in to them then we deceive ourselves about the truth, often with very dangerous results.

The resolution to this apparent dilemma lies in recognizing that these two beliefs are not, in fact, dissonant. We must learn that we can exist, and thrive, with the two notions side by side. We can, and in fact we must, recognize and accept that these events took place while also maintaining our sense of pride in our collective identities. If not, we risk substantial and potentially disastrous contortions of the truth. Many Serbs committed atrocities against ethnic Albanians in Kosovo. But Serbs are also, of course, a great people — with a proud and accomplished cultural and historical tradition. To say it seems obvious. But recognizing that we may be reluctant to acknowledge the truth because of what we fear it may say about our notions of self and identity — this may require deliberate attention and correction.

Combatting denial means teaching that these forces have the potential to act on all of us whenever we feel that our deeply held notions of identity, community, and self are threatened. We must recognize when this pressure may be distorting what we choose to believe and what we are prepared to accept.

We must hold people accountable to this high standard of truth; we know that we cannot accept denial in the face of such injustices. But we can also help them along. We can do so by making it clear that a strong sense of self identity, family, culture, and heritage can exist alongside a recognition that such acts were committed.

This is not an achievement without historical precedent. Germany has done a strikingly effective job of requiring its citizens to acknowledge and confront the reality of the Nazis and the Holocaust — perhaps the darkest national history one could imagine — while continuing to foster and build a strong sense of individual and collective identity. This has not been without its complications, of course, and there is no doubt that the passage of time has helped. But the passage of time itself is no guarantee of acceptance.

The Kosovo war crimes trials told a true story in which Kosovo Albanians were primarily victims and Serbs were primarily perpetrators. This is a story that many still do not want to hear. But in many ways Serbia has already begun to accept the reality of its recent past; more than any other country in the former Yugoslavia it has begun to confront and acknowledge the crimes that were committed on its behalf. It is Serbia that gave up Milošević, and a great many other war criminals, to the ICTY for prosecution. It is Serbia that has now taken up the fight, if slowly, to prosecute some of the worst individual offenders in its domestic courts. There is further to go, certainly, and "Serbia" does not speak with a single voice. The current generation, and the next, will need to lead the way in taking ownership over the dark parts of their history while still proudly embracing their culture and heritage.

# 15

# WHAT WAS FOUND

I

## The Forensic Examinations

The unearthing of bodies at Batajnica, for purposes of forensic investigation, began in June of 2001. Whereas the burials had been careless
and hurried, the final undigging was meticulous and slow. The first stage
of the process, given that the bodies were in Serbia, was conducted by
Serbian authorities. The new government seemed eager to distance itself
from Milošević and to capitalize on an important political opportunity to
implicate and condemn the old guard. With multi-million dollar foreign
aid packages on the line there were also clear incentives to being seen as
co-operative with the international community.

The discoveries made at Batajnica were presented at trial through
live witnesses and a significant number of documents. In court the
evidence came across as dry and technical, the detail sometimes excruciating — not surprising, at least in legal terms, given the need for
caution and scientific rigor in forensic reporting. The tenor of the

evidence, in this respect, stood in sharp contrast to the reality of what was actually uncovered.

Slobodan Mitrović, one of the members of the Serbian excavation team, would later provide a personal account of his early days at Batajnica and the effect the work had on him.[1] He was not a witness; I would only discover his account after the trial had finished. But his words seemed to put a more personal face on the forensic operation — an aspect I had been left wondering about. Mitrović described an overpowering stench sticking in the pockets of his nostrils every day he spent on the excavation, lingering long after he had left the site. He spoke of waking up in the middle of the night, panicked, trying frantically to locate a body in his bedroom before realizing he was at home and dreaming. For Mitrović, a Serb who described having thought of the Albanian population as the "immediate other" in the 1990s, the bodies and personal belongings he and his colleagues unearthed day after day had a "profoundly revelatory" quality.[2]

The first grave to be identified and unearthed was dubbed "Batajnica I." It was set somewhat apart from the others, lying just outside of the firing range. The initial forensic investigation into this grave was led by the head of the Belgrade Forensic Institute, Dušan Dunjić, although observers from the ICTY and the International Commission on Missing Persons came to oversee the operation as well. The second grave was excavated a month later. As more and more graves were found and unearthed, another professor at the Institute, Branimir Aleksandrić, had to take over. In the end, eight graves were discovered at Batajnica: five mass graves, two smaller sites, and one that was empty.[3]

The process of unearthing, cataloguing, and then repatriating the bodies had a strange symmetry to the way they had been concealed. For the purposes of forensic analysis the top layers of the mass graves were dug up using an excavator, but this time carefully and in thin layers. Once the excavator reached signs of bodies or a new type of soil the digging would be done carefully by hand.[4] Where the bodies had earlier been dumped into graves like cargo, they were now carefully unearthed, numbered and catalogued, and then placed into body bags.

Hips and spines, because they are easy to recognize, often proved the most useful to identify a body.[5] But some entire bodies were found wrapped in blankets, effectively mummified, and others were found rolled up in plastic sheeting. The graves contained bullets and shell cases, prayer beads and Korans, driver's licences and passports, personal items from pencils to bus tickets, and clothing pierced with gunshot holes.[6]

The team logged what they found as either a body (T, for *Telo*), a body part (DT, for *Deo Tela*), or an artifact (P, for *Predmet*).[7] Small bone samples were sawed off, usually from the femur if that was available, and placed in marked plastic containers. These were provided to an international team for DNA testing.[8]

The found bodies were stored in a tent as the team worked, then loaded into flatbed trucks and transported to a series of nearby tunnels. The tunnels could be sealed and thus kept secure; they maintained a relatively constant ambient temperature of 21 degrees celsius.[9]

The forensic evidence extensively corroborated the descriptions that had been given by the workers who had first buried the bodies at the site. But it also revealed some things that the men had apparently not wanted to talk about.

The forensic teams saw the marks of excavator teeth. They found the ramps the workers had made to dig gradually deeper into the ground. They noticed that the bodies in some of the graves were clustered, as if they had been slid in en masse.[10] They found the mechanical ramp door that had broken off and been buried, as well as the coffin that K88 had described.[11] They saw evidence that one of the truck trailers had fallen into one of the graves and then been extracted. The trailer itself was still sitting at the site.

What the workers who testified about the burials had *not* admitted to was attempting to burn the bodies. But the forensic evidence told a very obvious story. Several of the pits contained a large number of burnt tires, both over and under the bodies. Many of the bodies had been consumed by fire and were beyond recognition or entirely destroyed. The workers had tried to destroy the evidence before burying it.[12]

The forensic teams also found that a huge quantity of soil — twenty-two truckloads worth — had been trucked into the base and dumped over top of the graves. The new earth had helped to counter the swamp-like appearance that the terrain was starting to take on, and more importantly had created a "false horizon" that made it impossible to see where the graves had been dug. Once the burials were completed the entire area behind the firing range had been effectively re-landscaped.[13]

When the forensic process was completed the bodies were loaded, once again, into refrigerator trucks. Then they were driven back to Kosovo.

The Serbian authorities had certainly seemed willing to uncover the fact that the previous regime had been secretly hiding bodies. But officials still seemed reluctant to concede facts that would indicate or even suggest that the events in Kosovo had been a large-scale ethnic cleansing operation.

When the bodies arrived in Kosovo the OMPF began to see differences between the reports the Serbian authorities had provided and what they were finding in the body bags.[14] They conducted forensic examinations of their own and found some telling discrepancies. Most notable was that, in striking contrast to the evidence, the Serbian forensic authorities had reported that they couldn't determine the cause of death for *any* of the bodies they had autopsied. They claimed that to determine a cause of death they had to be able "to exclude all other causes," noting that since the bodies had decomposed, nothing could be said for certain. Even where piles of bodies were found together in mass graves, all with virtually identical bullet wounds to the head, the authorities claimed they couldn't determine how they had died.[15] It was a suspiciously self-serving approach, typical of the sort of bureaucratic obfuscation that would rear its head when the authorities sought to evade conclusions that didn't suit them.[16]

This was not to say, however, that conducting a forensic analysis in these circumstances was easy or straightforward. It was neither. With body parts so commingled, and many of them destroyed, reassembling and accounting for each victim proved an impossibly complex puzzle. The examiners set their goals instead on identifying a minimum number of bodies. The OMPF identified a minimum of 744 individuals from Batajnica, though there were surely more than this. They were able to identify the likely cause of death for 506 of them.

II

# Findings

The body of Jashar Berisha — everything but his leg — was found buried in Batajnica I. With him were the bodies of other members of the Berisha family, killed in the Suva Reka pizzeria. A thorough inventory of the site recorded what was found there. Amongst the items were various coloured sweaters, eyeglasses, a waistcoat, a small shoe, a sports jersey, a gold-coloured earring, a dark red tracksuit, a Seiko watch, and a child's underwear and diaper. The exhumations identified a minimum of thirty-six different bodies in the grave — seventeen female, sixteen male, and three that were too damaged to determine. Nine of the bodies were young children.[17]

An international team identified Jashar's body through DNA analysis; it matched with samples that had been provided by his brothers Halit and Eqrem.[18] With this discovery the journey his body had made could be fully reconstructed. Jashar had been taken from the gas station where he worked, brought to the pizzeria in downtown Suva Reka, and then executed. His body was tossed in with the others who were killed at the pizzeria, then transported by truck to the military firing range near Korisha in southern Kosovo. When that site was unearthed, however, it was found to contain only his leg and pieces of some of his clothing. With the discovery of the rest of his body at Batajnica, the final piece was now clear: the bodies from the Suva Reka massacre had been unearthed again from this temporary hiding place, then trucked hundreds of kilometres to Batajnica.[19]

Shyrete Berisha had also provided a DNA sample, along with her family tree. The results of the Batajnica excavation would bring some closure, perhaps, but certainly no relief. The remains of her son Redon and her daughters Majlinda and Herolinda were identified amongst the bodies in Batajnica I. Lirija Berisha, the twenty-four-year-old wife of Shyrete's cousin Nexhmedin, was found there as well, carrying an unborn child. In the end, twenty-four members of the Berisha family were identified in the same grave.[20]

The bodies found in mass graves II and V at Batajnica were identified as the victims of the killings that took place in Đjakovica, part of Operation Reka. Batajnica II held at least 269 identifiable bodies, all of them men. Batajnica V, which they found lined with a plastic sheet, held at least 287 bodies, many of them damaged by fire. Forensics suggested they had been brought in as many as a dozen different shipments.[21]

Amongst these many bodies were the family members of Lizane Malaj, whom she had last seen in the courtyard of her home, lying face down as she was forced to walk away. Their bodies were not all identified at once. She was first told they had found and identified the body of her husband Vat, whom she could finally lay to rest on April 17, 2004. Just over a year later she was told that her son Blerim had also been found and identified, along with her brother Nikoll and her nephews Arben and Andrush. The bodies were returned by the International Red Cross and then finally laid to rest in Meja on April 27, 2005.[22]

## III

# Petrovo Selo

Batajnica was the largest mass grave site found, but it was not the only one. A number of other sites where bodies had been hidden were identified in Serbia and across Kosovo.

At the special police centre in Petrovo Selo, located in eastern Serbia, two mass graves were found under a patch of newly grown grass. Their contents were exhumed and forensically examined by another Serbian team — this one from the Niš Institute of Forensic Medicine — under the watch of international observers, including the ICTY.

A few days after the delivery of the first batch of bodies to Batajnica, the Ministry of the Interior had redirected some of the trucks to Petrovo Selo. When the bodies arrived there, workers on site dug two deep pits and began filling them. The subsequent forensic examinations identified the bodies there as having originated from at least two sites in Kosovo: a village outside of Pristina and a timber mill in southern Kosovska Mitrovica.[23]

Like Batajnica V, the first of the two graves to be unearthed was lined with plastic sheeting. At the very bottom were thirteen bodies, all male and in an intertwined mass. Excavations also found a black garbage bag containing a number of surgical gloves, a range of clothing, and a gas mask — presumably from the workers involved in the burials. Above this was a layer of garbage, canvas sheets, and blankets, topped with a layer of soil. At the very top of the pit were three male bodies, arrayed neatly in a row, all with clear execution wounds.[24] The three bodies looked different, somehow set apart.

The three men, it turned out, were Americans — the Bytyqi brothers, Ylli, Agron, and Mehmet, who had left New York to join with the KLA's "Atlantic Brigade" and fight the Serbian forces in Kosovo. Weeks after the conflict ended, they had reportedly escorted a Roma family across the Serbian border and found themselves arrested by the Serbian police for having improper documentation. They were sent to jail in the town of Prokuplje, then released on July 8, 1999, and taken to the Petrovo Selo centre by a police officer named Sreten Popović. Đorđević would later admit that he had issued the order to Popović to take the men to Petrovo Selo. Once there, although the details of how it happened are not entirely clear, the brothers were bound, blindfolded, and shot, their bodies placed at the top level of the first mass grave and their documents tossed in alongside them.[25]

The second of the graves was larger, containing fifty-nine bodies. At the base, the bodies were in a jumble. At the top, they were cased in a range of mismatched body bags. Curiously, one of the bodies wore a KLA uniform while another wore the uniform of the Serbian special police.[26]

It was here that authorities ultimately found the bodies of those killed in Izbica, or at least thirty-one of them — mostly elderly and disabled men, but also several women who had been shot or burned to death on tractors.[27] The journey these bodies had taken was now clear enough: after the killings they had been buried by their fellow villagers in individual plots, then unearthed by Serbian forces and transported hundreds of kilometres to be hidden. But a curious veneer of bureaucratic procedure had been applied to the bodies from the Izbica massacre — one that served as an interesting lesson in the public relations tactics employed by the Milošević regime.

Following the killings, Liri Loshi's video had aired on CNN, showing the world the evidence of a massacre of elderly and infirm civilians. It seemed a virtual certainty that after the war the international community would go looking for the bodies, so to simply hide the evidence like so many of the other massacres would in this case have raised obvious questions. At the same time, to leave the bodies on site to be found and examined would clearly confirm that these unarmed, elderly, and infirm civilians had been executed en masse.

The improvised solution seemingly involved placing a facade of plausible deniability over top of an outright cover-up. The regime arranged for its own forensic team to conduct a token forensic examination and then buried (metaphorically at least) those findings. Dr. Gordana Tomašević, a forensic medicine specialist and a member of the Serbian forensic team, testified at the Kosovo 6 trial that her team had received an order from a District Court on May 31 that provided for the forensic examination of bodies from Izbica to determine time and cause of death. The team wasn't involved in the exhumation of the bodies; instead, 101 bodies were simply delivered to them in a truck by civilian workers.[28] They were only able to identify five bodies, which they did using grave markers and identity documents. Of course, had identification been the intention this wouldn't have been difficult — the bodies had been identified before they were buried, precisely recorded in a list and even labelled individually with grave markers.

Perhaps the most telling comment on the meaninglessness of this team's analysis came from Radomir Gojović, the president of the Military Court in Belgrade and a defence witness.[29] Confronted with the disappearance of the bodies from Izbica and their subsequent discovery in Petrovo Selo, even Gojović had to acknowledge that something wrong had happened. It was the final answer of his cross-examination:

> To the best of my knowledge, some investigation was done of the mortal remains. Disinterment was attempted, autopsies carried out, but what happened later I don't know. It's possible that — that may have happened, but it's unacceptable from any aspect, both criminal law aspects or other aspects. I don't know what the reasons were after the detection of such crime for the remains to be relocated. I don't know who — what guided those who relocated them because it has — serves no practical purposes. The criminal offence had been registered, procedures been initiated. There's no rational explanation for moving those mortal remains.[30]

There was, in fact, an entirely rational and rather obvious reason for moving these bodies: to hide the truth. But the cover-up had by now completely unravelled.

## IV

# Burnt, Exploded, and Hidden in Wells

Not all of the bodies of ethnic Albanians killed in Kosovo were transported and buried. Some were found where they were killed. But the bodies of the most nefarious civilian killings were consistently hidden in some fashion.

In addition to the bodies that had been transported away in trucks, the evidence of massacres in Kosovo was hidden in a range of different ways.

In late March 1999 in the town of Mala Krusha, for example, Serbian police had forced 114 ethnic Albanian men and boys into a barn owned by the Batusha family. They used a villager who was confined to a wheelchair to block the entrance, then positioned themselves at the doors and windows and opened fire on everyone inside. When the shooting was finished, they walked through and shot the survivors individually, then doused their bodies with an incendiary liquid, threw maize overtop of them, and burned the barn to the ground. Ten of the men inside managed to scramble away. Some were pursued and killed, but two of them — Mehmet Krasniqi and Lutfi Ramadani — survived and later testified at the ICTY. More than a hundred others were not so fortunate. Villagers returning to the site after the war found that explosives had been used to destroy what remained of the scene, leaving only two large craters and a number of damaged houses around the blast zone. All that remained to evidence the killings were the remnants of a wheelchair and a few bones.[31]

At around the same time, Serbian forces marched a group of ethnic Albanian men from the small village of Kotlina to the location of two dry wells. They beat and shot the men, then threw them into the wells. The Serbian forces then exploded TNT inside each of the wells, killing the men inside and causing the walls to collapse inwards. By the time the assigned international forensic team (from Austria) arrived at the scene in September, grief-stricken relatives were trying desperately to tunnel down into the wells, hoping to identify and properly bury the bodies. The jumbled remains inside the wells were ultimately identified as twenty-two bodies.[32]

In the end, the evidence painted a clear picture of a broad campaign to hide the truth. The more nefarious the killings, and the worse the potential optics, the more likely the acts were to be covered up. The bodies found in Batajnica's mass graves belonged to civilians from all across Kosovo, including the municipalities of Đakovica, Decani, Obilić, Kosovo Polje, Vucitrn, Prizren, Peć, Lipjan, and Suva Reka. In Petrovo Selo, bodies were found from Peć, Srbica (Izbica), Decani, Glogovac, Prizren, Obilic, and Malisevo.[33]

# V
# Lake Perućac

There was also the matter of the second submerged refrigerator truck — the one that had surfaced in Lake Perućac, discharging its bodies and sending them floating into the river, before being covered up again.

The Lake Perućac mass grave was found in the midst of a large and man-made gravel spit along the banks of the Derventa River, surrounded by the beautiful Derventa Canyon gorge. When a Serbian forensic team excavated the site they found a mass of forty-eight bodies.[34]

The excavation team also found broken pieces of the truck intermixed in the grave. Both the bodies and the remaining pieces of the truck showed clear evidence of having been burned, although there was no evidence of fire at the scene itself. The floor of the truck's cargo hold had suffered notably less damage, suggesting that the bodies had been inside the truck when the fire was lit and had protected the floor from the flames. The truck was probably driven into the lake after the burning efforts had failed.[35]

Years later, just as the Đorđević trial was wrapping up in the late summer of 2010, a Serbian work crew lowered the water in the Lake Perućac reservoir so that repairs could be conducted on the dam. As the water drained and the riverbed was exposed, workers began to find more bodies.

They were not, it turned out, bodies from Kosovo. The deeper levels of the artificial lake, effectively the catch-basin for the Drina River, held evidence of violence that had unfolded far away and then floated downriver. Most of these bodies, it soon became clear, were those of Bosnian Muslims who had been killed by Serb forces in Višegrad in 1992. The Missing Persons Institute of Bosnia and Herzegovina put out a call for volunteers to assist with exhumations, receiving a staggering turnout of regular civilians. Hundreds of Bosnian volunteers — many of them searching for still-missing family members of their own — took part in the seventy-four days of exhumations, spreading out across the newly revealed bottom of the large lake. The more they dug, the more bodies they found.[36]

By the end of September 2010, before the repairs to the dam were completed and Serbian authorities raised the water levels once again, authorities and volunteer workers had managed to recover the remains of 373 people. The bodies they found came from further back than the 1990s — several were identified as German Wehrmacht soldiers who had been lying beneath the river since World War II.[37]

VI

# The Unproven

There were a number of accounts describing the destruction of bodies in Kosovo that were never ultimately charged or proven. An early report by American Radioworks relied on insiders from the Serbian special police, who described collecting bodies from grave sites in Kosovo and trucking them to the Trepča mine, an enormous mining complex in northern Kosovo. There the bodies were incinerated in the blast furnace of the plant's lead refinery. The details the men gave were chilling — bodies of Kosovo Albanians being delivered once again in refrigerator trucks, only this time processed through industrial conveyors and incinerated to dust at ultra-high temperatures. Other Serbian industrial sites were implicated as well, including a copper smelting factory in Bor and a steel plant in Smederevo, not far from Belgrade.[38]

Years later, similar allegations surfaced in relation to the Mačkatica aluminum complex near Surdulica in southern Serbia. Again, details were provided by alleged participants who described trucks arriving at night with their lights off, then unloading bodies to be burned in blast furnaces. Sources who spoke to the director of the Humanitarian Law Centre, Nataša Kandić, and to reporters for the Institute for War and Peace Reporting, implicated senior police officials in the operation. This included Minister Stojiljković, Deputy Prime Minister Sainović, and most notably Đorđević, who had been born nearby in Koznica.[39]

The Tribunal, however, did not have sufficient evidence to lay charges in relation to these accounts.[40] Neither the Trepča mine nor the Mačkatica complex were made part of the ICTY's indictments. These industrial cover-up efforts, if true, may simply have been successful.

The fate of many of the bodies that disappeared in Kosovo remains a mystery to this day. Forensic science has its limits, and in many cases the efforts to destroy or conceal the physical evidence of mass executions appear to have worked. Attempts to conclusively identify missing persons on this scale face considerable practical and procedural challenges, and different accountings of missing persons in Korova show discrepancies in the number of people who have been reported missing and the number of people who have been identified. The International Commission on Missing Persons, which has continued its search to find and identify bodies that disappeared during the Kosovo conflict, produced a report in 2010 with an overview of its findings. Of the 4,500 persons they conservatively estimated had been disappeared in Kosovo, only half of those bodies were ever found and identified. The commission also pointed to hundreds more bodies that had been found but could not be connected to any persons who were officially reported missing. The vast majority of the progress in finding and identifying bodies was made in the years immediately following the conflict; by 2010, things had come to a virtual standstill.[41]

For many, having the fate and location of their children, parents, or close friends remain uncertain has meant existing in a prolonged state of agony. Such pain can also have implications on a broader level, serving as a barrier to the potential for some sort of closure, for reconciliation, or for the ability to move forward.

The hope some families still have that their relatives might somehow be alive has also drawn opportunists seeking to exploit them. In the years following the disappearance of those bodies, many villagers described men from other parts of the country descending on their towns with stories of having seen their relatives alive. The men would promise to share this information, but only for a steep fee. Once the fee was paid, the information would invariably prove elusive.

Public officials and local journalists have exploited these emotions in other ways, spreading stories of secret prison camps and torture centres on the basis of little to no evidence. Bizarre rumours continue to persist, though this should probably not be surprising. When the real is scarcely believable in itself, it can be hard to sort fact from fiction.

# 16

# FINAL JUDGMENT

I

## The Verdicts

The release of a final judgment at the ICTY tends to occur in a strange vacuum. There is seldom any timeline for how long one can expect to wait as the Trial Chamber goes about its enormous task of sifting the evidence and compiling it into a comprehensive final judgment. Inevitably, the victims and witnesses have long since returned home and resumed their lives. Many of the lawyers will have gone home as well, or at least moved on somewhere else.

The trial judgment for the Kosovo 6 case was released on February 26, 2009, shortly after the Đorđević trial had begun. It had walked a long road: more than two years of trial, 235 witnesses, and roughly 4,300 exhibits. The Kosovo 6 Trial Chamber found resoundingly that Serbian forces had planned and implemented a broad campaign of violence against the Kosovo Albanian population, with the aim of changing the ethnic balance of Kosovo. It summed up its findings this way:

Applying the legal elements of the crimes charged in the Indictment to the facts found proved in relation to each of the thirteen municipalities, the Trial Chamber finds that the crimes of: deportation, a crime against humanity; other inhumane acts (forcible transfer), a crime against humanity; murder, a violation of the laws or customs of war, and a crime against humanity; and murder, sexual assault, and wanton destruction of or damage to religious property, as forms of persecution on ethnic grounds, were committed by VJ and MUP forces in many of the locations alleged in the Indictment.[1]

The events had clearly occurred, though the criminal responsibility of each individual accused for those acts was a different question. The Kosovo 6 Trial Chamber acquitted Milan Milutinović, the president of Serbia, of all charges. For the Chamber, the evidence was not sufficient to establish beyond a reasonable doubt that he was involved in the formulation or implementation of the Kosovo plan.[2] The other five men, however, were convicted for their respective roles. Deputy Prime Minister Nikola Šainović, the lone remaining politician, was sentenced to twenty-two years. Dragoljub Ojdanić, the chief of the VJ General Staff, who had command and control over all units of the army in Kosovo, received a sentence of fifteen years. Nebojša Pavković, who commanded the 3rd Army and oversaw its role in Kosovo, received twenty-two years. Vladimir Lazarević, the commander of the Priština Corps, received fifteen years.

On the police side, Sreten Lukić, who reported to Đorđević and was the head of the MUP Staff for Kosovo, received twenty-two years. The Chamber found that Lukić had de facto command of police forces in Kosovo and had served as the bridge between the plans orchestrated in Belgrade and the events that took place on the ground.

With respect to the concealment operation, the Kosovo 6 Trial Chamber found that extensive efforts had been made to hide the killings of ethnic Albanians by unearthing, transporting, and reburying their bodies, noting that the fact this evidence was hidden underlined the criminal nature of the Kosovo operation. But the *responsibility* for these systematic cover-up operations was not established; the Chamber was not convinced on the evidence that Mr. Lukić had been involved.

That would be left to the Đorđević case.


The last day of the Đorđević trial proceedings came on May 20, 2010. The trial had heard testimony from 143 witness and admitted 2,518 exhibits, although the final day of this long journey saw little fanfare. After the last witness concluded, Judge Parker reiterated the timeline for the filing of final trial briefs and closing arguments and then stated, rather sparingly: "… it's been an interesting, long progress until now, but we've reached this point."[3] So it ended.

With the evidentiary stage of the court proceedings concluded, our prosecution team turned its full attention to the gruelling ordeal of drafting the final trial brief — synthesizing all of our factual and legal arguments into a single document and then revising and refining it in cycles to bring it down under the word limit. After our final brief was filed, the closing arguments were presented. And then we were done.

With the all-consuming world of the trial finally and rather suddenly giving way, I found myself confronted squarely with the prospect of leaving the Tribunal and returning home. It was a somewhat tortured decision — it meant leaving the job I had always wanted to do, the teammates and friends I had been through so much with, and this institution that I wanted so badly to succeed. I have never had a particularly easy time sleeping, but as the decision about what to do loomed ever larger, I found myself lying awake and staring at the ceiling more than usual.

To live and work in The Hague as a war crimes prosecutor is a temporary and somehow displaced existence. Whether you're there for six months or ten years you can still somehow feel like you're living month to month; you're never quite at home, never quite settled, and always thinking about what might be next or whether you should return to a regular life. To work at one of these courts is to live in one bubble inside of another — as a foreigner amongst other foreigners, at an international institution that deals with events that took place thousands of kilometres away, at a time that remains fixed and unaffected by anything that may be changing or evolving around you. The result is that your life can feel like it was put on hold. In truth, of course, nothing has stopped moving.

The compensation for this stopped-out state of existence is the chance to do intensely meaningful work, surrounded by people who have chosen to walk this same path with you, for a limited window of time.

In the end, deciding to come home seemed as inevitable as deciding to work for the Tribunal in the first place. This was a temporary job, after all, and now the ICTY itself was winding down, employees already flooding out the door. I had a permanent job as a prosecutor back in Toronto that was calling me home. To give up that career position for an indeterminate extension at an ad-hoc Tribunal, already in its final stages and with few cases left to try, seemed ill-advised.[4] Perhaps most important of all, I had a relationship back in Toronto. I had been gone for almost two years, and though we had been able to make things work — or so it seemed — we needed to be in the same place. Now that the case was over, it was time to come home. I spent the following months wrapping up at the Tribunal and preparing to head back to Canada.

By the end of 2010 I was back in Toronto, sleeping in my old bed, and prosecuting Canadian criminal trials and appeals. It was strange to return, and in truth much harder than I had expected. It wouldn't last. Within two years my relationship had ended, I had left Toronto again, and I had stepped away from my career as a prosecutor. But that wouldn't come until the end of 2012.

On February 23, 2011, the day of the Đorđević trial judgment, I was temporarily living out of a hotel room in wind-chilled Sudbury, Ontario, prosecuting a police officer charged with multiple sexual assaults. That morning, preparing to cross-examine the accused in the culmination of what had already been a gruelling two-week trial, I live-streamed the ICTY's video feed alone in my office. I watched the Trial Chamber enter the courtroom as they had day after day for nearly two years, now for the last time. The defence team, the clerks and chambers staff, and a few remaining members of my prosecution team were all there. As I watched the Trial Chamber read the prepared summary of their final decision, I felt as far away as I was.

The Trial Chamber found Mr. Đorđević guilty. He had power and effective control over the police in Kosovo and knowledge of what was happening on the ground. He played a key role in coordinating police actions throughout what was found to be a deliberate campaign of violence and terror. Deportation and forcible transfer was established across all thirteen Kosovo municipalities that were listed in the indictment and in sixty specific locations.

At the end of its judgment, the Trial Chamber provided detailed "Schedules," listing the names of the victims who the facts specifically established were killed as a result of the crimes charged. Schedules A through J were sorted by the locality in which the crimes occurred, identifying the name, age, and gender of each victim and the place and date of their murder. In the end, the Chamber found that 724 individual murders had been specifically proven.[5]

The crimes committed, including mass deportation, murder, persecution, and the destruction of religious property, were not the result of "isolated incidents perpetuated by random individuals," as the defence had argued.[6] Nor were the actions of the military and police actually directed at terrorist forces, as the authorities had tried to claim. The Chamber found that they had been directed at the Kosovo Albanian civilian population. A pattern across multiple crime sites was established: the army would shell, residents would flee, then police would enter on foot, often setting houses on fire and looting as they went, in many cases executing the men and older boys and then deporting everyone else en masse, directing them to the borders on foot, by road, even by rail. The Chamber found that Serb forces had taken away their identification documents and licence plates before they crossed; the intention was to make it as difficult as possible for them to return.

The evidence established that it was Đorđević who had directly incorporated the notorious Scorpions into a unit of the police under his direct control, had overseen these men being armed and equipped for war, and had then knowingly sent them into Kosovo, where within minutes they committed the killings in Podujevo. It was also Đorđević who, after the Scorpions were withdrawn from Podujevo, rearmed and deployed them back to Kosovo once again.[7]

Đorđević was also convicted for his role in directing the operation to unearth and transport bodies to be hidden en masse — in Batajnica, in Petrovo Selo, and at Lake Perućac. The Trial Chamber found that the operation had been a coordinated campaign to clear the terrain of the evidence of crimes being committed against the ethnic Albanians. It was directed by Đorđević and assisted by Dragan Ilić, at the direction of the now-deceased former Minister Stojiljković, and pursuant to an order from Slobodan Milošević.[8] Mr. Đorđević received a sentence of twenty-seven years in jail.

## II

# Appeals

When a trial decision is released, the process feels like it has come to a final conclusion, the end of a long and exhausting road. But this is not the final word. There are, in fact, two stages of final judgments for every case at the ICTY. Beacuse the Tribunal, virtually every case is appealed as a matter of course, with a new five-judge panel appointed to sit in review of the initial trial decision.

The Kosovo cases at the ICTY didn't actually come to an end until 2014. The appeal judgments for the Kosovo 6 and for Đorđević were released a few days apart, Kosovo 6 coming on January 23 and Đorđević on January 27. By this time, the longest-serving of the accused had already been in the Tribunal's custody since 2002, almost twelve years.[9] Nearly five years had passed since the Kosovo 6 trial judgment, and it had been almost three years since the Đorđević judgment.

I flew back to The Hague for both appeal judgments, my first return since 2010. I watched the delivery of each judgment from the other side of the fishbowl, sitting in the gallery with the public and peering in through the glass at the proceedings. The experience left me with two very distinct impressions. The first was just how privileged I had been to sit on the other side of that glass, representing the public in the courtroom. The second was how curiously disconnected these proceedings and their sometimes impenetrable legal language can feel from regular life.

In the end, both the Kosovo 6 Appeal Chamber and the Đorđević Appeal Chamber upheld almost all of the original convictions.[10] Although Đorđević extensively challenged his convictions in relation to the operation to transport and conceal bodies, the Appeals Chamber dismissed all of these arguments in their entirety.[11] On one count, addressing allegations relating to charges of sexual assault, the Appeals Chamber actually entered a new conviction for persecutions through sexual assault as a crime against humanity.[12]

Most notably for the victims and members of the public, however, the Appeals Chambers reduced all but one of the sentences under appeal. Mr. Sainović's twenty-two-year sentence was reduced to eighteen years.

Mr. Pavković's sentence was left at eighteen years. Mr. Lazarević's sentence was reduced from fifteen to fourteen years. Mr. Lukić's sentence was reduced from twenty-two years to twenty. In the case of Đorđević, the Appeals Chamber set aside his twenty-seven-year sentence and imposed an eighteen-year sentence instead.[13]

III

# The Meaning of a Judgment

Sentencing in international criminal law is a strange and seemingly separate world. Viewed in comparison to the sentences imposed in any country's domestic courts, the quantum of sentences imposed by international courts and tribunals seem to make little sense. In most Western countries, a single murder earns you a life sentence. Internationally, where committing murder, rape, or destruction on a massive scale is usually prerequisite to being brought to trial, a life sentence tends to be reserved for the worst offenders. Any one of these offenders, if the scale and scope of their crimes were judged against the acts of regular criminals, would seem to warrant the heaviest sentence possible. But at the international courts and tribunals, this often doesn't happen.

I have long suspected that this difference is attributable to a strange notion of internal consistency and parity. We all share the belief that the severity of a sentence should reflect the seriousness of the crime. What seemingly causes the disconnect is a matter of institutional perspective: for the international courts and tribunals, war criminals are being compared against each other — to give a life sentence to nearly every war criminal would seemingly fail to distinguish between them.

But even within these curious parameters, many were stunned to learn that the apparent tariff for the acts that took place in Kosovo — mass murder, cover-up, the burning of homes, the destruction of religious sites, the deportation of hundreds of thousands — was between fifteen and twenty-two years. Such sentences may reflect a belief that crimes directed from a distance are fundamentally different, and should be accorded lesser punishments, than crimes committed by one's own hand.

Although the sentencing regime in international law often leaves people frustrated, it is not — in my view at least — where the central importance lies. What matters most is proving the acts that were committed, identifying those most responsible, and then meaningfully condemning their actions. A criminal sentence can surely reach a quantum where it seems so grossly inadequate that it doesn't constitute a meaningful condemnation. But eighteen years is still a very long time for any human being to spend locked in prison, particularly for an elderly offender already in the final stages of his life.

There is, after all, surely no punishment to be meted out against one person, or a handful of people, that could hope to be commensurate with the suffering that was endured. What is now unmistakably clear, however, is that these acts have been proven, they have been judged and condemned, and a new ordering of right and wrong has been asserted.

## IV
# From the End, Looking Back

The inevitable question to ask, at the end of a trial process like this, is whether it was worth it. Witnesses flown thousands of kilometres, sometimes multiple times, to testify in a foreign courtroom. Traumatic memories not just unearthed but actively challenged. Leaders forced from office, driven into hiding, extradited to stand trial, housed in a detention centre for years on end. Millions upon millions of dollars — money that could have been earmarked for victims, hospitals, schools, and roads — spent on Western courtrooms, administrative staff, lawyers, and judges. Proceedings stretched out over years, only concluded long after the events have faded from the headlines. And then, in the end, the summary of a final judgment read aloud in a courtroom, only partially understood by the public and finished before the first court break. A comprehensive and voluminous written decision that follows, spelling out the evidence and factual findings in painstaking detail, but which virtually no one will actually read.[14]

If the only thing the Đorđević trial had achieved was the punishment of this one man at its conclusion then it would be difficult to see it as worthwhile. But this type of exercise — a significant undertaking, without question — is not only worthwhile but *necessary* for the many other things it achieves. It is necessary because it brings a fair, impartial, and rigorous process to bear on the determination of what actually took place and who can be held accountable. It is necessary because it makes the declaration, on behalf of an ordered and right-seeking world, that these acts were immoral, indefensible, and wrong. It is necessary because — hopefully — it gives a voice to victims, allowing them to speak out against the injustices they suffered, but within a broader context — one that is not about one group against another but is, instead, about all of us together, on the side of shared moral and ethical values. Many of these things are in fact about *process*, not about a final result. None of these things are automatic.

International criminal law clearly has a long way to go. It remains entirely dependent on the investment and acceptance of the world around it. It needs individual nations to get offenders before its courts — no small challenge. It functions within a broader and ever-shifting context of state influence and power, and although its roots seem deeper now, it still sways dramatically with shifts in the political wind. The way it is understood and interpreted, both by the world at large and by the societies who make up its victims and perpetrators, is crucially important to the success or failure of the whole endeavour.

We shouldn't lose sight of how young this movement still is; the fact that the option of a war crimes prosecution is even up for discussion, and that journalists and world leaders speak casually now of indictment and prosecution in The Hague, was unthinkable just twenty-five years ago. Still, whether we will be speaking optimistically about the International Criminal Court twenty-five years from now, or lamenting its irrelevance, seems an open question.

V

# A Legacy of Local Trials

Some have criticized the international criminal courts and tribunals for focusing only on high-level perpetrators; for taking a top-down approach instead of prosecuting the individual men or women who physically committed the crimes on the ground.[15] These criticisms have a point: the men and women at the top of the command structure generally *have* been the focus of the international courts, which intentionally pursue the highest-level perpetrators available. What this means is that the individual offenders whom victims often think about every day — the policemen who executed their husbands and sons, the soldiers who raped them, the militiamen who destroyed their town — are seldom the ones in the dock.

But this is not the entire story. A vitally important part of the ICTY's legacy is that it has enabled and encouraged local courts to pursue justice against a number of the individual perpetrators who did the actual killing. This is a work in progress — these local trials have moved slowly, and the results have been mixed. But they are a vitally important step.

Many of the direct perpetrators of the crimes Mr. Đorđević oversaw were prosecuted in local trials.

## Suva Reka

Beginning in 2006, a number of perpetrators were prosecuted in the Belgrade District Court for their role in the murders of forty-eight civilians in Suva Reka, including the killings that took place in the pizzeria. The trial was plagued with a number of problems — one of the judges was replaced in the midst of the hearing, delays were extensive, and there were allegations of tampering. Nonetheless, on April 23, 2009, the Belgrade court sentenced Radojko Repanović and Slađan Cukarić to twenty years in prison, Miroslav Nišević to thirteen years in prison, and Miroslav Petković to fifteen years in prison. Commander Radoslav Mitrović, Assistant Commander Nenad Jovanović, and Zoran Petković were acquitted.[16]

## Ćuška

In April of 2010, while the Đorđević trial was still proceeding, a man named Milić Martinović was arrested in Sweden and prosecuted there, pursuant to domestic war crimes legislation, for his alleged involvement in the Ćuška massacre. Martinović was convicted and sentenced to life in prison. In December of 2012, however, the Swedish appeal court expressed concerns with the evidence identifying him and quashed his conviction.[17]

After the Đorđević trial was completed, the Belgrade War Crimes chamber commenced proceedings against eleven alleged perpetrators of the Ćuška massacre. On February 11, 2014, Judge Snezana Garotić convicted nine of these men, members of a paramilitary known as the Jackals, for killing more than 120 ethnic Albanian civilians — not just in Ćuška but also in the nearby towns of Zahac, Pavljan, and Ljubenić.[18] The trial heard insider testimony from Zoran Rasković, a member of the unit, who described the brutality in detail and rejected suggestions that the men were actually fighting against terrorists.[19] The court concluded that the men had "committed murders, rapes and robberies in an extremely brutal way, with the main goal to spread fear among Albanian civilians in order to force them to leave their homes and flee to Albania."[20]

One of the most notorious perpetrators in Ćuška was missing from the Jackals trial. Nebojša Minić, described as the Jackals' "Commander of Death," and also a commander of the notorious Munja ("Lightning") brigade, had gone into hiding after the war. Born in a Kosovo village just east of Peć, Minić had evolved from a middling domestic criminal to a rather notorious war criminal who had raped, tortured, and murdered his way across both Bosnia and Kosovo.[21] In 2005, Minić was found hiding in Argentina, where he had assumed a new identity as "Vlada Radivojević" and even opened a pizza parlor. He was identified and arrested by a local police investigator and was to be deported to stand trial in Serbia, but he never made it. Minić died in hospital at the age of forty-one, barely able to speak, from complications stemming from cancer and AIDS.[22]

## Podujevo

The 2005 trial of Saša Cvjetan was not the only local case against the Scorpions. The Belgrade District War Crimes Chamber also prosecuted five Scorpions — Slobodan Medić (Boca), Aleksandar Medić, Branislav Medić, Pera Petrasević, and Aleksandar Vukov — for their involvement in the execution of Muslim men in Trnovo, Bosnia, in 1995.[23] Four of the five men were convicted, with Boca receiving a twenty-year sentence.[24]

Beginning on September 8, 2008, the Belgrade Chamber also prosecuted Dragan Medić, Željko Đukić, Dragan Borojević, and Miodrag Šolaja for their involvement in the Podujevo killings. The trial included testimony from Spasoje Vulević ("Vuk"), the SAJ officer who had first come to the children's assistance after he heard the shooting. Vulević, who had become the SAJ's commander by the time of the trial, implicated the accused men in the killings.[25] All four men were convicted, and on June 18, 2009, Dragan Medić, Đukić,[26] and Borojević received twenty-year jail sentences, while Šolaja received a fifteen-year sentence.[27]

Perhaps the most impactful local event to take place in Belgrade, and in many respects the most encouraging, happened outside of the courtroom. In 2013, the Bogujevci children put together an art exhibit telling the story of their lives, both before and after the killings. The exhibition was hosted at the Belgrade Cultural Centre and sparked significant controversy. It was reportedly banned by the Ministry of the Interior — until pressure from non-governmental organizations caused it to quickly relent — and when the show opened it drew angry protestors, many of them brandishing photographs of crimes committed against Serbs. But the show went on, and to the great surprise of many of the onlookers, Serbian Prime Minister Ivica Dačić was amongst the exhibition's first attendees.[28] SAJ Commander Vulević attended the show as well.

VI

# The Unwritten Chapter

As I alluded to at the outset of this book, the most significant chapter that has yet to be written, and at present the most contentious one, concerns violence committed by ethnic Albanians against Kosovo Serbs. This is an area fraught with question marks and controversy, and one that speaks to both the importance of our international justice system and the dangers inherent in our attempts at justice.

Although the KLA disbanded after the war, its members remained a powerful force in Kosovo. In December of 2004, Ramush Haradinaj — the KLA's commander for their Western District — was elected prime minister. His tenure was brief, however — by March of 2005 he was indicted for war crimes by the ICTY, along with Idriz Balaj and Lahi Brahimaj, for actions that took place in 1998. The three men were charged with removing and mistreating Serbs and perceived collaborators from their region and overseeing a detention centre in Jabllanicë where captives were beaten and executed. The men surrendered to the Tribunal and were prosecuted together beginning on March 5, 2007.[29]

On April 3, 2008, Haradinaj and Balaj were acquitted, while Brahimaj was convicted for acts of cruel treatment and torture and sentenced to six years in jail. The Trial Chamber found that a number of the alleged crimes had been committed by members of the KLA but that the evidence wasn't sufficient to find Haradinaj or Balaj responsible. It was readily apparent to anyone watching the trial that many of the witnesses had been scared and were unwilling to testify.[30]

The prosecution successfully appealed the acquittals. The Appeals Chamber ruled that in that climate of witness intimidation and threats surrounding the trial, the Trial Chamber should have allowed the prosecution more latitude to protect its witnesses.[31] The court ordered a partial retrial, but it played out in much the same way. On November 29, 2012, all three accused were acquitted on the remaining charges.[32]

The acquittals — both the first round and the second — left many people outraged, particularly in Serbia. It didn't help, surely, that the case seemed to bear key similarities to the preceding trial of KLA members Fatmir Limaj, Isak Musliu, and Haradin Bala, which was also pervaded by fear and intimidation.[33] In Kosovo, on the other hand, the acquittals were met with celebrations — Haradinaj's final trial verdict was shown on a giant screen in Pristina, where crowds of ethnic Albanians celebrated with cheering and fireworks.[34] These celebrations, broadcast back to Serbia, only worsened the anger — as did the fact that just weeks earlier an ICTY appeal panel had acquitted Croatian general Ante Gotovina, who was celebrated like a hero on his return to Croatia.[35]

The reactions to such judgments tell a story of their own. It is understandable, certainly, that acquittals for such individuals will leave some — if not many — to feel that justice was not done. What is more troubling is the degree to which these judgments are also used to tell broader stories about *collective* blame and responsibility, or collective vindication and justification, along broad lines of ethnicity and nationhood. When cast this way, these trials can become part of a framework that sees ethnicities pitted against each other and injustices used to stoke anger and exacerbate conflict.

As Serbian President Tomislav Nikolić stated after the final Haradinaj acquittal, stoking the very flames he was condemning the Tribunal for igniting: "If somebody wanted to turn us against one another, they have found the right way."[36]

These reactions suggest how much is at stake — both inside and outside the walls of the ICTY — as broader stories of collective injustice are continually reframed throughout the Balkans.

It is against this backdrop that allegations of injustices that took place in Kosovo *after* the war have continued to fester. They have included claims about persecution, murders, and disappearances perpetrated by the KLA against the Serb and Roma populations. They have also included more lurid allegations that the KLA was harvesting, transporting, and selling the organs of ethnic Serbs after the war. These latter claims seem to have a certain symmetry, at least on their face, to the Serbian operation to transport and hide the bodies of murdered Albanians. It has thus far proven difficult to sort fact from fiction.

The ICTY does not have jurisdiction to pursue crimes that were committed outside of the armed conflict in the region, which in Kosovo ended in June of 1999. In September of 2011, therefore, the European Union set up a Special Investigative Task Force (SITF) to investigate allegations of crimes committed by the KLA after the war.[37] On July 29, 2014, following an investigation that spanned almost three years, the SITF announced its preliminary findings and indicated that it would be filing indictments against senior members of the KLA. The crimes alleged include unlawful killings, abductions, enforced disappearances, and illegal detentions in camps.[38] With respect to claims of organ harvesting, the SITF announced that it found evidence that the practice had in fact occurred, though on a "very limited scale," with only a "handful" of individuals subjected to the crime.[39]

Kosovo's Parliament has approved a new EU-backed special court to prosecute these alleged crimes. The court will operate pursuant to Kosovo's laws but it will be staffed by international prosecutors and judges.[40] The court is expected to commence its operations in 2015.

# 17

# THE JUSTICE WE SEEK

I fell beside him — his body taut,
tight as a string just before it snaps,
shot in the back of the head.
"This is how you'll end too; just lie quietly here,"
I whispered to myself, patience blossoming into death.
"*Der springt noch auf*," the voice above me said
through caked mud and blood congealing in my ear.
— Miklós Radnóti, "Postcard 4"[1]

## I

## Tell It to the World

Miklós Radnóti's final words to the world were found scrawled in a notebook, hidden in a pocket of his overcoat. He had continued to write, whenever and however he could, even as he endured brutal conditions of forced labour in Serbia and an excruciating forced march through a barren wasteland. His notebook, and the poem above, were discovered by his wife when his body was exhumed from a mass grave in the aftermath of the war. He had been writing up until his eventual and predictable execution.

Radnóti was not a victim of the Balkan wars of the 1990s. He died fifty years before they began. But his experiences, his hopes, and his words resonate as if they were just written. Thinking about the atrocities that took place in the Balkans in the late 1990s, and about the importance of memory, testimony, and the hope for some sort of justice, I often came back to Radnóti.

Mr. Radnóti was a Hungarian Jew, a passionate writer and poet with dreams of greatness who had the misfortune to spend the prime of his life in Hungary during World War II. As the particularly ruthless Hungarian phase of the Holocaust began to unfold, Radnóti was sent to do forced labour, first within Hungary, then in German-occupied Yugoslavia. His third and final internment was to a labour camp in what is now Serbia, near the town of Bor — not far from where the first refrigerator truck was discovered in 1999. Radnóti was sent there with six thousand other conscripts, principally to build a railroad to service a local copper mine. It was a death sentence and he knew it.

In spite of the harsh conditions — or perhaps because of them — Radnóti continued to write poetry. Drawing on a reserve of energy somehow reawakened in the midst of excruciating labour and deprivation, in conditions designed to break the body and the mind, he scribbled his words in stolen moments, using all the focus he could summon. Many of his poems were smuggled out from the barracks by other men.

As the Russian army advanced, Radnóti and his fellow inmates from the Bor labour camps were forced on a brutal fourteen-day march towards western Hungary. Massacres of the sick and fading Jews around him began shortly thereafter. They were killed by the hundreds.

Radnóti grew increasingly aware that his execution lay ahead, his body to be disposed of in a newly dug hole, piled with the bodies of his fellow men. In November of 1944 he found himself sick and unable to walk. He was loaded onto a cart along with about twenty other men and taken to the river. The men were ordered off of their carts, forced to dig a ditch, and then systematically shot and killed.

After the war, Radnóti's body was exhumed from a mass grave. Inspecting his pockets, his wife found several poems that he had written just before his death and had carried with him. "Postcard 4," above, was the last thing he ever wrote.

The poem describes what he had seen befall others, and the fate that he knew was waiting for him: an anonymous extermination, his body to be disposed of en masse with the bodies of other men. This was the reality of being shot in the back of the head, piled with others, and left hidden in the ground. The fate that befell Miklós Radnóti was disturbingly similar to the fate that would befall many in the Balkans, once again, fifty years later.

What seems most striking about Radnóti's words is not their descriptive potency — eloquent and powerful though they are — but the very writing of them, voiced as they were in a context of inhumanity and suffering, by a man on the precipice of an anonymous death.

His writing raises a question: for whom were these words intended? He entitled his final four poems "Postcards." Who were these postcards intended for, and why?

The answer, I came to think, is that they were written for some broader conception of humanity — some idea of all of us, in other words, who would see the evil he suffered for what it was: an injustice. His writing spoke, and continues to speak now, to some profound value that we see in the human voice. A power to identify cruelty and injustice and an accompanying hope that we can reclaim our humanity by communicating and sharing that experience.

Radnóti's final words don't expressly moralize. They don't declare, or argue, that these acts were unjust. They just describe. They tell us what happened, and that is somehow enough to engage our sense of justice.

Radnóti was bearing witness. He was speaking to some virtuous and properly ordered notion of humanity in which this behavior was not acceptable and these acts should not have happened. He was perhaps seeking some sense of reassurance, even if only within himself, that the madness and randomness, the wrongness he had encountered in these twisted circumstances, might one day be identified and denounced in the right-thinking world. Radnóti's words resonate powerfully today because we are still, collectively, his intended audience.

This is the deep-rooted and remarkably powerful impulse we have to seek justice. It is an impulse that seems to exist in all of us, and can be activated in vastly different ways. It often begins with the need to be heard — to tell what happened, to speak the truth. We seem to seek some reaffirmation that such acts were, and are, a transgression. We need to know that they should not have happened. That they were wrong.

I encountered very different expressions of this will to communicate injustice as I watched witnesses from Kosovo arrive in The Hague to provide accounts of the darkest moments of their lives. This was the United Nations, after all — an international tribunal. It was intended to listen, to judge, and to condemn on behalf of the world.

It was an insanely ambitious enterprise, an attempt to bring justice and accountability to a region and a conflict that had once seemed lost. There were times, certainly, that it seemed perfunctory: bureaucratic and artificial. But in the end, the process held more meaning, and had more impact, than I could have imagined.

II

## The Justice We Seek

The events in Kosovo were but one part of the larger tragedy that unfolded in the Balkans, which was itself one of a long list of violent and large-scale atrocities that took place throughout the twentieth century.

Injustice is an ever-moving target, and new versions of such violence are unfolding in other corners of the globe. Each orchestration of violence is born in a context very much its own, with its own agenda, its own set of grievances and practicalities, its own perpetrators and victims, and its own groups of insiders and outsiders. Yet the paths to mass violence have a surprising amount in common.

We seem to have a strong and shared sense of morality; we know right from wrong in broad strokes. But this competes alongside another predisposition: our easy tendency to group people, to categorize some as insiders who are entitled to our morality and others as outsiders who are not.[2] We are prone to draw these lines of distinction based on the many things that divide us: ethnicity, religion, and nationhood among them. A crucially important question, then, is *what* makes us overemphasize these divisions, and what enables us to feel justified in diminishing the humanity of others.

Our human drive for justice is a powerful and curious thing. The very concept of justice offers itself as wholly noble; we envision it as an almost unquestionable force for good, a sort of benevolent compulsion that should be indulged and pursued at almost any cost. But the impulse to seek justice also has a darker aspect, with a potential for inversion. Once engaged, our sense of injustice can animate the most profound strivings for peace and stability. But it can also mobilize us to bloodshed and war, perpetuate cycles of violence, and justify and seemingly entitle the most unjust and inhumane acts one could possibly imagine. We seem rarely to speak of justice in this second way, or to recognize the connection between the justice we seek and the injustices we commit.

A look into the recent past suggests that we ignore this darker potential of justice at our peril. Narratives of past injustice, misdirected, can all too easily lead us down a path that sees us render other human beings, even neighbours and friends, as outsiders and as a *type* — a Muslim, a Croat, a Serb, a Hutu, a Tutsi, a Jew, a member of the privileged ruling class, a Shiite, a Sunni, a Hindu. As a two-dimensional role-player, in other words, in a story of historical grievance that cries out for recompense and may seemingly justify using violence to obtain it.

We need, therefore, to walk two paths simultaneously. We must, absolutely, recognize and give voice to injustice when it occurs. This means identifying and exposing unjust acts that have taken place, telling these stories, and judging and denouncing what happened. But we also need to guard zealously against the potential for our sense of injustice and victimhood to be rallied in furtherance of new injustices. This means watching for, and protecting against, those who invoke a sense of injustice and victimhood in order to enable and justify violence.

In broad scope, the international war crimes trial should tell a story of shared human perspective. It should function as a concrete expression of the notion that we all stand together on the side of a common and ordered view of humanity, one that agrees that these acts should never happen and that they can never be justified. It should work against the counterpull of the sort of tribalism that calls us to divide along various lines and thereby diminish and readily violate the human rights of outsiders. This symbolism, and this perspective, matter.

It has been said, persuasively, that the foundation for human rights is "imagined empathy," the belief and understanding that the "other" is in fact someone just like us.[3] It surely follows, then, that our approach to questions of human rights, dignity, politics, even war, shouldn't pull us apart into groups divided by race, ethnicity, culture, class, or religion, but instead rally us to a shared perspective that reaffirms that such things were a violation of the values common to all of us.

This, really, is as much about how we choose to *view* mass violence, and the courts that indict and prosecute it, as it is about the cases and court procedures themselves. It should not be Serb versus Albanian, or one group against another, but right-thinking humanity on the same side, condemning a transgression of what we all value.

As the arbiters of justice who propose to determine guilt and innocence in the eyes of the world, the international criminal courts and tribunals unavoidably walk this terrain in their day-to-day operations. We hope, I think, that the societies to whom these war crimes trials directly pertain will buy into our view that we are enforcing a shared moral code. We hope and believe that these trials are speaking to the broader perspective of humanity to which Miklós Radnóti seemingly addressed his final words. But if we aren't careful, these trials can instead be viewed from within the same prism of ethnic and national divisions, and can reinforce the same view of insiders and outsiders that led to the violence in the first place.

The International Criminal Tribunal for the Former Yugoslavia is still too often viewed through this divisive lens by the ethnic groups of the former Yugoslavia — Serb, Croat, Bosnian Muslim, Kosovo Albanian. As the rest of the world checks in occasionally, confirming that justice and the rule of law has been brought to bear on another tragedy, the stakeholders to the conflict are in many cases looking to the Tribunal's judgments for condemnation of the others and redemption for themselves. Pronouncing judgment in these circumstances can be a two-edged sword. We should not ignore the narratives that are being advanced and perpetuated, both inside and outside of the courtroom. If we aren't careful, we may pay too little attention to the broader picture into which our attempts at justice are cast.

This is not to suggest that there is no such thing as actual justice or that there is no role for truth — far from it. Justice matters. Truth is essential. There are real victims and real injustices, just as there are falsehoods and distortions. Understanding and recognizing the truth of what took place is a necessity and the conduct of a fair trial is an absolute prerequisite to ensuring that happens. Just because someone is charged does not mean that he is guilty. We know all of this, I think — and in this respect the international courts aren't so different from their domestic counterparts. But dealing with mass violence that invariably has such collective and historical impacts means that people can be invested in the process and outcomes of these trials in vastly different ways. In this respect, it is not only the stories we tell that matter, but also why — and to what ends — we tell them.

The international courts and tribunals are part of this discussion, but the issue is much larger. Outside of the courtroom, in the dialogues we engage in and the discussions we have, we should be asking ourselves continually whether the stories we tell divide or unite. If we are casting ourselves collectively as victims, to what end are we doing so? Is there a way in which this is seemingly entitling us to collectively diminish others or to sanction acts that we wouldn't otherwise feel entitled to endorse?

The hopeful path, I think, lies in embracing, nurturing, and endlessly encouraging a shared perspective on humanity, while resisting the urge to turn each other into outsiders or enemies. This means being sensitive to the ways in which people naturally seek to protect their own self-perceptions and identities, and avoiding the subtle tricks that cognitive dissonance can play in making us resist the acceptance that crimes have been committed. It means being sensitive — oversensitive, even — to the temptation to wield justice as a sword.

One of the most valuable narrative acts is to tell the stories of our seeming adversaries. Hutus telling the stories of Tutsis, Croats telling the stories of Serbs, Palestinians telling the stories of Jews. Real listening is perhaps the best start. This is the Bogujevci children's art show being hosted in Belgrade and attended by the prime minister of Serbia. It is Israeli Jews visiting Palestinian refugee camps and Palestinians visiting Auschwitz. It is growing up in modern Germany, which has owned its dark history and taken on the responsibility for telling the story of the Holocaust in its school system, its memorials, and its museums.

To do this means recognizing that the darkness in one's collective past — or present — is not actually dissonant with a sense of pride in one's identity. To the contrary, the recognition should itself be a source of pride. Accepting and owning the worst parts of one's collective history is a necessity, because it is from the very human temptation to deny and obfuscate that darkness — by blaming others, by accepting only victimhood status, by stoking fear — that the greatest collective distortions to our ethics are often born.

# ACKNOWLEDGEMENTS

A heartfelt thank you to my agents at Transatlantic for their tireless support of this book: to Meggie MacDonald, for embracing and driving the book forward from the beginning, and to David Bennett for picking up the cause enthusiastically, even through some challenging times. Thank you as well to the hardworking staff at Dundurn, in particular my editor Dominic Farrell, and to cover designer Ingrid Paulson and map designer Andrew O'Driscoll.

Many thanks to Benjamin Berger for endlessly making time to read, revise, and challenge me with questions, and for pushing me in ways that always made me a better writer and thinker. To Laura Harris, for real inspiration, deeply held ideas, and an approach to the creative process that I have carried with me. To Daniela Kravetz, for your very generous help and always sound judgment through this process, and to Paige Petersen for all your support, input, and thoughtful advice.

To the indomitable Graham Reed, whose ideas and keen insight I have continued to seek since our first collaboration. To Amy Stulberg, Tina Horwitz, and Amanda Betts for your invaluable early help. To

Emily Brady, Arianne Robinson, Chris Jackson, Jessica Braun, Melissa Chandler, Alexa Engelman, Nadia Thomas, and Veronica Lemcoff — your ideas, encouragement, feedback, and help are throughout this book. To my brother Mark, your opinions, thoughts, and point of view are always somewhere in whatever I write.

To all of my teammates in the Office of the Prosecutor at the ICTY, who walked every moment of this case in lockstep with me, so often guiding and helping me along, I owe you not just my sanity through almost two years of long hours and intensely heavy human experience but also the best professional experience of my career. I count you not just as colleagues but among the closest and most valued friends I could ever have hoped for.

Finally, to the victims and witnesses who travelled to The Hague to testify about what you experienced, and who bore the weight of re-opening and exposing the darkest and most traumatic moments of your lives, I have never stopped being amazed at your courage and determination. I can only hope that I have not done your stories any great injustice, and that you might understand where my desire to tell these very real stories came from.

# NOTES

## 1.

1    See for example: Samuel Moyn, *The Last Utopia: Human Rights in History* (Cambridge, MA: Belknap Press, 2012).

2    Ibid., 1–10.

3    I would later go back to look for these images. I believe the footage I remembered was recorded by Allied forces at Bergen-Belsen, immediately following its liberation.

4    Sam Berger, *The Face of Hell* (*Die unvergeblichen sechseinhalb Jahre meines Lebens, 1939–1945*) (New York: Carlton Press, 1994).

## 2.

1    See *Updated Statute of the International Criminal Tribunal for the Former Yugoslavia*, as amended July 7, 2009, by Resolution 1877.

2    These are more than niceties; without evidence being digitized, scanned, and (roughly) sorted, cases of this size and scope would take years longer to prepare, argue, and decide.

# 3.

1 This is a common strategy in war crimes trials. Many defendants end up pursuing one of these two tacks, if not both.

2 See *Prosecutor v. Vlastimir* Đorđević, Case No. IT-05-87/1-T, Public Judgement, February 23, 2011, paras. 1288, 1301, and 1358–59.

3 Ibid., Transcript, T.1656–T.1759; Exhibit P00352.

4 Ibid., Transcript, T.1740. And see footnote 5023 of Public Judgement, para. 1300.

5 Ibid., Transcript, T.1738.

6 Ibid., Public Judgement, para. 1308.

7 Ibid., paras. 1287–88; 1301.

8 Ibid., paras. 1301–07. Golubović's claim that they had waited to conduct the operation at night in order to avoid the NATO bombing was also firmly rejected by the Đorđević Trial Chamber [*Prosecutor v.* Đorđević, Public Judgement, para. 1303].

9 Ibid., para. 1288. See also para. 1301: "The Chamber observes that this witness gave the clear impression of trying to adapt his account of the events to assist the Accused, but was not at all convincing in his manner as he did so, nor in the explanations he attempted for the changes in his story."

10 Ibid., para. 1313.

11 Ibid., para. 1314.

12 I'm not sure what the reverend was pointing to or asking about in the gallery, although I assumed he was likely being told who was sitting where and what role each of us was playing.

13 David Wippman, "Notes and Comments: The Costs of International Justice," *American Journal of International Law* 100, no. 4 (October 2006): 861–81; "The Cost of Justice," UN: ICTY, *www.icty.org/sid/325*.

14 There has been friction about this over the years, particularly from the lawyers trained in civil law systems. The reality is that although the Tribunal purports to employ a hybrid common law/civil law system, the trials employ an only slightly modified adversarial common law system, to which common law litigators are generally better suited. There have, of course, also been a great number of exceptionally talented civil lawyers at the ICTY. And some of the judges enforce procedures in their courtrooms that are more civil in

nature. If you sit in on enough meetings, or just linger around the Lavazza machine, you're bound to hear some arguments about this.

15  That is, unless the accused in your case has successfully managed to sandbag the proceedings through one of the many age-old tactics: claims of various physical or mental illnesses (sometimes true, often false or exaggerated); arguing endlessly about how he wants to be represented; engaging in repeated rounds of contempt of court; or just refusing to come to court at all.

16  These were pronounced, respectively, as "Moop," "Oop," and "Soup."

17  The ICTY, at least, recognizes that the languages are all essentially the same. When the representatives of Serbia, Croatia, and Bosnia met in Dayton, Ohio in 1995 to negotiate the Dayton Accords, the live translation system had a separate channel for each language — Serbian, Croatian, and Bosnian — except that the exact same translation appeared on each channel. When Richard Holbrooke (who brokered the negotiations) pointed out the absurdity, he was told that "Serbo-Croatian" no longer existed and that distinctive and separate vocabularies were being intentionally and aggressively developed for each ethnic group. As Holbrooke observed at the time: "Language, which had once helped unify Yugoslavia, was now another vehicle through which people were being driven apart." [Richard Holbrooke, *To End a War* (New York: Random House/ Modern Library Paperback Edition, 1999), 232.]

18  Having said this, I have worked with interpreters at many levels of court, and the interpreters at the ICTY were by far the most patient, accurate, and thorough that I have ever worked with.

19  "The March on the Drina," a patriotic march composed during World War I that drew on the beauty of the Drina River, was embraced by many Serbs as a symbol of national and ethnic identity. The song was prohibited in Communist Yugoslavia but embraced anew during the surge of ethnic nationalism in the 1990s. It became known as a sort of "unofficial anthem" among Serbian forces conducting ethnic cleansing operations. For an interesting read, see Neil MacFarquhar, "Ovation, Then Apology, for Serbian Song," *New York Times*, January 17, 2013, *www.nytimes.com/2013/01/18/world/ europe/united-nations-apologizes-over-serbian-song.html.*

20  See for example: *Prosecutor v. Milan Lukić* and *Sredoje Lukić*, Case No. IT-98-32/1, Judgement; *Prosecutor v. Mitar Vasiljević*, Case No. IT-98-32-T, Judgement; Rachel Irwin, "Visegrad in Denial Over Grisly Past," *Institute for War and Peace Reporting*, February 24, 2009, *http://iwpr.net/report-news/visegrad-denial-over-grisly-past*.

21  See for example: *Prosecutor v. Radislav Krstić*, Case No. IT-98-33-T, Judgement; *Prosecutor v. Erdemović*, Case No. IT-96-22-Tbis, Sentencing Judgement; *Prosecutor v. Dragan Obrenović*, Case No. IT-02-60/2-S, Judgement; *Prosecutor v. Vidoje Blagojević* and *Dragan Jokić*, Case No. IT-02-60-T, Judgement.

22  The Đorđević Trial Chamber weighed this directly when it assessed Keric's evidence:

> It appears to the Chamber that more than one factor may have influenced the accounts given by Kerić. If so, these factors may well have pulled him in different directions, and with differing degrees of force, at different times.... Kerić knew Đorđević as his superior, and also personally over a number of years. A significant factor may well be a concern not to implicate him in criminal conduct or to place ultimate responsibility for it on someone else. Having regard to these matters, the Chamber has approached the evidence of Đorde Keric with caution. For all these reasons, and for reasons dealt with in greater detail in what follows, the Chamber has decided it can only rely with full confidence on certain parts of Kerić's evidence.... Despite discrepancies, the Chamber has found many aspects of the evidence of Đorde Keric to be entirely persuasive, and is prepared to rely on these aspects of his evidence.
> [*Prosecutor v. Đorđević*, Public Judgement, paras. 1358–59.]

23  *Prosecutor v. Đorđević*, D00316, para. 7.

24  This general description is consistent with evidence from both Kerić and Đorđević, and as confirmed by the Trial Chamber, though it also relies on a more detailed hearsay account provided by Mitricević (see: D00316) and a previous statement by Kerić (P01212).

25  On this issue, Kerić's evidence differed from an initial statement
    he had provided at the Tribunal. In an earlier statement, Kerić
    had declared that despite being in communication with Đorđević
    about what to do, he and the other men had decided on their own
    to bury the bodies. This characterization made little sense and was
    ultimately not accepted by the Trial Chamber. But it made for a
    tense cross-examination. [See for example: *Prosecutor v. Đorđević*,
    Transcript, T.7847–52, and Judgement, paras. 1358–59.]

# 4.

1  Whether the prosecution could rely on evidence of the deporta-
    tions from Ćuška as part of their allegations concerning the Munic-
    ipality of Peć became the subject of dispute on appeal. The Appeal
    Chamber ultimately concluded that it could not be. [See *Prosecutor
    v. Đorđević*, Appeal Judgement, paras. 638–44.]
2  The accounts below are based on the following public sources: *Prose-
    cutor v. Đorđević*, Transcript, T.4712–87 and T.4599–T.4673; Exhibits
    P00796, P00797, P00803, and P00804; and Public Judgement, paras.
    743–64. See also, Fred Abrahams, Gilles Peress, and Eric Stover, *A
    Village Destroyed: May 14, 1999* (Berkeley, CA: University of Califor-
    nia Press, August 2002), portions of which were relied on at trial.
3  *Prosecutor v. Đorđević*, Public Judgement, para. 749; Transcript,
    T.4718–20, 4770; Exhibit P00803, paras. 25, 27, 28.
4  See for example: Matthew Kaminski and John Reed, "NATO Link
    to KLA Rebels May Have Helped Seal Victory," *Wall Street Journal*,
    July 6, 1999. On March 10, 2006, Agim Çeku became the prime
    minister of Kosovo.
5  The statement review process was addressed in court: *Prosecutor v.
    Đorđević*, Transcript, T.4713, l.20–T.4715, l.12.
6  Ibid., Transcript, T.4618.
7  Ibid., Transcript, T.4618–19.
8  Ibid., Transcript, T.4619.
9  Ibid., Public Judgement, paras. 743–64.

## 5.

1   The witness experience at the ICTY has been the subject of academic study, which I often found to dovetail quite well with what I experienced first-hand. Eric Stover's excellent book *The Witnesses* documents intensive interviews that he conducted with witnesses who had testified at the Tribunal — an opportunity that would be denied to prosecutors, who are necessarily circumscribed in their interactions with witnesses. [Eric Stover, *The Witnesses: War Crimes and the Promise of Justice in The Hague* (Philadelphia: University of Pennsylvania Press, 2007).]

2   For a thoughtful treatment of this notion, see Benjamin Berger, "On the Book of Job, Justice, and the Precariousness of the Criminal Law," *Law, Culture and the Humanities* 4, no. 1 (February 2008): 98–118.

3   Beverly Beaver, "A Comparison in Nazi Litigation Strategies from Nuremberg to the Present: A Paper Trail v. A Trail of Tears," *Rutgers Journal of Law & Religion* 12 (Fall 2010): 145–47; 154–56; 160–61.

4   Ibid., 151–52.

5   Ibid., 162.

6   Deborah E. Lipstadt, *The Eichmann Trial* (New York: Random House, 2011), 61.

7   Beaver, "A Comparison in Nazi Litigation Strategies from Nuremberg to the Present": 165–67.

8   Ibid., 1–4.

9   Devin O. Pendas, *The Frankfurt Auschwitz Trial, 1963–1965: Genocide, History and the Limits of the Law* (New York: Cambridge University Press, 2006), 249–58.

10  Peter Weiss, *The Investigation: Oratorio in 11 Cantos* (London: Marion Boyars, 2012).

## 6.

1   Video, accompanying images, summaries, and findings: *Prosecutor v. Đorđević*, Exhibits P00288, P00289, P00290, P00291, P00293; Public Judgement, paras. 626–28.

2   The defence spent much of its cross-examination seeking to establish that many of the able-bodied men had already left to join the KLA. Thaqi denied any knowledge of this.

3   *Prosecutor v. Đorđević*, Transcript, T.608–09.

4   Ibid., Transcript, T.699.

5   Ibid., Exhibits P00288, P00289, P00290, P00291, P00293; Public Judgement, paras. 626–28.

6   See for example: "U.S.: Massacre video matches mass grave evidence," CNN.com, May 19, 1999, *http://edition.cnn.com/WORLD/europe/9905/19/massacre.02/*.

7   "The Promise of Justice: Burning the Evidence — A Calculated Risk," *American RadioWorks, http://americanradioworks.publicradio.org/features/kosovo/burning_evidence/story3.html*.

## 7.

1   For a succinct overview of an extensive history, see Alastair Finlan, *Essential Histories: The Collapse of Yugoslavia, 1991–1999* (Great Britain: Osprey Publishing, 2004).

2   Noel Malcolm, *Kosovo: A Short History* (New York: New York University Press, 1998), 334–37.

3   Ibid., 338.

4   Louis Sell, *Slobodan Milošević and the Destruction of Yugoslavia* (Durham, NC: Duke University Press, 2002), 78.

5   Malcolm, *Kosovo*, 339.

6   Sell, *Slobodan Milošević and the Destruction of Yugoslavia*, 79.

7   Ana S. Trbovich, *A Legal Geography of Yugoslavia's Disintegration* (New York: Oxford University Press, 2008), 195–96.

8   Malcolm, *Kosovo*, 341.

9   For a clear assessment of these events it is hard to do better than the original footage. Much of my account here is based on that footage as obtained and compiled by the BBC, along with a number of remarkably clear interviews with the protagonists that it obtained for its documentary *The Death of Yugoslavia: Enter Nationalism*. The documentary intermixes video footage of key events with surprisingly candid interviews of Stambolić, Milošević, and Kosovo Serb leader Miroslav Solević, among others. The documentary and its extensive footage were often referenced directly at the Tribunal.

10  Some have translated it as, "You will not be beaten again."

11  David Bruce MacDonald, *Balkan Holocausts? Serbian and Croatian victim-centred propaganda and the war in Yugoslavia* (New York:

Manchester University Press, 2002), 69.

12  Mesut Uyar and Edward J. Erickson, *A Military History of the Ottomans: From Osman to Atatürk* (Santa Barbara, CA: Greenwood Publishing Group, 2009), 24–27.

13  Caroline Finkel, *Osman's Dream: The History of the Ottoman Empire* (Cambridge, MA: Basic Books, 2005), 21.

14  MacDonald, *Balkan Holocausts?*, 75–76.

15  Ibid., 71.

16  One of our witnesses, Veton Surroi, covered the amendments as a journalist and testified at the outset of the Đorđević trial. [*Prosecutor v. Đorđević*, T.245–T.368.]

17  The term "hearts and minds" itself has an intriguingly loaded history. See for example: Elizabeth Dickinson, "A Bright Shining Slogan: How 'hearts and minds' came to be," *Foreign Policy*, August 24, 2009, *www.foreignpolicy.com/articles/2009/08/13/a_bright_shining_slogan*.

18  Donald Black, "Crime as Social Control," *American Sociological Review* 48 (February 1983): 35.

19  Ibid., 34–45.

20  Ibid,, 38.

21  In the ordinary context of an individual offender committing a single criminal act, Black's approach adds an interesting dimension of analysis, though there are invariably a wide range of different motivations for the commission of various crimes. I nonetheless think we would do well to recognize that a significant portion of crime is born of misguided justice-seeking behaviour, because this has a number of social and sociological implications. Individuals who feel fundamentally disenfranchised from the legal system they live within, for example, will more often tend to pursue what they see as "justice" themselves. We would expect to see more such acts in criminal cultures that cannot turn to societal mechanisms like the police for enforcement, like criminal gangs, drug dealers, and organized criminals. Where individuals reject the justice system as illegitimate or inaccessible, or where it does not function or does not exist, they may more often take this perceived pursuit of justice into their own hands.

22  MacDonald, *Balkan Holocausts?*, 7.

# 8.

1  *Prosecutor v. Đorđević,* Exhibit P00272.

2  Ibid., Transcript, T.485.

3  Ibid.

4  *Prosecutor v. Milutinović et. al.,* Transcript, T.7462.

5  Weiss, *The Investigation,* 198.

6  *Prosecutor v. Đorđević,* Transcript, T.7042.

7  Ibid., Transcript, T.7066.

8  "It may strike you as illogical, but I realised that the order was illegal, therefore I refused to carry it out": *Prosecutor v. Đorđević,* Transcript, T.7069.

9  *Prosecutor v. Đorđević,* Transcript, T.7071–74.

10  Ibid., Transcript, T.7044.

11  Ibid., Transcript, T.7078.

12  Ibid., Transcript, T.7079–80.

13  Ibid., Transcript, T.7051–52.

14  Ibid., Transcript, T.7052.

15  Ibid., Transcript, T.7049; T.7053; T.7055.

16  Ibid., Transcript, T.7053.

17  Ibid., Transcript, T.7054.

18  Ibid.

19  Ibid., Transcript, T.7054–55.

20  Ibid., Transcript, T.7063.

21  Ibid., Transcript, T.7062–63.

22  Ibid., Public Judgement, paras. 667; 685.

23  The information here is derived from the following public trial sources: *Prosecutor v. Đorđević,* Public Judgement, paras. 654–79; 682; 685; 1404; 2089; Transcript, T.370–96; T.399–455; *Prosecutor v. Milutinović* et. al., Transcript, T.3937–T.4005.

24  *Prosecutor v. Đorđević,* Transcript, T.387.

25  Ibid., Transcript, T.389.

26  Ibid., Transcript, T.408.

27  Ibid., Transcript, T.394.

28  *Prosecutor v. Milošević,* IT-02-54, Transcript, T.7503–04.

29  There was no forensic evidence tendered with respect to Sedat's cause of death, although given the other evidence the Trial Chamber

had little hesitation in accepting that he was shot by local police in Suva Reka. [*Prosecutor v.* Đorđević, Public Judgement, para. 1405.]

30  *Prosecutor v.* Đorđević, Exhibit P00593.

31  Ibid., Transcript, T.3347–48.

# 9.

1  Samantha Power, *A Problem From Hell* (New York: HarperCollins, 2007), 444.

2  Tim Judah, "The Kosovo Liberation Army," *Perceptions* (September–November 2000): 67–68.

3  Ibid., 68–69.

4  *Prosecutor v.* Đorđević, Public Judgement, paras. 271, 1990.

5  Ibid., Exhibit P00741; Human Rights Watch Report, "Humanitarian Law Violations in Kosovo," *www.hrw.org/legacy/reports98/kosovo/*.

6  *Prosecutor v.* Đorđević, Public Judgement, paras. 300–01.

7  Ibid., Public Judgement, paras. 288–93.

8  *The situation in Kosovo (FRY).* SC Res. 1199, September 23, 1998.

9  *Specijalna Anti-teroristička Jedinica*, in Serbian.

10  *Prosecutor v.* Đorđević, Public Judgement, paras. 396–401.

11  Ibid., Public Judgement, paras. 396–409.

12  Ibid., Public Judgement, paras. 409–15.

13  Ibid., Transcript, T.13085–87.

14  Roland Paris, "Kosovo and the Metaphor War," *Political Science Quarterly*, Volume 117, Number 3 (2002): 437.

15  Ibid., 433–38; 440–43.

16  Ibid., 442.

17  MacDonald, *Balkan Holocausts?*, 73–76; 80–84; 91.

18  Ibid., 83, quoting Dobrica Cosic, "L'éffondrement de la Yougoslavie," 44.

19  *Prosecutor v.* Đorđević, Public Judgement, para. 432.

20  Ibid., Public Judgement, paras. 435–39.

21  Ibid., Public Judgement, para. 433.

22  Benjamin S. Lambeth. *NATO's Air War for Kosovo: A Strategic and Operational Assessment* (Santa Monica, CA: RAND, 2001), 66–67.

23  Francis X. Clines, "NATO Opens Broad Barrage Against Serbs as Clinton Denounces 'Brutal Repression,'" *New York Times*, March 25, 1999, quoted in Lambeth, *NATO's Air War for Kosovo*, 84.

# 10.

1  *Prosecutor v. Milutinović et. al*, Public Judgement, Vol. I, paras. 930–40.

2  The name is derived from the Turkish, dating back to the Ottoman Empire, for what other Muslims know as Eid-al-Adha. The festival commemorates Abraham's willingness to sacrifice his son Ishmael.

3  The men's bodies were later found by the OSCE, buried with a number of other bodies in the Podujevo Cemetery. [*Prosecutor v. Đorđević*, Public Judgement, para. 1454.]

4  *Prosecutor v. Đorđević*, Transcript, T.1887–88.

5  It was Fatos who described the vehicle as a Pinzgauer, an all-terrain, four-wheel drive vehicle: "It's like a minivan but it's with iron, like a combat vehicle," he explained. This sort of knowledge, it seems, was often a reality for young children growing up in Kosovo. [*Prosecutor v. Đorđević*, P00381, 4.]

6  *Prosecutor v. Đorđević*, P00381, 3.

7  Ibid., Exhibit P00380 (08:40–09:30).

8  Ibid., Exhibit P00380 (09:35–10:28).

9  A video showing some of the killings committed by the Scorpions in Trnovo, after the fall of Srebrenica, subsequently garnered a significant amount of attention. The video shows members of the Scorpions, including their commander, Boca (Slobodan Medić), transporting six Bosnian Muslims in a truck, their hands bound. The men show clear signs of having been beaten. The Scorpions take four of the men into a field and shoot them. They make the two surviving men move those four bodies, and then they shoot and kill those two men as well. [See *Prosecutor v. Zdravko Tolimir*, IT-05-88/2-T, Judgement, December 12, 2012, paras. 547–51; and Tim Judah and Daniel Sunter, "How video that put Serbia in dock was brought to light," *The Guardian*, June 4, 2005, *www.theguardian.com/world/2005/jun/05/balkans.warcrimes*].

10  The Serbian town of Šid suffered the first major assault of the war when it was shelled by Croat forces at the beginning of November, 1991. ["Serbs Accuse Croatia of 2nd Attack," Reuters, *Reading Eagle Newspaper*, Nov. 5, 1991; Chuck Sudetic, "Yugoslav Fighting Breaks Cease-Fire," *New York Times*, November 7, 1991.]

11 "Massacre at Podujevo, Kosovo," *CBC News*, March 29, 2004, *www. cbc.ca/news2/background/balkans/crimesandcourage.html.*

12 The money for tours of duty in Kosovo was not to be underestimated. Stoparić described that as of 1998 he had begun to notice members of the police force returning from tours of duty with hoards of cash and jewellery. [*Prosecutor v.* Đorđević, P00493, para. 32.]

13 *Prosecutor v.* Đorđević, P00493, para. 55.

14 Ibid., P00493, para 61.

15 It remained unclear on the evidence exactly how many of the Scorpions were redeployed, and why some of the men were not. The defence argued that the men who were involved in the incident were not redeployed, but this did not appear consistent with other evidence — particularly given that the men thought to be involved in the incident had not even been identified at the time the Scorpions were redeployed. See for example: *Prosecutor v.* Đorđević, Public Judgement, para. 1964.

16 Also admitted to the Pristina Hospital, the day before the shootings took place, was the SAJ's commander Živko Trajković. Trajković's Jeep had driven over an anti-tank mine on March 27; he survived but his driver was killed instantly. After the incident, Trajković — who also testified for the prosecution in Đorđević — was told about what happened in Podujevo. That account, although it was hearsay, suggested a particular motivation for the killings: Trajković said he was told that some of the Scorpions had come across civilians in the town and were provoked by the police to "do away with these people," to revenge the injury of their commander. [See *Prosecutor v.* Đorđević, Transcript, T.9093–94.]

17 *Prosecutor v.* Đorđević, P00493, para. 73.

18 The documentary provided a view into the life of the surviving children in England, and powerful visual evidence of Saranda walking through the scene of the massacre and explaining it. The video was tendered as an exhibit at the Đorđević trial. [*Prosecutor v.* Đorđević, P00380.]

19 *Prosecutor v.* Đorđević, Public Judgement, para. 1965; Transcript, T.2843.

20 One NGO, Natasa Kandić's Humanitarian Law Centre, played a significant and very influential role in working with witnesses and ensuring that the trial went forward. The Centre produced a comprehensive report about the trial proceedings. See: *Podujevo 1999 — Beyond Rea-*

*sonable Doubt*, Humanitarian Law Centre, *www.hlc-rdc.org/wp-content/uploads/2013/07/Podujevo-1999-Beyond-Reasonable-Doubt.pdf.*

21 *Prosecutor v. Milutinović et. al.*, Transcript, T.706–07; *Prosecutor v. Đorđević*, Transcript, T.2846–47.

22 I do not know the details of this identification process, nor am I able to assess how reliable it may have been. It was reported that all of the children positively identified him.

23     When he started shooting I was in the middle of our group, near the wall. I leaned against the wall and slid down to the ground. When I slid down to the ground he was still shooting and he shot me twice in the leg. He kept shooting, he only stopped after a while. One person could not breathe normally so her heavy breathing was heard. Then they started shooting again. During that shooting I was shot in the arm and in the back. After a while the shooting stopped. I could not hear anything and I don't know for how long this went on.

    Then I lifted my head to look around. Since I was not lying down, but was in a sitting position, my brother Sekim, who was lying down, had his head where my legs were, so I could see half of his face. My cousin Fatos, who was lying on the ground, was in front of me. There was something in his back that indicated that he had been hit because something was coming out of his back. At first I thought he was dead, but then I saw that he was alive because he lifted his head, I did not know if he was sick. Then I saw Enver's oldest son whose name is Arbar, I think his name is Arbar. He was shot in the face and his face was disfigured. Then I saw my grandmother, Sekira, who was facing me. She was all yellow and her eyes were protruding. She was facing our group, we were in the back, she was in the front. Then I saw Farije, my aunt's daughter-in-law. I could not see her face, but I saw her body. She was lying down and she was dark blue.

    Genc was near her and he lifted his head. "Saranda, look what they did to Spetin," referring to my brother. Then I heard some voices and shouting and I told Genc to lie down, and I went back to where I was earlier. Then I closed my eyes, but I heard that someone was next to us, around us. Then I heard one of my cousins moaning with pain very quietly. I did not know what was happening, but I decided to open my eyes because I assumed they thought I was dead. When I moved, I think two men came and pulled me out. [Examination of Saranda Bogujevci, from the Trial of Sasa Cvjetan: *Prosecutor v. Đorđević*, P00374, 4–5.]

24    Then we saw our mother for the second time, she was crying. One of them grabbed her by the shirt, then she said something, but I only understood that she said 'They are only children.' Then they grabbed her and sent her to a place which was a bit further away from us and then they shot her in the back. Then my sister and I screamed, then we saw another soldier walking in front of us and then they took us to the edge of the courtyard. After that I just heard shooting and we all fell to the ground. So first shooting was heard, then there was a pause, and then shooting was heard again.

…

When I said that I fell down, it was because everyone started moving in the same direction and falling over each other. I was knocked to the ground because they pushed me from the back and after that they shot at me. They shot at us. The shots were coming from at least two directions, but I cannot say how many of them there were because they were shooting from automatic weapons, it didn't last long. First they fired and then they probably changed weapons or they reloaded and put in a new cartridge. [Examination of Fatos Bogujevci, from the Trial of Sasa Cvjetan: *Prosecutor v. Đorđević*, P00382, 4; 6.]

25  Bogdan Ivanisević and Jennifer Trahan, "Justice at Risk: War Crimes Trials in Croatia, Bosnia and Herzegovina, and Serbia and Montenegro," *Human Rights Watch* 16, no. 7(D), (October 2004): 11.
26  See for example: TRIAL, "Sasa Cvetan: Legal Procedure," *www.*

*trial-ch.org/en/resources/trial-watch/trial-watch/profiles/profile/624/*
*action/show/controller/Profile/tab/legal-procedure.html.*

27 The bodies of those killed in Podujevo, including the fourteen women and children murdered in the courtyard, were subsequently exhumed and documented by an OSCE team in July 1999, and then re-exhumed and autopsied by the British Forensic Team in August 2000. Evidence showed the cause of death as gunshot wounds to the chest, neck, and head. [*Prosecutor v.* Đorđević, Exhibits P01142, P01150, Public Judgement, paras. 1452–58.]

28 The trial heard from a range of witnesses on this issue, most notably SAJ Commander Živko Trajković, Scorpions member Goran Stoparić, and defence witnesses Zoran Simović and Radislav Stalević, the SAJ commanders on the ground in Podujevo.

29 *Prosecutor v.* Đorđević, Public Judgement, para. 1228.

# 11.

1 This was well chronicled in the Đorđević Final Judgement. See for example: paras. 852–1012.

2 Stojanović testified for the defence and denied this, but his denials did not withstand cross-examination. As the Đorđević Trial Chamber concluded: "The Chamber was left with the clear impression that the evidence of both Milos Dosan and Momir Stojanović, at least in part, was influenced by self interest to minimise their own roles in Operation Reka and to present it as solely an operation directed against KLA fighters." [*Prosecutor v.* Đorđević, Public Judgement, para. 943.]

3 *Prosecutor v. Milutinović et. al.*, Transcript, T.2644.

4 The victims were: Tringa Vejsa, Dorina Vejsa, Marigona Vejsa, Shihana Vejsa, Rita Vejsa, Arlind Vejsa, Fetije Vejsa, Hysen Gashi, Shahindere Hoxha, Flaka Hoxha, Valbona Čaka, Dalina Čaka, Delvina Čaka, Diona Čaka, Valbona Haxhiavdia, Doruntina Haxhiavdia, Egzon Haxhiavdia, Rina Haxhiavdia, Shirine Nuci, and Manushe Nuci. [*Prosecutor v.* Đorđević, Public Judgement, para. 889.]

5 *Prosecutor v. Milutinović et. al.*, Transcript, T.2646.

6 Ibid., Transcript, T.2652.

7 This wasn't the only close call with police who were suspicious of Dren's injury, perhaps on the lookout for survivors who should not

have survived. Dren and his family had an encounter in a random police spot check on their way to the border: "Well, there was an incident that happened before we went to the border, a police officer in the middle of the night was checking cars and he saw my arm was wrapped up and he had asked my aunt's husband what happened. And he's like, 'Oh, he just hurt himself playing.' And the guy asked to unwrap my arm. And he's like, 'Come on, he's just a kid, he's sleeping, just leave him alone.' And nothing — like, I didn't get woken up, so I guess everything had went okay." [*Prosecutor v. Đorđević*, Transcript, T.8649.]

8 This was confirmed by forensic evidence. See for example: *Prosecutor v. Đorđević*, Exhibit P01161, 2–10; Public Judgement, para. 898.

9 The information contained here was provided in open session and/or included in public court judgments, in particular: *Prosecutor v. Đorđević*, Public Judgement, paras. 987; 1275–85; 2099; Transcript, T.8918–84; *Prosecutor v. Milutinović et. al.*, Transcript, T.5315–45.

10 *Prosecutor v. Đorđević*, Transcript, T. 8924.

11 *Prosecutor v. Milutinović et. al.*, Transcript, T.5333.

12 In the strange atmosphere of wartime Kosovo, K72 had also found himself assisting Kosovo Albanians after a NATO bomb accidentally hit a column of Albanians on the road between Dakovica and Prizren. He had received orders from the local MUP to report to the site of the bombing and fill up the hole in the road with gravel and earth, but once there he was asked by Albanians to help them transport victims of the bombing with his excavator. He agreed, taking five or six bodies in the shovel of his excavator across a nearby bridge, where he transferred them to a smaller vehicle. [*Prosecutor v. Đorđević*, Transcript, T.8946–47, 8971–72.]

13 See for example: *Prosecutor v. Đorđević*, Public Judgement, paras. 898; 985–86.

# 12.

1 George Orwell, "Revenge Is Sour," in *George Orwell: In Front of Your Nose, 1946–1950*, eds. Sonia Orwell and Ian Angus (Jaffrey, NH: Nonpareil, 2000), 3–6.

2 Ibid., 5.

3 See for example: *Prosecutor v. Đorđević*, Public Judgement, para. 1698; and P00734, 4. These numbers were thoroughly corrobo-

rated by statistics that the Serbian police tracked themselves and published in daily situation reports. See for example: *Prosecutor v. Đorđević*, Exhibits P00718, 5; P00721, 6; P00694, 8.

4    Power, *A Problem From Hell*, 450.

5    See for example: *Prosecutor v.* Đorđević, Public Judgement, para. 1690. Defence witness Milutin Filipović, who temporarily commanded the VJ Pristina garrison during the NATO bombing, emphatically denied that the Serbian police or military had exerted any pressure on the ethnic Albanians to leave their homes, and instead claimed every possible alternative reason for why the Albanians left Kosovo: that they were afraid of the NATO bombing, that they were fleeing the KLA, that they weren't really sure why they were leaving, that they were only pretending to leave and forming columns to present a false image to the international media, that the columns were formed to hide terrorists, and that they were fleeing depleted uranium ammunition dropped by NATO. The Đorđević Trial Chamber devoted a separate subsection to emphatically reject this testimony [see *Prosecutor v.* Đorđević, Public Judgement, paras. 842–51].

6    See for example: *Prosecutor v.* Đorđević, Public Judgement, paras. 1798–1855.

7    Lambeth, *NATO's Air War for Kosovo*, 29–30.

8    See for example: Michael Ignatieff, *Virtual War: Kosovo and Beyond*, (New York: Picador, 2001).

9    Lambeth, *NATO's Air War for Kosovo*, 21, 80, 86, 95–96.

10   Ibid., 22–23.

11   Ibid., 113–19.

12   Ibid.

13   Daniel Williams and Bradley Graham, "Yugoslavs Yield to NATO Terms," *Washington Post*, June 4, 1999; R. Jeffrey Smith and Molly Moore, "Plan for Kosovo Pullout Signed," *Washington Post*, June 10, 1999; "Crisis in the Balkans: 2 Generals' Remarks on Pullout Pact," *New York Times*, June 10, 1999, *www.nytimes.com/1999/06/10/ world/crisis-in-the-balkans-2-generals-remarks-on-pullout-pact. html*; Lambeth, *NATO's Air War for Kosovo,*141–47; 200–24.

14   Lambeth, *NATO's Air War for Kosovo*, 22.

15  See for example: Marlise Simons, "War Crimes Tribunal Expands Milosevic Indictment," *New York Times*, June 30, 2001, *www. nytimes.com/2001/06/30/world/war-crimes-tribunal-expands-milosevic-indictment.html*; Marlise Simons, "Milosevic, Indicted Again, Is Charged With Crimes in Croatia," *New York Times*, October 10, 2001, *www.nytimes.com/2001/10/10/world/milosevic-indicted-again-is-charged-with-crimes-in-croatia.html*. For a good overview of the procedural history, see *ICTY Case Information Sheet*, IT-02-54, *Prosecutor v. Slobodan Milošević, www.icty.org/x/cases/slobodan_milosevic/cis/en/cis_milosevic_slobodan_en.pdf.*

16  Jonathan Steele, "Serbian War Crimes Suspect Shoots Himself," *The Guardian*, April 11, 2002, *www.theguardian.com/world/2002/apr/12/balkans.warcrimes*; "Top Serb Suspect Dies," *BBC News World: Europe*, April 14, 2002, *http://news.bbc.co.uk/2/hi/europe/1928491.stm*; "Former Serbian minister's suicide note," *BBC News*, April 12, 2002, *http://news.bbc.co.uk/2/hi/world/monitoring/media_reports/1925931.stm.*

17  Cables and reports to this effect were published by the controversial site Wikileaks, though I cannot confirm their accuracy. See for example: *www.wikileaks.org/plusd/cables/07PODGORICA215_a.html* and *www.scoop.co.nz/stories/WL0706/S01713/cablegate-montenegro-arrests-pifwc-vlastimir-djordjevic.htm.*

18  Alexander Hinton, *Why Did They Kill? Cambodia in the Shadow of Genocide* (Berkeley, CA: University of California Press, 2004), 51, 59.

19  Ibid., 52.

20  As Pol Pot put it in a seminal 1977 speech: "… the key problem, the fundamental problem which was decisive for victory [was to] arouse the peasants so that they … burned with class hatred and took up the struggle." The "struggle" that followed involved identifying and vilifying people based first on affiliation with the previous regime and then more broadly along perceived lines of socio-economic class, searching for "hidden enemies," including intellectuals and members of the "elite," which for them included teachers, landlords, and policemen. Cambodians who lived in cities were identified as wealthy and corrupt urbanites and imperialists, exploiting and otherwise victimizing the rural poor. [Hinton, *Why Did They Kill?*, 52 (quote), 78, 81–83; 87–89.]

21  Hinton, *Why Did They Kill?*, 82.

22  Ibid., 138. For a remarkably comprehensive accounting of the confession process, see David Chandler, *Voices From S-21: Terror and History in Pol Pot's Secret Prison* (Berkeley, CA: University of California Press, 1999).

23  See for example: Power, *A Problem From Hell*, 331–35.

24  See for example: Philip Gourevitch, *We Wish to Inform You That Tomorrow We Will Be Killed With Our Families* (New York: Picador, 1998), 47–62.

25  Alison Des Forges, *Leave None to Tell the Story: Genocide in Rwanda* (New York: Human Rights Watch, 1999), 75–95, *www.hrw.org/reports/pdfs/r/rwanda/rwanda993.pdf.*

26  This approach — imputing your enemy with the intention to commit the injustice that you yourself intend to commit — has been previously identified as an effective propaganda tactic. In her 1999 Human Rights Watch report, Alison Des Forges refers to the tactic as "Accusation in a mirror," taking the term from a how-to propaganda pamphlet that was found in Butare. Des Forges describes how this technique was used extensively in Rwanda. See Des Forges, *Leave None to Tell the Story,* 75–76, *www.hrw.org/reports/pdfs/r/rwanda/rwanda993.pdf.*

27  Des Forges, *Leave None to Tell the Story,* 75–95, *www.hrw.org/reports/pdfs/r/rwanda/rwanda993.pdf.*

# 13.

1  *Prosecutor v. Đorđević,* Public Judgement, paras. 74, 1325.

2  Both K88 and K87 were codenamed witnesses who testified in public session. The information that follows is from public materials, in particular *Prosecutor v. Đorđević,* Public Judgement, paras. 74, 1325–52, 1972; Exhibits P01415 (Redacted witness statement of K87), P00370A (Redacted witness statement of K88).

3  *Prosecutor v. Đorđević,* P00370A, paras. 14–16.

4  Ibid., Public Judgement, paras 1328–29; P01415, paras. 12–13.

5  Ibid., Public Judgement, para. 1329.

6  Ibid.

7  (Peter Zeković) *Prosecutor v. Đorđević,* Public Judgement, paras. 1332, 1349.

8  It bears noting that ramped graves like this were found in a number of sites across the Balkans. It is difficult to know if these similarities were a function of simple practicality or of common instructions.

9  *Prosecutor v.* Đorđević, P00370A, paras. 19–21; P01415, paras. 18–20; Public Judgement, para. 1328.

10  Ibid., P00370A, para. 22.

11  Ibid., P00370A, para. 23; Public Judgement, para. 1340.

12  Ibid., Public Judgement, para. 1351.

13  Ibid., P00370A, paras. 22, 27, 29–31.

14  Ibid., P00370A, paras. 27–28.

15  Ibid., P00370A, para. 30; *Prosecutor v. Milutinović et. al.*, Transcript, T.10450.

16  *Prosecutor v.* Đorđević, P00370A, para. 16; *Prosecutor v. Milutinović et. al.*, Transcript, T.10448.

17  *Prosecutor v.* Đorđević, P00370A, para. 35; Public Judgement, para. 1345.

18  Ibid., P00370A, para. 25.

19  K87 tried to claim that the trailer was left there intentionally to mark the site, but the Trial Chamber rejected this claim as a fabrication intended to support his claim that the authorities had some intention to dig up and rebury the bodies after the war. The claim was internally inconsistent and did not fit with the facts. See *Prosecutor v.* Đorđević, P00370A, para. 24 and Public Judgement, para. 1340.

20  *Prosecutor v.* Đorđević, Transcript, T.9125–27; Public Judgement, para. 1352.

21  Christopher Hitchens, "Body Count in Kosovo," *The Nation*, June 11, 2001, *www.thenation.com/article/body-count-kosovo*.

22  *Prosecutor v.* Đorđević, Exhibit P00364.

23  Ibid., Exhibit P00364.

24  Ibid., Exhibit P00364.

25  Ibid., Exhibit P00365.

26  There were some specific discrepancies in the account from the evidence as it would later emerge in court. Zika, for example, described the truck as having license plates, and with an inscription on the side from Peć, not Prizren. But the core of the account was generally consistent with what would later emerge at trial from a range of sources, corroborated by physical evidence. [See for example: *Prosecutor v.* Đorđević, Exhibit P00365; Public Judgement, para. 1292.]

27  *Prosecutor v.* Đorđević, Exhibit P00365.

28  See for example: "Milosevic Arrested," *BBC News*, April 1, 2001. *http://news.bbc.co.uk/2/hi/europe/1254263.stm.*

29  *Prosecutor v.* Đorđević, Public Judgement, paras. 1371–72.

30  Ibid., Public Judgement, para. 1373.

31  Ibid., Public Judgement, para. 1374.

## 14.

1  For interesting reflections on Arendt and Eichmann and how perceptions of the two have shifted over the years, see Mark Lilla, "Arendt & Eichmann: The New Truth," *The New York Review of Books*, November 21, 2013, *www.nybooks.com/articles/archives/2013/nov/21/arendt-eichmann-new-truth/* and Jennifer Schuessler, "Book Portrays Eichmann as Evil, but Not Banal," *The New York Times*, September 2, 2014, *www.nytimes.com/2014/09/03/books/book-portrays-eichmann-as-evil-but-not-banal.html.*

2  Alain De Botton, *The News: A User's Manual* (London: Penguin Books, 2014), 193. De Botton applies this perspective to the news, but I think it also has much to lend us with respect to the criminal trial.

3  Adam Philips, *Missing Out: In Praise of the Unlived Life* (New York: Picador, 2012), 93.

4  From Lawrence Weschler, "Inventing Peace: What can Vermeer teach us about Bosnia?" *The New Yorker*, November 20, 1996, *www.pbs.org/wgbh/pages/frontline/shows/karadzic/genocide/inventing.html.*

5  The two results that seem to cause the most frustration are *Prosecutor v. Gotovina et al.* and *Prosecutor v. Ramush Haradinaj et al.*

6  Leon Festinger, *A Theory of Cognitive Dissonance* (Stanford, CA: Stanford University Press, 1957).

## 15.

1  See Slobodan Mitrović, "Fresh scars on the body of archaeology," October 10, 2006, *http://traumwerk.stanford.edu/archaeo-log/2006/10/fresh_scars_on_the_body_of_arc.html.*

2  *Ibid.*

3  *Prosecutor v.* Đorđević, Exhibits P00507, P00526; Public Judgement, paras. 1479–83.

4  Ibid., Exhibit P00507, para. 7.
5  Ibid., Exhibit P00815, para. 39.
6  Ibid., Exhibit P00815, paras. 17–18, 20, 26.
7  Ibid., Exhibit P00815, para. 15.
8  Ibid., Public Judgement, paras. 1481–83; Exhibit P00526, para. 9; Exhibit P00507, para. 13.
9  Ibid., Exhibit P00815, para. 28.
10  Ibid., Exhibit P00507, para. 8.
11  Ibid., Public Judgement, para. 1341; Exhibits P00370 (Redacted statement of K88), P00815, para. 38, 23.
12  Ibid., Exhibit P00507, para. 9; Public Judgement, paras. 1335, 1340; Exhibit P00815, paras. 39, 52.
13  Ibid., Public Judgement, para. 1340; Exhibits P00370 (Redacted statement of K88), P00815, paras. 13, 53–54; 66.
14  Ibid., Public Judgement, para. 1462.
15  Ibid., Public Judgement, paras. 1459, 1463.
16  When asked by the defence about the discrepancy between his team's findings and the findings of the international team, Dunjić seemed to accidentally tip his hand, describing that he "knew" that the victims were killed in clashes between terrorist forces and the police/military:

> So what facts did I have? I had the fact that the bodies had been brought there from somewhere else; that they had been transported using various vehicles or means of transport; that some of them had been buried else-where, before; *and that those persons were killed in var-ious clashes between the terrorist forces, the KLA actions targeting the police and the regular military*; and these are all the facts that I had in my head.
> — [Italics added. *Prosecutor v.* Đorđević, Transcript, T.3268; and see Public Judgement, para. 1479.]

17  Ibid., Public Judgement, paras. 1377, 1484–85.
18  Ibid., Exhibit P00799.
19  Ibid.

20  Ibid., Exhibit P00799; Public Judgement, paras. 1486–91.

21  Ibid., Public Judgement, paras. 1492–95, 1498–1502.

22  Ibid., Transcript, T.830–31.

23  Ibid., Public Judgement, paras. 1353–56.

24  Ibid., Exhibit P00815, 30–31.

25  Popović and Miloš Stojanović were later charged with the murders by the Serbian War Crimes Prosecutor's Office. Unusually, Đorđević himself was called to testify at that hearing, in the midst of his trial in The Hague. Popović and Stojanović were ultimately acquitted. But as noted here, Đorđević admitted to directing Popović to take the brothers to Petrovo Selo. [*Prosecutor v.* Đorđević, Transcript, T.9973–75; Public Judgement, para. 1978; Exhibit P00815, 30–31.]

26  *Prosecutor v.* Đorđević, Exhibit P00815, 31.

27  Ibid., Public Judgement, paras. 620, 1409–10.

28  It may be noted here that at least 135 bodies were buried — it is not clear what happened to the remaining bodies.

29  According to Gojović, the investigation into the killings in Izbica was initiated on May 29, 1999. As of the date of his testimony in the Đorđević trial — in 2010 — the investigation was "still pending." [*Prosecutor v.* Đorđević, Transcript, T.10460–61]
Gojović had sought to describe the existence of a robust military court system that had existed to charge and punish crimes committed during wartime. However, it became clear through his testimony that the court had directed all of its focus to crimes committed against the army, such as desertion, refusal to obey orders, and petty theft. So what of the failure to lay charges for the mass deportation of hundreds of thousands of ethnic Albanians from Kosovo, which would have constituted the crime of "expulsion" in Serbia? Gojović's explanation was quintessentially bureaucratic:

> … the prosecutor found that there was no intention to expel them across the border because it is impossible pursuant to effective laws of Yugoslavia to expel one's own citizens. This would be [a] legally unacceptable formulation, and it's true that some segments of the population of all ethnic background in Kosovo and Metohija left

their places of residence because of combat activity. This is a relatively small area with quite substantial military effect on both sides. And naturally, the civilian population moved away from such fighting.

[*Prosecutor v. Đorđević, Transcript, T.10454–55.*]

In other words, it was impossible legally to expel one's own citizens, therefore it could not have happened. And if people did leave, it must just have been a natural response to combat activity.

30  *Prosecutor v. Đorđević*, Transcript, T.10461–62.

31  Ibid., Public Judgement, paras. 480–98, 1395–1402. The journalist John Sweeney ventured to Mala Krusa and reconstructed the massacre in a powerful video. He later testified at trial as well.

32  Ibid., Exhibit P01167; Public Judgement, paras. 1428–38, 1445.

33  See *Prosecutor v. Milutinović et. al.*, Exhibit P02798; Transcript, T.26801–02.

34  Although Serbian authorities identified a minimum of forty-eight bodies, subsequent examination by an international team reportedly identified the remains as belonging to at least eighty-four people. None of the bodies exhumed and identified from Lake Perućac were named in the Schedules of the Đorđević Indictment. [*Prosecutor v. Đorđević*, Public Judgement, paras. 1379, 1459–68, 1515–20; Exhibit P00815, 33–38.]

35  *Prosecutor v. Đorđević*, P00815, 33–38; Public Judgement, paras. 1459–68.

36  For an affecting and personal account of the exhumations and the volunteers who participated, see Dijana Muminović, *Secrets of Lake Perucac, http://issuu.com/dijanam/docs/lake*.

37  "Scores of bodies found at Perucac Lake," *Channel 4 News*, August 12, 2010, *http://blogs.channel4.com/world-news-blog/scores-of-soldiers-bodies-found-at-perucac-lake/13688*; Miran Jelenek, "Balkan river still bleeds the dead of wars past," Aug 9, 2010, Reuters, *www.reuters.com/article/2010/08/09/us-bosnia-river-dead-idUS-TRE6782Q320100809*; Nidzara Ahmetasević, "Lake Perucac's Watery Grave," *International Justice Tribune*, Radio Netherlands Worldwide, no. 114, October 6, 2010, *http://sites.rnw.nl/pdf/ijt/ijt114.pdf*.

38  See Michael Montgomery and Stephen Smith, "American Radio-works, The Promise of Justice: Burning the Evidence," *http://americanradioworks.publicradio.org/features/kosovo/burning_evidence/index.html.*

39  "Investigation: Serbia: More Mackatica Body Burning Revelations," Institute for War and Peace Reporting, BCR Issue 553 (August 2, 2005), *http://iwpr.net/report-news/investigation-serbia-more-mackatica-body-burning-revelations.*

40  I should add here that I was not involved in these decisions, nor do I have any specific information about why such charges were not laid. But it certainly seems apparent — both from the published accounts and from the fact that charges were not laid — that the available evidence was simply not sufficient to found criminal charges.

41  "The Situation in Kosovo: A Stock Taking," International Commission on Missing Persons, September 14, 2010, *www.ic-mp.org/wp-content/uploads/2007/11/icmp-dg-264-4-doc-general.pdf.*

# 16.

1  International Criminal Tribunal for the former Yugoslavia, "Judgement Summary for Milutinović et al.," February 26, 2009, *www.icty.org/x/cases/milutinovic/tjug/en/090226summary.pdf.*

2  To put it another way, the evidence was insufficient to show that he made a significant contribution to the joint criminal enterprise.

3  *Prosecutor v. Ðorđević*, Transcript, T.14361.

4  Although none of us knew at the time that General Ratko Mladić would soon be captured, thus requiring a number of additional prosecutors in short order to prepare for that trial.

5  The breakdown, by my count, was as follows: Bela Crkva — 60; Mala Krusa — 117; Suva Reka — 45; Izbica — 135; Ðakovica — 24; Meja — 296; Vucitrn — 4; Kotlina — 23; Slatina — 4; Podujevo — 16.

6  *Prosecutor v. Ðorđević*, Public Judgement, paras. 2002, 2132.

7  See *Prosecutor v. Ðorđević*, Public Judgement, paras. 1926–29.

8  Ibid., Public Judgement, paras. 1980–81.

9  Sainović and Ojdanić surrendered into custody in 2002, Milutinović in 2003, and Pavković, Lazarević, and Lukić in 2005. Mr. Ðorđević was arrested and transferred to the ICTY in 2007.

10  For a good — if still rather technical — overview of what happened on appeal, see ICTY, *Prosecutor v. Šainović et. al.*, Appeal Judgement Summary, January 23, 2014, http://icty.org/x/cases/milutinovic/acjug/en/140123_summary.pdf; and *Prosecutor v. Đorđević*, Judgement Summary, January 27, 2014, http://icty.org/x/cases/djordevic/acjug/en/140127_summary.pdf.

11  See *Prosecutor v. Đorđević*, Appeal Judgement, paras. 400–33.

12  This was a significant development. I have not written much about the sexual assault elements of these trials because this information was largely confidential and subject to publication ban. However, I hope the reader will not mistake my silence here for a lack of appreciation of the significance of the issue.

13  The Kosovo 6 appeal was also significant from a purely legal perspective, as it reversed the current and troublesome state of the law for the requirements to aid and abet an offense. In brief, the court held that a conviction for aiding and abetting an offense would no longer require the prosecution to prove that an accused's acts were "specifically directed" to assist the crimes. This was a very important legal point, though a rather technical one. For a good overview of the "specific direction saga" in international law, see for example: Manuel J. Ventura, "Farewell 'Specific Direction': Aiding and Abetting War Crimes and Crimes Against Humanity in Perišić, Taylor, Šainović et al., and US Alien Tort Statute Jurisprudence" in S. Casey-Maslen, ed., *The War Report 2013* (Oxford: Oxford University Press, 2014).

14  The fact that so few people read these judgments certainly can't be laid at the feet of the Tribunal's ever-improving outreach efforts, which see the judgments made available online, printed and bound in hardcopy, and made freely available to the public, alongside shorter summaries and all sorts of complementary background resources. It is, I think, more a question of who has the time or the dedication to read a one-thousand-page legal judgment. What seems stranger is why historians don't seem to read and cite these judgments more frequently, given that they provide as thorough and authoritative a historical account as one could hope to obtain. This, I hope, will change.

15  For an interesting expression of this perspective, see Phil Clark, "All Justice Is Local," *New York Times*, June 11, 2014, *www.nytimes.com/2014/06/12/opinion/all-justice-is-local.html*.

16  The sentences were upheld on appeal. Although a retrial was ordered for Repanović, he was convicted once again and on December 15, 2010 received another twenty-year sentence. See: "New sentence for Radojko Repanović in the Suva Reka War Crime Case," *Humanitarian Law Centre (Online)*, December 17, 2010, *www.hlc-rdc.org/?p=13097&lang=de*, and Miloš Teodorović, "Suva Reka Trial in Trouble," *Institute for War and Peace Reporting*, April 18, 2008, *http://iwpr.net/report-news/suva-reka-trial-trouble*.

17  "Sweden Acquits Serbian Policeman of Kosovo Crimes," *Balkan Transitional Justice*, December 20, 2012, *www.balkaninsight.com/en/article/swedish-court-acquits-policemen-for-crimes-in-kosovo*.

18  "Serbian ex-paramilitaries guilty of Kosovo killings," *BBC News Europe*, February 11, 2014, *www.bbc.com/news/world-europe-26146224*; Safet Kabashaj and Ivana Jovanović, "War crimes verdicts improve Kosovo-Serbia relations, experts say," *SETimes.com*, March 6, 2014, *www.setimes.com/cocoon/setimes/xhtml/en_GB/features/setimes/features/2014/03/06/feature-01*.

19  See for example: "Cuska — a 'brave and patriotic' trial," *Radio Netherlands Worldwide*, January 18, 2012, *www.rnw.nl/international-justice/article/cuska-a-"brave-and-patriotic"-trial*; and Marija Ristic, "Serbian Paramilitary Describes Massacre of Kosovo Villagers," *Balkan Transitional Justice*, April 23, 2013, *www.balkaninsight.com/en/article/ex-jackal-testifies-about-war-crimes-in-kosovo*.

20  "Serbian ex-paramilitaries guilty of Kosovo killings," *BBC News Europe*, February 11, 2014, *www.bbc.com/news/world-europe-26146224*; Safet Kabashaj and Ivana Jovanović, "War crimes verdicts improve Kosovo-Serbia relations, experts say," *SETimes.com*, March 6, 2014, *www.setimes.com/cocoon/setimes/xhtml/en_GB/features/setimes/features/2014/03/06/feature-01*.

21  For a comprehensive account of Minić's life of crime, see Matthew McAllester, *Beyond the Mountains of the Damned: The War Inside Kosovo* (New York: New York University Press, 2002).

22  See Colin McMahon, "Fleeing past, meeting his death," *Chicago Tribune*, October 23, 2005, *http://articles.chicagotribune.com/2005-*

10-23/news/0510230495_1_kosovo-mendoza-police-investigator; Colin McMahon, "His thirst for justice confronts arid past," *Chicago Tribune*, November 18, 2005, *http://articles.chicagotribune. com/2005-11-18/news/0511180157_1_argentina-war-crimes-argentine-jews*; Matthew McAllester, "Serb soldier unapolegetic to the end," *Chicago Tribune*, October 23, 2005, *http://balkanupdate. blogspot.com/2005/10/serb-soldier-unapolegetic-to-end.html*.

23  This was addressed in the Đorđević trial, see *Prosecutor v.* Đorđević, Public Judgement, para. 1953. See also Nicholas Wood, "4 Serbs Guilty in Execution of 6 Bosnians," *New York Times*, April 11, 2007, *www.nytimes.com/2007/04/11/world/europe/11serbia.html*.

24  Branislav Medić also received a twenty-year sentence. Pero Petrasavić, who pled guilty, received a thirteen-year term. Aleksander Medić received a five-year sentence. Aleksander Vukov was acquitted. See: Nicholas Wood, "4 Serbs Guilty in Execution of 6 Bosnians," *New York Times*, April 11, 2007, *www.nytimes. com/2007/04/11/world/europe/11serbia.html*.

25  See for example: "'Scorpions' Tried in Serbian Court for Massacring Women, Children, Elderly," Associated Press, October 7, 2008, *www.foxnews.com/story/2008/10/07/scorpions-tried-in-serbian-court-for-massacring-women-children-elderly/*.

26  The Appeals Chamber ordered a retrial in the case of Željko Đukić, though in September of 2010 he was again convicted and sentenced to twenty years in prison. [Republic of Serbia Office of the War Crimes Prosecutor, Public Relations Service: "Željko Đukić Receives 20 Years in Prison for a Podujevo War Crime," September 22, 2010, *www.tuzilastvorz. org.rs/html_trz/VESTI_SAOPSTENJA_2010/VS_2010_09_22_ENG.pdf.*

27  See for example: "Four Scorpions sentenced to severest punishment for war crimes against Albanian civilians," Humanitarian Law Centre, June 18, 2009, *www.hlc-rdc.org/?p=13002&lang=de*; Republic of Serbia Office of the War Crimes Prosecutor, Public Relations Service, "Verdicts Passed in the Podujevo War Crimes Case," June 18, 2009, *www.tuzilastvorz.org. rs/html_trz/VESTI_SAOPSTENJA_2009/VS_2009_06_18_ENG.pdf.*

28  Ivana Jovanović, "Exhibit is a step forward in Serbia-Kosovo relations, officials say," *SETimes.com*, January 14, 2014, *www.setimes.com/ cocoon/setimes/xhtml/en_GB/features/setimes/features/2014/01/14/fea-*

*ture-02*; Marija Ristic, "Kosovo Massacre Children Demand Truth at Art Show," *Balkan Transitional Justice*, December 20, 2013, *www.balkaninsight.com/en/article/children-of-war-debate-in-belgrade*; Nataša Kandić, "Albanian children extend their hand to us," Danas.rs, *www.zarekom.org/press/Albanian-children-extend-their-hand-to-us.en.html*.

29  Haradinaj was in fact granted provisional release from the detention centre in June of 2005, allowing him to return to Kosovo until the trial. He returned to The Hague in February of 2007, just before the trial began.

30  See for example: *Prosecutor v. Ramush Haradinaj, Idriz Balaj, Lahi Brahimaj*, IT-04-84-A, Public Judgement, July, 19 2010, para. 6.

31  *Prosecutor v. Ramush Haradinaj, Idriz Balaj, Lahi Brahimaj*, IT-04-84-A, Public Judgement, July 19, 2010.

32  *Prosecutor v. Ramush Haradinaj, Idriz Balaj, Lahi Brahimaj*, IT-04-84bis-T, Public Judgement with Confidential Annex, November 29, 2012.

33  The Trial Chamber expressly noted this in their judgment: "The Chamber further observed that a significant number of witnesses requested protective measures at trial, and expressed concerns for their lives and those of their family. This context of fear, in particular with respect to witnesses still living in Kosovo, was very perceptible throughout the trial." Limaj and Musliu were acquitted, while Bala received a thirteen-year sentence. [*Prosecutor v. Fatmir Limaj, Isak Musliu & Haradin Bala*, IT-03-66, Public Judgement, November 30, 2005, para. 15.]

34  See for example: "Kosovo ex-PM Ramush Haradinaj cleared of war crimes," *BBC News Europe*, November 29, 2012, *www.bbc.com/news/world-europe-20536318*; Christine Spolar, "Kosovo celebrates leader's acquittal," *Chicago Tribune*, April 4, 2008, *http://articles.chicagotribune.com/2008-04-04/news/0804030981_1_kosovo-serbs-ramush-haradinaj-ethnic-albanians-and-serbs*.

35  As in the case of Haradinaj, the Gotovina verdict was met with jubilation as it was watched in Zagreb's Central Square. See for example: Bruno Waterfield, "Croatian hero Ante Gotovina acquitted of war crimes," *The Telegraph*, November 16, 2012, *www.telegraph.co.uk/news/worldnews/europe/croatia/9682855/Croatian-hero-Ante-Gotovina-acquitted-of-war-crimes.html*; "Hague war court acquits Croat Generals Gotovina and Markac," *BBC News Europe*, November 16, 2012, *www.bbc.com/news/world-europe-20352187*.

36  Amra Zejneli, Branka Mihajlović, and Miloš Teodorović, "Serbian Fury at Haradinaj Verdict," Institute for War and Peace Reporting, TRI Issue 767 (December 3, 2012), *http://iwpr.net/report-news/serbian-fury-haradinaj-verdict.*

37  Statement of the Chief Prosecutor of the Special Investigative Task Force, July 29, 2014, *www.sitf.eu/images/Statement/Statement_of_the_Chief_Prosecutor_of_the_SITF_EN.pdf.*

38  Ibid.

39  "Statements that have been made by some implying that hundreds of people were killed for the purpose of organ trafficking are totally unsupported by the information we have and that Dick Marty had. If even one person was subjected to such a horrific practice, and we believe a small number were, that is a terrible tragedy and the fact that it occurred on a limited scale does not diminish the savagery of such a crime." Statement of the Chief Prosecutor of the Special Investigative Task Force, July 29, 2014, *www.sitf.eu/images/Statement/Statement_of_the_Chief_Prosecutor_of_the_SITF_EN.pdf.*

40  Fatos Bytyci, "Kosovo parliament votes for a new war crimes court," Reuters USA, April 23, 2014, *www.reuters.com/article/2014/04/23/us-kosovo-warcrimes-idUSBREA3M0YD20140423*; Edona Peci, "Kosovo MPs Approve New War Crimes Court," *Balkan Transitional Justice*, April 23, 2014, *www.balkaninsight.com/en/article/kosovo-mps-approve-set-up-of-war-crime-tribunal*; Marija Ristic, "New Tribunal to Prosecute Kosovo Guerrillas in 2015," *Balkan Transitional Justice*, July 23, 2014, *www.balkaninsight.com/en/article/special-kosovo-court-fully-functional-in-2015.*

## 17.

1  Miklós Radnóti, *Clouded Sky* (New York: Sheep Meadow Press, 2003).

2  For an excellent treatment of the scientific evidence underlying this perspective, see Emily Esfahani Smith, "As Babies, We Knew Morality," *The Atlantic Online*, November 18, 2013, *www.theatlantic.com/health/archive/2013/11/as-babies-we-knew-morality/281567/.*

3  See Lynn Hunt, *Inventing Human Rights: A History* (New York: W.W. Norton & Company, 2007), 32; 82.

# INDEX